D1206536

POETS ON
STREET
CORNERS

POETS ON STREET CORNERS

PORTRAITS OF FIFTEEN RUSSIAN POETS

BY OLGA CARLISLE

RANDOM HOUSE
NEW YORK

Acknowledgment is hereby made to the following for permission
to reprint from their works:

Atheneum Publishers for *Selected Translations 1948–1968*, by W. S. Merwin. Copyright © 1968 by W. S. Merwin. "When Psyche Who Is Life" appeared originally in *The Southern Review*. "I Am the Last Poet of the Villages," "Wind Whistles Through the Steep Fence," and "It's Done; I Have Left the Home Fields" were first published in *The Hudson Review*, Vol. XXI, No. 1, Spring, 1968.

The Atlantic Monthly for several adaptations of Osip Mandelstam by Robert Lowell, first published in the June, 1963, and October, 1964, issues. Copyright © 1963, 1964 by The Atlantic Monthly Company, Boston, Mass.

Basic Books, Inc. for *Antiworlds and the Fifth Ace*, by Andrei Voznesensky, edited by Patricia Blake and Max Hayward. Copyright © 1963 by Encounter, Ltd. Copyright © 1966, 1967 by Basic Books, Inc., Publishers, New York.

Farrar, Straus & Giroux, Inc. for *Imitations*, by Robert Lowell. Copyright © 1958, 1959, 1960, 1961 by Robert Lowell.

Life for Yevtushenko's "The Restaurant for Two" translated by John Updike. Copyright © 1967 by Time, Inc.

Little, Brown and Company for *Pages from Tarusa*, by Andrew Field. Copyright © 1964 by Andrew Field.

Vladimir Nabokov for the translation of Pushkin's "Exegi Monumentum," first published in *Three Russian Poets*, translated by Vladimir Nabokov. Copyright 1944 by New Directions Publishing Corporation.

The New York Review of Books for the "Journal of Anne Akhmatova," published in the December 23, 1965, issue. Copyright © 1965 by The New York Review. For several adaptations of Osip Mandelstam by Robert Lowell, first published in the December 23, 1965, issue. Copyright © 1965 by Robert Lowell.

New American Review #2 for "The Last Entry" in *Mayakovsky Notebooks*, translated by Frederick Seidel.

Random House, Inc. for *Voices in the Snow*, by Olga Carlisle.

ACKNOWLEDGMENT   The author wishes to express her heartfelt thanks for the generous grant of the International Poetry Forum of Pittsburgh, Pennsylvania. Without its timely assistance, *Poets on Street Corners* could not have been published in its present form.

ACKNOWLEDGMENTS.—The above figure is copyrighted by Lloyd's
Register for the encouragement of the International Jury Forum
of 1879(7?). Reproduction without its timely endorsement—
copyrighted liberal figures could not have been published in
the US.

FOR HENRY

FOREWORD

Poets on Street Corners does not pretend in any way to
be a definitive anthology of contemporary Soviet poetry.
It is no more than a personal effort, dictated by my own
preferences in an immensely rich field. Naturally these
preferences reflect to some degree those of my family. It
is from them, and especially from my father, the Russian
poet Vadim Andreyev, that I have acquired my love and
my knowledge of Russian poetry. (It is well known that
poets may be prejudiced in their literary tastes and that
Russian families are given to passionate likes and dis-
likes.)

Deliberately, I have chosen to stress one particular aspect of contemporary Russian poetry—the poets' involvement with the flow of everyday life as it is symbol-
ized by *the street*, whether it is Mayakovsky's Square,
where Yevtushenko read his "Babi Yar" publicly for the
first time, or Yesenin's murderous "bent streets of Moscow," the scene of his private wanderings. (Thus, for
example, there are no patriotic poems in this book, although many very good ones were written in the period
it encompasses.)

Personal encounters with Soviet poets played an important role in my choice of materials. Literary friendships influenced me. Subtle yet powerful, special affinities between Russian and American poets were decisive in establishing who was to be included in this book. Certain contemporary Russian poets fascinate their American counterparts, and they usually prove eminently "translatable"; this is the case for example of Osip Mandelstam and Andrei Voznesensky. Others, equally important Russian poets, seem to leave American poets cold. I am particularly unhappy at my omission of two major poetic voices—Gumilev's and Khodasevich's. However, despite several attempts I was unable to arrange for good adaptations of these poets' works. I also regret my failure to represent the Soviet "war poets," a generation which has great moral authority in the U.S.S.R. and includes several important writers: Tvardovsky, Martynov, Semelyakov, Tarkovsky, Samoylov, Mezhirov, Khorzhavin, Okudjava. It does appear, however, that this generation might make its strongest statement in prose. I am thinking of novelist Alexander Solzhenitzin, a wonderful, many-faceted writer whose literary and moral prestige in the U.S.S.R. today is greater even than Pasternak's before his death.

There is no need for me to dwell on the difficulties of poetic translation—of "imitations," as Robert Lowell so aptly calls them. A superb article on the subject was published by George Steiner in *Encounter*, August, 1966, and those interested in the subject are urged to read it. No matter what approach is taken, a translation is always an approximation, a black-and-white projection of a colorful, complex whole. Opinions are sharply divided on what constitutes a good poetic translation. For example, the eminent Soviet critic Kornei Chukovsky, a close friend of mine, was greatly displeased, even angered by Robert Lowell's renditions of Mandelstam because of their lack of faithfulness to the originals. On the other hand, Madame Osip Mandelstam, the poet's widow, who knows English as well as Mr. Chukovsky (which is to say, very well), takes delight in Mr. Lowell's "imitations." She wrote in a letter to him in March 1967: "There are two different kinds of poetic translations. One kind is the rendering of verse with great skill but rather mechanically. It is pure translation and nothing else. . . . The other is a great moment, the meeting of two poets writing in two different languages. There is sudden recognition between them, as if the poet and his translator had struck up a close friendship. In such translations everything is unexpected, and only they belong to literature as such. Generally, they are quite free. . . And that is why I greatly liked your translations of my husband's verse."

While reading Robert Lowell's or Jean Valentine's free adaptations it is important to remember that what sometime appears as a mistranslation in English is an attempt on the part of the adapter to recapture the concreteness of the Russian original. There are dozens of such instances in this book, although there are unquestionably some genuine mistranslations as well. Thus in his adaptation of "Stalin" by Mandelstam, when Mr. Lowell chooses to write that:

> After each death, he is like a Georgian tribesman,
> putting a raspberry in his mouth.

it is not because he is unaware of the exact Russian text:

> Every execution is a delight for him,
> And the chest of the Ossitian is wide.

However, it is his preference to emphasize the expression which Mandelstam uses to depict Stalin's delight, a colloquial expression by which, in Russian, what is good is "someone's raspberry." And to describe an Ossitian

(Georgian mountain tribesman) simply as a "Georgian tribesman."

In other cases, the translators have replaced peculiarly Russian concepts by others less quaint in English. Thus in Tsvetayeva's "Poems for Blok," Poem 3, the line "and the familiar grass lifting in the wind," is actually "and the familiar red cotton cloth from the district of Kaluga billowing and lifting in the wind." Certain poems were shortened in English. Personally—and especially since the Russian texts are facing the English ones, making checking and comparing easy—I feel that the reader is best served when poetic translations are freest and most imaginative.

The fact that there are nine poems by Pasternak and two by Blok should not be taken for my assessment of the relative importance of these poets, but rather as an admission that matchmaking between translators' talents and Russian poetry is anything but an exact science.

Since—with the exceptions of Alexander Andreyev and Henry Carlisle—none of the adaptors whose work is included in this book knows any Russian, each had to work with collaborators who provided them with literal Russian texts. Professor Wladimir Weidlé worked with W. S. Merwin on his six Brodsky adaptations; Andrew Field assisted Miss Levertov in translating "A Letter," "Autumn in Tarusa," and "No Need for talk . . ."; Max Hayward helped William Jay Smith with "Winter at the Track." I myself worked on most of the other adaptations. In some instances I consider myself as co-translator of the poem. Where extracts of poems are quoted in the text without attribution, I am responsible for the adaptation, except in the cases of quotations from poems which appear in full elsewhere in the book.

OLGA CARLISLE

Washington, Connecticut

I wish to thank the many Russian and American poets who helped create *Poets on Street Corners*. Some of them also acted as patient and indispensable editors, notably Rose Styron, Jean Valentine, Olga Lang, Henry Carlisle, and Mrs. S. Erlich. Professor Clarence Brown kindly checked my Mandelstam chapter, while innumerable Russian friends helped with advice and moral support. I want also to thank Mrs. William Vanderheuvel, Miss Galen Williams of the New York Poetry Center and Dr. Samuel Hazo of the International Poetry Forum for their faith in my attempt to make Russian poetry more accessible and more enjoyable for the American reader. My greatest debt, though, is to my parents, Olga and Vadim Andreyev. Without their help this book could not have existed.

O.C.

CONTENTS

INTRODUCTION

A SEA OF young people with ecstatic open faces; here and there middle-aged women in drab clothes, with gray faces, some with eyes filled with tears — they all press against one another on hard auditorium benches, trying to make room for those jammed in the aisles. Young men are precariously perched on window ledges halfway up to the ceiling; students are crowding to the very footlights of the brightly lit stage.

A pretty woman walks out onto the stage. She is wearing pumps with high heels. Her navy silk dress is extremely short, her reddish hair set according to the latest fashion. She looks like a doll with her heavily made-up wide-open dark eyes. She stands there a bit unsteadily, clutching the microphone, lifting an unseeing immobile face to the public. After six or seven outbursts of acclaim, she raises her left arm in a timid, rounded gesture — and perfect silence settles over the audience within seconds. Bella Akhmadulina is having a solo public reading for the first time in many months. This young woman, who was admitted into the Writers' Union as a translator rather than as a writer, whose single slim volume of verse was published in 1962, is Russia's most famous young poetess. This evening at the Journalists' Club is one of the great events of the literary season in Moscow in the spring of 1967.

Akhmadulina recites her "Volcanoes" from memory, her eyes now almost closed, emphasizing the rhythm

2

and assonances of her poem. Her voice is melodious and grieving. She seems on the verge of dissolving into tears as she addresses Pompei:

> What future did you assume,
> What were you thinking of and whom,
> When you leaned your elbow thus
> Thoughtlessly on Vesuvius?

—TRANSLATED BY W. H. AUDEN

Poetry readings are a popular form of entertainment today in the U.S.S.R., second only to soccer games. While soccer is the Soviet Union's national sport, poetry is without any doubt its national art. In a country where religion is discouraged and the visual arts underdeveloped, poetry plays an all-important social and spiritual role. This has been so for many years.* From its very beginnings, from the days of Pushkin, Russian poetry has slowly but steadily grown into a popular art, an ever-growing wave that now carries hundreds of poets and millions of readers.

Traditionally, lyric self-expression is the Russians' greatest artistic gift. The roots of Russian poetry and music are buried deep in Russian history — a history of oppression and violence. As secret as music yet more explicit, poetry is the perfect means of expression for a suffering people. Lack of freedom does not seem to stifle poetry; rather, it lends it a sense of urgency. Most Russian poetry has a markedly "nonliterary" tone, which is emphasized in translation when its melodic aspect is necessarily altered or lost. For Russians, poetry is an attempt to discover order in a raw, chaotic world. It is a *cri de coeur*, an incantation. All of Pasternak's poetry is a hymn to life, yet in his "Breakup" he wrote:

---

* Poetry recitals were first fashionable in Russia in the years immediately preceding the Revolution. Limited to a small circle, they were an expression not only of love for poetry, but also of revolutionary feelings and of *fin de siècle* exhibitionism.

3

Werther's already had his day.
By now the air itself reeks of death—
Opening a window is like opening a vein.

Even in young Yevtushenko's and Voznesensky's
sometimes almost bombastic tone—a tone erroneously
taken by some non-Russians to be the sole mode of expression of Soviet poetry today—a sense of the tragic
may be felt. The tragedy is less that of mortality than
that of history as it affects Russian people and Russian
poets. The great poet Osip Mandelstam expressed his
anguish in the face of Russian history in this ominous
poem, adapted here by Robert Lowell:

Preserve my words forever for their aftertaste of
    misfortune and smoke,
for their tar of collective patience and conscientious work—
water in the wells of Novgorod must be black and sweetened
to reflect a star with seven fins at Christmas.

O my Fatherland, my friend, my rough helper
remember your unrecognized brother, the apostate from the
    people's family
I have promised to build you forest and log wells,
such as the Tartars built to lower the princes in
    wooden buckets.

If only your executioners, the frozen blocks, could love me
as the Tsar Peter, a deadly marksman, loved the balls he
    bowled on the lawn—
for your love I'll walk through life in an iron shirt,
for my execution, I'll walk the woods like Peter and find a
    handle for the ax.

On the whole, formal and stylistic preoccupations
have seldom been a major concern of Russian poets.
Such questions were absorbing only for certain writers
during the rich Revolutionary, confused years, and before that, at the turn of the last century, at the time when

4

Symbolism flourished in Russia.* Today the work of many of these poets stands on its own merits, while the schools that claimed them are all but forgotten. Most Russian poets would subscribe to Pasternak's words:

The most extraordinary [poetic] discoveries are made when the artist is overwhelmed by what he has to say. In his urgency he uses the old language and the old language is transformed from within.

Since 1953, when Stalin's death ended an age of political and cultural terror that had lasted for almost twenty-five years, a tremendous poetic proliferation has taken place in the Soviet Union. It is clearly a nationwide phenomenon. Whole printings of books by popular poets are sold out in a few hours, and printings of as many as three hundred thousand volumes are not uncommon.** Throughout the country, huge crowds congregate whenever a public poetry reading is given. More than twelve thousand people attended a reading at the Luzhniki Stadium in Moscow in the fall of 1962. Well-known, rebellious young poets like Yevgeny Yevtushenko, Andrei Voznesensky, and Bella Akhmadulina took part in this recital. It was such a triumph that the Soviet government, ever anxious to keep all cultural activities under

---

* The latter is sometimes called the Silver Age of Russian literature, a period considered secondary to the Golden Age of Pushkin and his contemporaries. The Silver Age was marked by a variety of literary and mystic trends; some were inspired by Western Symbolism, others were nationalistic in spirit. Fyodor Sologub, Vyacheslav Ivanov, Konstantin Balmont, Valery Bryusov, Zinaida Hippius, Maximilian Voloshin, Andrei Bely, and Alexander Blok were the best-known Symbolists.

** For a long time books were published in the Soviet Union exclusively on the basis of political acceptance, with arbitrary rules regarding reprintings. As a result, millions of books remained unsold in state-run stores, while most popular books were impossible to obtain. In recent years, Soviet publishing has begun to think in terms of profit; bigger printings of books by sought-after authors are issued every year. This is particularly true of poetry, both classical and contemporary, but nonetheless books by fashionable contemporary Soviet poets are usually hard to buy in the U.S.S.R.

close ideological control, seems to have made it its policy since then to limit the size of poetry audiences. Even so, an attendance of several thousand at a poetry reading in a big city is usual. "In my opinion two or three thousand listeners make for the very best audience as far as size is concerned," Yevtushenko has said, praising the feeling of intimacy given by such "small" audiences. It is as if a whole nation were searching for itself through poetry; during a visit in Paris in 1963, Andrei Voznesensky attempted to explain this phenomenon, in a conversation:

> The vogue of poetry in Russia demonstrates that Communists are nowadays concerned with "inner man." For us poetry is above all a group experience. A poet creates in solitude, but when he reads his poems to a crowd he and his public commune. Together they partake of something new and deep.

Andrei Voznesensky and Yevgeny Yevtushenko, now in their midthirties, are the most famous young poets in Russia today—two of a group of five or six who have brought a certain kind of declamatory, candid, youth-oriented poetry into the open.* In their poems they have asserted their faith in a new Russia. To do so during the Khrushchev years, marked by political uncertainty, certain young poets actually went out into the streets of Moscow to read their work—an act of defiance unheard of in the U.S.S.R. since the twenties. Thus in November, 1961, Yevtushenko read his "Babi Yar" for the first time beside Mayakovsky's statue in the heart of Moscow.**

---

* Other well-known poets of that generation are Bella Akhmadulina, Robert Rozhdestvensky, Novella Matveeva, Yuna Moritz, Victor Sosnora, and Rimma Kazakova.

** Statues of Mayakovsky and Pushkin, situated near each other on Gorky Street, are rallying points for protesting, literary-minded Muscovite youths. In December, 1966, fifty students brandishing hand-painted banners demanded the release of the writers Sinyavsky and Daniel. Although they were not molested by the police, several of them were arrested afterwards.

6

Yevtushenko is an intrepid young poet. Through determination and persistence and a fine flair for politics he manages to publish poems on topics regarded as being taboo in the Soviet Union, such as the inhumanity of bureaucracy, and anti-Semitism in Russia. He was both cunning and outspoken in the early stages of de-Stalinization, and he continues to take up a variety of thorny social and political themes in his verse. He is liked in Russia for his generosity as a man and as a writer. Unfortunately, his best poems have proved difficult to translate into English because of their evanescent melodic quality. In contrast with his public diatribes, these delicate, lyric poems such as "The White Snows Fall," published in the magazine *Yunost* (*Youth*), June, 1965, are in the tradition of Russian folk songs; at their best they remind one of the peasant-poet of the Revolution, Sergei Yesenin.*

Andrei Voznesensky, unlike the *engagé* Yevtushenko, is essentially a "literary" writer, despite the rhetorical tone of some of his poems.** Voznesensky's impact as a poet is to be felt in the field of poetic techniques. He is a virtuoso of form, a resolutely modern poet continuing the tradition of the great innovators of the twenties, Pasternak and Mayakovsky.

The role of Voznesensky and Yevtushenko is not only literary but social and political as well. Alone among the young Russian intelligentsia today, they are allowed to travel extensively outside of Russia, to meet with foreign writers and to debate international issues with Western

* Two million copies is the usual printing of this Soviet magazine second only to *Novy Mir* in literary excellence.

** Yevtushenko's and Voznesensky's "public-style"—an attempt to reach out to the masses—is also in part a political necessity. They are imitating Mayakovsky. One of several major writers nurtured by the Revolution, Mayakovsky was a dedicated Communist. He was the only poet to combine modern literary techniques and political orthodoxy in his highly rhetorical "public" poems which are intensively studied in Soviet schools today.

diplomats. When they are at home, their lives are as glamorous and comfortable as is possible under present circumstances in the Soviet Union. Not that they have forsaken their ideal of a more open, more liberal Russia that would introduce more humanity into Communism — the platform that earned them their great popularity with Soviet youth a few years ago. Rather, it is the government, or at least certain members of it, who have come to share their views. Or perhaps, more simply, a government faction now recognizes that their ideal is necessary to the perpetuation of the Soviet state. Their value as trustworthy diplomats is now acknowledged, and Voznesensky was quickly forgiven his recent act of defiance against the Writers' Union — a letter published in the West denouncing this organization as "dishonest."* But this very acceptance creates new difficulties for Yevtushenko and Voznesensky. They, who in times of political reaction depended on their notoriety for survival, are now presented with a problem that commonly affects Western and notably American writers: how to live with such widespread adulation and go on being a writer dedicated to his work. Shortly after the publication of *Doctor Zhivago* in the West, Pasternak expressed his anxiety regarding the effects of celebrity on a poet's life:

Everyday life has grown very complicated for me now. It must be so anywhere for a well-known writer, but I am unprepared for this role. I don't like a life deprived of secrecy and quiet. It seems to me that in my youth work was an integral part of life, which illuminated everything else in it. Now it is something I have to fight for.

Because it is a mass phenomenon, contemporary Soviet poetry is hard to explore and to evaluate. The writing of poetry in the U.S.S.R. is not the prerogative of

* July, 1967.

8

members of the Writers' Union, nor is its appreciation
limited to a literary milieu. For every Andrei Voznesensky, how many poets are there, as gifted, who for political reasons cannot be heard internationally or even
nationally? It is still very difficult for a Soviet writer
totally unwilling to conform politically to be published
in the U.S.S.R. Thus, Joseph Brodsky, an excellent
young poet, to date has had only a couple of short poems
printed in his country. Yet, even if we consider only those
who are officially recognized and published, there is a
remarkable number of accomplished poets in the Soviet
Union. Among the older poets — those who could be Voznesensky's and Yevtushenko's fathers — several managed to live through Stalinism while retaining their integrity as writers: Pavel Antakolsky, Leonid Martynov,
Arseni Tarkovsky, Alexander Tvardovsky, Yaroslav
Semelyakov, Olga Bergholz, Victor Bokov.*

The serious poets now in their forties are David Samoylov, Alexander Mezhirov, Bulat Okudjava, Boris
Slutzky, Naum Khorzhavin, Vladimir Kornilov, Nikolai
Panchenko, Yuri Levitansky, Yevgeny Vinokurov, Vladimir Sokolov, and a half dozen others. As very young men
they fought in World War II — the Patriotic War, as it is
known now in Russia. Many of their generation perished; a dramatization of poems by "those dead at
twenty" in the war was produced recently by the Lubimov Repertory Theater in Moscow, which made clear
that several promising young poets were killed between

---

* To this group one may add those who had had at one time authentic
poetic voices but who have become literary officials in recent years,
like Nikolai Tikhonov and Ilya Selvinsky. Others, important poets of
that generation, have died: Nikolai Aseyev, Eduard Bagritsky, Mikhail
Svetlov, Nikolai Zabolotsky, Pavel Vasiliev, Boris Kornilov, Vladimir
Lugovskoy. Equally distinguished, a school of Russian poetry flourished outside of the U.S.S.R. in the twenties and thirties, notably in
Paris. Its two major poets were Marina Tsvetayeva and Vladislav Khodasevich, but Georgi Ivanov, Vladimir Nabokov, Boris Poplavsky,
Anna Prismanova, Alexander Ginger, and Vadim Andreyev were all
original, talented writers.

9

1941 and 1945—notably Pavel Kogan, Mikhail Kulchitsky, Vsevolod Bagritsky, and Simon Gudzenko.*

Those of this younger war generation who survived are still haunted by war, but paradoxically these poets shaped by military life have failed so far to make a definitive statement about their experience. They are unable to give full expression to their feelings, which are pacifist rather than patriotic — and genuine, unconditional pacifism is frowned upon in the Soviet Union. Moreover, these artists belong to a generation which carries a burden of guilt concerning Stalin, in whom many had an absolute faith at one time. With them a Russian poetic tradition is coming to an end; Alexander Blok — who could see Christ leading the twelve mythical Red Army men through revolutionary Petersburg — was its last major voice.

Born in the middle of last century, this tradition is that of an exalted, mystical patriotism. Dostoevsky was one of its representatives; another was Nikolai Nekrasov (1821–1877), who celebrated the Russian people in his famous poem "Russia":

> You are the barren one,
> And the abundant one,
> O mighty country,
> Powerless yet powerful
> Dear Mother Russia!
>
> Through years of servitude
> The heart of the people
> Remained proud and free.
> The golden heart of the people
> Remained proud and free.

* This extremely dynamic show demonstrates the increasingly important role played by poetry on the Soviet legitimate stage today. The Lubimov group has recently produced a superb *Mayakovsky* and is now working on an adaptation of Sergei Yesenin's *Pugachev*, a lyrical, loosely built drama about one of Russia's most famous rebels, executed in 1775 by Catherine the Great.

10

> The power of the people
> Is the only power:
> Clear purity of conscience,
> Truth indestructible,
> The golden heart of the people!

But truth no longer can be found in the heart—the spoken heart—of the Russian people, not after the Stalinist years. While younger poets seek it elsewhere, many among those who fought for Russia in World War II are left without a faith. Some are fascinated by the Civil War, presumably because right and wrong were clearly defined then. Thus Bulat Okudjava, a poet and songwriter who is also the author of a well-known pacifist novella about World War II, celebrates that "distant civil war" in traditional metrics, preferred by his generation of poets:

> Hope, I will come back again to hear
> The bugler sounding Taps
> When he lifts up the bugle to his lips,
> A sharp elbow to the air.
> Hope, I will remain untouched and sure
> The damp earth's not for me;
> Rather I'll bear your trials, anxiety,
> The sweet world of your care.

> Yet if death should win, should one day spread
> Above me its wide wing,
> Though strange fresh battles go on pounding
> Till the world is waste,
> I in my dreams shall still have bled
> In that bygone Civil War
> And silently over me a commissar
> Will bow in his helmet of dust.

> —ADAPTED BY ROSE STYRON

Although World War II is a recurrent theme with Soviet poets, there are only a few completely successful works about it. The wholeheartedly patriotic, realistic "Vasily Tyorkin," a portrait of the average soldier, by Alexander Tvardovsky, is such a poem. Another is "The Russian Gods," a lengthy visionary work by Daniel Andreyev, a remarkable poet, who is still unpublished in Russia. (Andreyev (1907–1958) died after a ten-year incarceration in a Stalinist prison.) It describes the desperate solidarity which led the Russians to victory in 1945:

> Night winds! Dark mountainous skies
> Over the snowy bier of Leningrad!
> You are our trial and our great reward,
> And I keep, treasured as a medal won,
> The memory of that evening when my stubborn
> Steps I mixed on the black ice
> Road with steps of the Russian race
> Somber, covered in steel to its eyes.
>
> From Moscow's hills, from Saratov's meadows,
> Where waves of rye vibrate in summer
> From *tayga's* heartland where centenary cedar
> Trees give birth to a deep
> Howling,
> For a bitter military deed
> The law welded as one our races.
> From drifts of snow to floating glaciers
> We stretched like a long live rope.

> —ADAPTED BY ROSE STYRON

Traditional forms and themes are used by the poets who fought in the war — possibly because anything resembling modernism was regarded as a crime in the Soviet Union during the formative years. Thus Yevgeny Vinokurov celebrates nature in a charming, yet conventional manner; his poem may be considered as the *art poétique* of his generation:

12

Place midnight in the care of my hands
where fresh wet lilac rustles;
its delicate petals I'll not distress
but accent, soft, its sounds.

Give me the lightning of May, dense rain,
far dawns and secret woodland:
no leaf shall I crumple nor frail grass bend,
but rhyme the birch trees' murmuring.

Lend me a full river, flowing with stars,
sharp fins, sky and steep clearings;
no fields of night will I touch, but lightly
punctuate here and there.

—ADAPTED BY ROSE STYRON

The history of Russian poetry in the last fifty years cannot be separated from that of the Russian people as a whole. It is an extraordinarily cruel history, marked by civil war, political terror, prisons, and concentration camps on a gigantic scale, and the almost incredible devastation of World War II, which was followed by more terror. Entire social classes were destroyed during that time, such as the kulaks, the prosperous peasants of Russia. Similarly, whole literary schools were annihilated during those years. This was the case, for example, of the Oberiuti,* a highly original, satirical-minded group of Surrealists who wrote in the late twenties. Out of five or six important poets, like Zabolotsky, Harms, Olenekov, and Vaguinov, Zabolotsky alone survived. He spent many years in a concentration camp; he is said to have lived only because he was assigned, in place of hard labor, to a clerical job connected with the running of the camp. This good fortune filled him with a sense of guilt that nothing could erase afterwards.

Although I was brought up on contemporary Soviet

---

* This name is a nonsense word; it has no meaning in Russian, but it does have a mysterious sound.

poetry, the Oberiuti other than Zabolotsky were unknown to me until 1967. At that time, some of their poems (those which had not been lost throughout the years of persecution) began circulating in Moscow in typescript. Surrealism is the dominant literary fashion in Russia today, and an interest in Oberiuti experiments is natural at this time, particularly among painters who use Surrealistic techniques. But there is every reason to believe that whole segments of Soviet poetry are permanently lost to us. Certain works, such as the late poems of Osip Mandelstam, were saved from destruction only through a combination of good luck and courage on the part of friends and relatives of the writer. Some of them are still part of an underground literature, which is passed from hand to hand, usually in typescript.

The poetry of the Stalinist years in Russia is extraordinarily rich and varied, and this book can only give a limited introduction to it. Despite the fantastic sufferings which filled this period, it will be remembered as a great age for poetry. In fact, as we study it, we discover that while revolution and terror were destroying people and particularly writers, it also heightened their creative powers. (Psychologically, this is quite plausible. It is said in Russia that political terror heightened people's sexual drive; intense love affairs blossomed during these catastrophic times.)

Today, despite its spectacular growth in the comparatively safe political climate now prevailing in the U.S.S.R., Russian poetry appears to have entered a period of decline qualitatively. There are no young poets who show promise of equaling Blok or Mandelstam. It is as if poetry was becoming weakened by its extraordinary popular appeal, taking place at the expense of a development in depth. The poets themselves are instinctively aware of this, notably Voznesensky, who had a great sensitivity for new trends. He said recently:

I know when things were going badly with me, personally and publicly, I wrote my strongest work. I am not looking to be hurt but I know that a sense of danger is beneficial to artists. Perhaps Russian poets have come to depend too much on this . . .

Poetry is now an essential part of Soviet contemporary life, and poetic vitality is to be found in new, popular art forms, notably in folk songs, or rather, in the sophisticated, rebellious variety. This is not unlike the coming together of folk songs and poetry taking place in the West today, except that the interdependence of poetry and folklore is an old Russian tradition; while poets such as Pushkin and Nekrasov borrowed from the folklore, they also contributed to it by writing poems which were taken up by the people as their own songs. And many of Yesenin's poems have become folk songs. Last fall in the vicinity of the Pushkin monument I heard several beat-niklike young men, so much like their Western counterparts with their beards and guitars, sing his menacing lyrics:

> I too will cut a throat
> to the whistling of autumn.

Certain singers continue this tradition; they write their own songs in the popular vein, drawing mostly on contemporary urban folklore. Okudjava (who is also a poet), Visotsky (an actor), and Galich (an engineer) are famous now not only among the intellectuals but also in student and working-class circles—even though their works are never recorded officially. These artists give an expression to the harsh mood of skepticism now spreading in the U.S.S.R. Their public admires Pasternak and Mayakovsky, is curious about the Oberiuti, and tends to have no respect for Voznesensky and Yevtushenko, accusing them of political opportunism. After fifty years of dictatorship, thoughtful Russians are severe towards those who are successful.

It is impossible to overemphasize the importance of the oral tradition in Russian poetry. Poetry continued to be written and read during Stalinist persecutions. It could be circulated orally with ease and was consequently the art which suffered least from censorship. And Russians are as a rule well trained to memorize poetry; this is an ancient heritage. Until the eighteenth century, all Russian lay poetry was oral—only Slavonic devotional texts were recorded in writing.

Transmitted from individual to individual, forbidden poems were whispered throughout the Soviet Union—in the depths of Siberian concentration camps, in the far north, on the front lines during the war, in Georgia, where a flourishing school of poetry was all but destroyed by Stalin. The contemporary oral trend of the *blatnoi*, (thieves' songs) developed further in this climate. The *blatnoi* songs and poems are anonymous, the creation of soldiers, of concentration camp inmates, of convicts. Although they remain unpublished, these songs are popular today in students' and workers' circles, where they are sung commonly in attenuated versions. They are not unlike the Russian convicts' songs of the seventeenth and eighteenth centuries, but they are usually more obscene and more terrifying than the old songs. They tell of the immensity of the Russian people's suffering under Stalin, suggesting that the soldiers and the convicts who built "modern" Russia under Peter the Great, and Ivan Denisovich, Alexander Solzhenitzin's hero, the innocent peasant laboring in a Stalinist camp, had similar lyrical voices.

Today, it is fairly common for Russians to gather at each other's homes to listen to poetry. It may be recited by a poet himself, or be played on a tape recorder, an all-important means of communication in the Soviet Union. Or, more simply, guests will read their favorite poems. This kind of entertainment is hard for us to conceive of

16

on a large scale. One must bear in mind, however, that besides the fact that many Russians look to poetry for political and philosophical answers, there is a relative lack of nightly entertainment in the Soviet Union. (And, of course, the average Soviet citizen is quite well read today. To have a lucrative or interesting career without a university education is impossible; this encourages all those who qualify in terms of grades to seek an education — and education is free.)

Almost always, a good part of a private poetry reading is dedicated to newly published works by the Russian poets of the revolutionary years. With the exception of Mayakovsky, who has enjoyed the unchallenged status of "Greatest Socialist Poet" since his death in 1930, many of them had been virtually out of print until the early sixties. (One poet, Mandelstam, is still unpublished, although public readings of his works are occasionally held in universities and there is some indication that his *Selected Works* might at last be issued in 1968.) But now at last the greater part of Pasternak's, Tsvetayeva's, Akhmatova's writings are available to Soviet readers, who are discovering for the first time the extraordinary, almost Elizabethan, scope of these artists. The grayness of most Soviet official literature helps by contrast to light up their uninhibited, profound works. These poems are read with passion, as if they had been written the day before. Yet they also fill their readers with nostalgia for the early twenties, when art and revolution went hand in hand.

The country's past provides an explanation of the Russian's identification of poetry with revolution and freedom—an attitude on the part of poets and readers alike that has existed as long as Russian poetry itself has existed as a national art, for about two hundred years. Long before that, in the Middle Ages, the Russian people had found their identity through the Orthodox religion. Orthodoxy held the country together for centuries. Russia was amorphous, an immense, bleak expanse of land dotted with small fortified towns and monasteries. Its boundaries were ill defined and it was constantly being invaded from all sides—by the Tartars, the Teutonic knights, the Swedes. After the fall of Constantinople and the final destruction of Byzantium, Moscow—that small kremlin, or fortified town—lost in the middle of an endless wooded plain, began to be looked to by Orthodox theologians as the third and final embodiment of Rome, the homeland of authentic Christianity, the source of all spiritual and temporal authority. However, in the eighteenth century, with the advent of Peter the Great, the Orthodox Church began to lose its power to an autocratic centralized state, and Moscow ceased to be the Russian capital. Peter wanted to bring his country abreast of other European nations; through will power and ruthlessness and an extraordinary imagination, he created for himself an opulent new capital, a Western City. St. Petersburg is the embodiment of imperial grandeur, and its churches are an expression of worldly authority more than of devotion.

But the Age of Enlightenment was coming to Europe. Slowly, revolutionary ideas penetrated even remote Russia. While the Orthodox Church was becoming ossified, these ideas were bringing a promise of human dignity and freedom to a people more and more miserable under tsarist rule. Throughout the nineteenth century the role played by poetry for many cultivated Russians resembled to some degree that of religion in former times. It was experienced as an intimation of spiritual order, a promise of hope for an enslaved people.

Three writers of the age of Catherine created prosody in the eighteenth century: Lomonosov, the great scientist-poet; Sumarokov, the playwright-poet, and Derzhavin, one of the greatest of all Russian poets. Until then

18

poetry had existed in Russia only as folklore, or as a Slavonic religious literature. These two traditions were clearly differentiated, each concerned with its own genres; however, it is important to stress that both reached all classes of Russian society—hence their many-sidedness and their vitality, as well as their influence upon subsequent literary developments. The writers of Catherine's time derived their inspiration from the French, the language which the Russian aristocracy was to speak almost exclusively until the Revolution, but they took into account the richness and melodiousness of Russian as it existed then, both in its spoken vernacular and written Old Church Slavonic forms. A new literary language was born soon afterwards with Alexander Pushkin (1799-1837). Many influences met to create this new language; eclecticism was its main characteristic. Russian folklore, Slavonic liturgy, Baroque influences from Poland and Germany, and of course French Classicism, joined to form a sonorous, beautiful idiom. Starting with Pushkin, who was a Classicist in some of his poems, a Romantic in others, a Realist in his prose, eclectism of style has remained a significant aspect of Russian literature.

Pushkin was the main literary figure of a period known as the Golden Age of Russian poetry, which lasted roughly from 1810 to his death in 1837. With him, a whole pleiade of poets came into their own for what was to be a short-lived, brilliant literary and intellectual blossoming.* He and his contemporaries shared a passionate love for Russia and compassion for its people. In this respect the poets of the Golden Age initiated a noble tradition. The poets who followed them never lost sight of the fate of the Russian masses; they never ceased to

* They included Karamzin, Zhukovsky, Krylov, Batyushkov, Vyazemsky, Griboyedov, Ryleyev, Kuchelbecker, Delvig, Baratynsky, Yazykov— to cite only a few.

protest the Tsars' tyranny, and later Stalin's. A rare example of a Russian poet who identified himself with the authorities was Vladimir Mayakovsky, who killed himself in 1930. About this death, which had a variety of causes, both political and personal, Pasternak said simply:

It seems to me that Mayakovsky killed himself out of pride, because there was in him, or around him, something with which his sense of honor could not be reconciled.

Perhaps as a result of the poets' concern for the people, love of poetry spread through Russia very quickly. In 1837 as many as fifty thousand Russians paid homage at Pushkin's funeral. He had been killed at the age of thirty-seven by a French royalist in the service of Tsar Nicholas I, Baron Georges D'Anthès, in a duel that possibly had been secretly prearranged by Nicholas the First. The Tsar was anxious to be rid of a freedom-loving, dangerously influential poet. The vast majority of Pushkin's mourners were illiterate, but his verse and his concern for the people had reached the masses. Here is an account of an eyewitness, the widow of the poet Karamzin, Ekaterina Karamzina:

It was touching to see the huge crowd seeking to pay homage to his body; it is said that more than 20,000 people passed through his house on that day—clerks, officers, merchants—who walked in reverent silence, with deep feeling. Pushkin's friends were made happy by this. . . .

One old man impressed Zhukovsky [the poet Vasily Zhukovsky, a friend of the family] by the deep concentration with which he looked for a long time at Pushkin's face, which was altered by then. He even settled down across the room and went on looking for a quarter of an hour, sitting there, immobile. As he left, Zhukovsky sent someone after him to ask his name. "Why should you want to know my name?" he said. "Pushkin didn't know it, and I have never

20

seen him until today, but I'm heartbroken because of the loss of Russia's brightest glory." In general, the "second society" [the people] show such enthusiasm, such sympathy, such regrets that Pushkin's soul must be happy if an echo of worldly life reaches it now. There is a wave of indignation against Pushkin's assassin, threats are heard—but all this takes place in the "second society" and among the young people. In our circle, D'Anthès has a number of defenders.*

Alarmed by this display of popular feeling, the Tsar hastened to have Pushkin's body taken out of his house. Another friend of the poet wrote:

The people have been duped. It has been said that Pushkin's funeral was to be held in Saint Isaac [Petersburg's largest cathedral]—this was announced on the cards sent out by his widow. Yet his body was carried out of his apartments at night and taken for a hasty service to the small Church of the Stables. On that day strict orders were given to the professors at the university not to leave their classrooms. Students were obliged to attend all lectures.

Pushkin's spirit was to live on, as he had predicted himself in his *Exegi Monumentum*," translated here by Vladimir Nabokov:

No hands have wrought my monument; no weeds
will hide the nation's footpath to its site.
Tsar Alexander's column it exceeds
in splendid insubmissive height.

Not all of me is dust. Within my song,
safe from the worm, my spirit will survive,
and my sublunar fame will dwell as long
as there is one last bard alive.

* The Baron D'Anthès eventually returned to France and served as a *sénateur* under Napoleon III. He lived to be ninety. According to Vladimir Nabokov: "When an inquisitive Russian traveler once asked the grand old man how he had found it possible to deprive Russia of her greatest poet—'*Mais enfin*', answered the Baron rather testily, '*moi aussi* [I too am something]; *je suis Sénateur!*'" (as recounted by Nabokov in his *Three Russian Poets*).

Throughout great Rus' my echoes will extend,
and all will name me, all tongues in her use:
the Slavs' proud heir, the Finn, the Kalmuk, friend
    of steppes, the yet untamed Tunguz.

And to the people long shall I be dear
because kind feelings did my lyre extol,
invoking freedom in an age of fear,
    and mercy for the broken soul.

Obey thy God, and never mind, O Muse,
the laurels or the stings: make it thy rule
to be unstirred by praise as by abuse,
    and do not contradict the fool.

In Pushkin's works, the sumptuous Russian folklore
had joined with a grace and a strength reminiscent of
Mozart, with "Voltairianism," as Western liberal ideas
were then known in Russia. These elements formed not
only a new literary language but also a new sensibility.
The latter was akin to Western Romanticism, yet it had
less sentimentality and more concern for social issues. It
grew into an all-encompassing humanism, serving as an
inspiration to Dostoevsky and Tolstoi, and to Russian
poets to come—and more particularly to those who came
almost a century later. In the interim, several magnificent, isolated poets such as Lermontov, Tyutchev, Fet,
and Nekrasov preserved the essence of Pushkin's heritage. But on the whole, Pushkin's age was followed by a
period of social criticism, in which prose predominated.
(To a degree Russian literature appears to be a cyclical
affair; a generation of poets is followed by a generation
of prose writers. Thus, each new generation of poets is
forced to reinvent a poetic idiom for itself and is consequently spared to some degree the inheritance of
clichés.)

By the middle of the nineteenth century the "beautiful" became unpopular at the expense of the "useful" and
the well-meaning. This puritanical attitude was dictated

22

by the political situation; a fierce reaction followed the spreading of revolutionary ideas in Russia in the first half of the nineteenth century. It was an age of heavy censorship—government-enforced but also self-imposed by conscience-stricken radical writers. Tolstoi's renunciation of literature at the end of his life is characteristic of this attitude. So are these remarks by the celebrated anarchist Peter Kropotkin, writing in his *Autobiography* about himself and his brother Alexander when they were young in the middle of the century:

"Read poetry, it makes men better," wrote my brother in his letters. How often later in life I realized the truth of his remark! He was himself a poet and had a wonderful facility for writing most musical verse; indeed, I think it was a great pity that he abandoned poetry. But the reaction against art which arose among the Russian youth in the early sixties (and which Turgenev has depicted in Bazarov [in his *Fathers and Sons*]) induced him to look upon his verse with contempt and to plunge headlong into the natural sciences.

Pushkin's heritage was rekindled by poets who grew up with the twentieth century. A poetic renaissance took place in the years immediately preceding and following the Revolution in 1917. These years may be compared to Pushkin's age: the same passionate readership, the same exalted role assigned to the poet by the intelligentsia of the day, the same hopes for social changes. The poets of the turn of the century were viewed as the redeemers of their age; some of them were working for a revolution, as Pushkin and his aristocratic friends had worked for the overthrow of the government, which culminated in the abortive 1825 Decembrist uprising. This period too was followed by an era of oppressive censorship in the arts—one of unprecedented rigor.

Among the ten or twelve superb poets who came up with the 1917 Revolution, six stand above the rest. Each in his own way—Pasternak, Akhmatova, Tsvetayeva,

Yesenin, Mandelstam, Mayakovsky—was a prophet of his time. A seventh poet, Alexander Blok, born some ten years before these, may be included in this group, although technically he belonged to the Symbolists, an earlier school of poets. Blok did not survive the Revolution, but "The Twelve," his last long poem, is one of the masterpieces of that time. Other major poets of that extraordinary age had been Innokenty Annensky, Fyodor Sologub, Vyacheslav Ivanov, Maximilian Voloshin, Andrei Bely, Velemir Khlebnikov, Nikolai Gumilev, Vladislav Khodasevich.

In the works of the poets of the Revolution, worship of Pushkin's memory and the values he embodied runs like an unbroken thread. These poets had all been friends in the "fabulous years," as Blok had called the beginning of the century. (Pushkin and his contemporaries too had been linked in strong friendships.) Two of these poets lived on into our time: Pasternak and Akhmatova were dominant figures who survived wars and persecutions, writing poetry until their deaths—1960 and 1966 respectively. Except for Mayakovsky, who was a political poet—"the archangel of public squares," Tsvetayeva called him—these writers upheld the tradition of humanism that had been created in Russia by Pushkin and his contemporaries. They had a great love of freedom. Their devotion to Russia did not blind them to the rest of the world and their awareness of their own worth was tempered by humor. They were hopeful about the Revolution:

> The arguments of freedom shall not die,
> The Roman senate testifies to this!

Mandelstam's Decembrist had said this; yet Mandelstam was fully aware of the cataclysmic turn that the Revolution was taking:

> Those who have heart, must know, O Time,
> Your boat is sinking to the bottom.

With Anna Akhmatova's death in March, 1966, a gap between past and present suddenly opened in Russian letters. Pushkin, who had continued to be the symbolic patriarch of Russian letters, receded into the past.

> Alexander Sergeyevich, it's hardest
> when one can't even mourn!

Mayakovsky had thus addressed himself to the spirit of Pushkin when life was becoming unbearable for him. But Mandelstam, who had a clairvoyant awareness of the times, was grieving the progressive cooling of "yesterday's sun," Pushkin, as early as 1921:

> A man dies, the heated sand cools down,
> And yesterday's sun is carried out on a black litter.

Pushkin's bright presence was being swept away by the great post-Revolutionary wave of disasters.

Not that the Revolutionary generation had lived in the past; quite the contrary. In essence, Pushkin's legacy is an acceptance of change. "One must live and write restlessly with the help of the new reserves that life offers," Pasternak said in 1960. "I am weary of the notion of faithfulness to a point of view at all cost." And Akhmatova has said: "In my poems lies my link to our times, to the new life of my people. As I wrote them I lived with the very rhythms that resounded through my land." These two were members of an intelligentsia that had hoped that revolution and humanism could be reconciled. Above all, the poets of that generation had been revolutionary in their writings. Mandelstam had revolutionized the world of poetic perceptions, breaking away from nineteenth-century intellectual and psychological concepts. Tsvetayeva, Mayakovsky, and Pasternak had created new, daring forms. As for Akhmatova, her innovating spirit is to be found in the realm of sentiment. She taught herself, and all of Russian womanhood (for her popularity was immense from her very first book of poems) to shed the coy Victorian attitudes with which she began life —to find inner freedom.

As far as we can judge by what is published today in Russia—an enormous amount of "fair" poetry, well-written and often unexciting works by hundreds of poets— Andrei Voznesensky is the most accomplished official young Soviet poet. He has the gift of fresh, witty perceptions; he works with unusual images and modern rhythms. His poetry is dynamic; he has an excellent feeling for movement in poetry. In contrast with his earlier works, his recent poems have a new, more intimate tone. Voznesensky has undergone a mutation as a poet in the last year or two. His low-keyed laments for himself and all those wounded by contemporary life are moving, though they lack the sparkling energy of his early poems. They were heralded in "Autumn in Sigulda," written in 1961:

> From the last platform of the moving train
>   I lean out:
> goodbye,
> goodbye, my summer!
>   The hour has come.
>   The sound of axes echoes outside the summer houses.
>   Already the wooden boards have nailed shut my door.
> Goodbye!

> My woods are shorn of their leafy crowns.
> Empty and melancholy they stand
>   like an old accordion case
>   from which the music has gone.

> Do you remember, love, the time you came upon me
> in the autumn woods
>   and asked me, oh, something,

dragging by the collar that silly dog
who wouldn't budge?
My thanks.

I came to life then.
And for the fall,
and for explaining me to myself,
for the landlady who got us up at eight
and for the noisy jazz, the hipster songs
on holidays,
my thanks.

But now you are leaving, leaving
like a train going out, leaving,
departing through my hollow pores.
We go out of each other as if this house
were bad for us.

You are still here, yet somehow far away,
almost in Vladivostok now.
We shall repeat ourselves, I know,
in friends and lovers,
in blades of grass —
one, and then another, will replace us.
Nature abhors a vacuum.

And last, my thanks
for the wind-shredded crowns of my forest —
a million leaves
will come here in our place
and grow, and learn your laws.

But look! There! down the long slope
a woman runs like a leaf of fire
behind the train —
Save us!

—ADAPTED BY ROSE STYRON

Despite his gifts, Voznesensky as a poet is not in the
same league as his teachers, Pasternak and Mayakovsky.
He is typical of a new Russian generation of writers, one

which is interested in individual rather than collective experience. The older poets, notably Pasternak, were also interested in the individual, but they generalized their experience, viewing it in the light of history and ethics. Voznesensky's poetic shifts and jumps seek to reveal the immediate, the unique. Born and brought up in Soviet Russia, Voznesensky accepts his society as it is. When he is hurt, it is life itself which is wounding him, rather than the particular political system under which he lives. Voznesensky is no rebel. A clear indication of his point of view is his recent poem about an earthquake—a blindly inflicted, completely meaningless disaster, against which there is no effective protest.

This is a significant aspect of contemporary Russia. In the works of Joseph Brodsky, another promising young poet—one who has no outward resemblance to Voznesensky—the reader detects the same existential aspirations and the same underlying passivity that can be found in Voznesensky's poems. But there is another dimension to Brodsky's poetry. His religious preoccupations reflect those of a growing body of Russians today who are rediscovering religion, usually in a mystical, individualistic manner. On the whole, Russians are trying to come to terms with their own conscience. They have never been told that they as a nation were guilty of Stalinist horrors; they are discouraged even from thinking about them. Those who are guilt-stricken—and many are—look into their own souls, and they listen avidly to poets who are able to reach them intimately, echoing their self-questioning and self-pity. The latter is a new note in Soviet poetry, but one suspects that it may become recurrent in the works of tomorrow's poets. Now that the heroic dreams are over, Russians are discovering how much they suffered—and allowed others to suffer. They cannot escape introspection with its pangs of terror and regret.

ALEXANDER ALEXANDROVICH BLOK

(1880–1921)

Like the tales of the Stuarts
the tales of our fathers,
farther away than Pushkin
the figures of dream.

Boris Pasternak, *1905*, 1926

BEAUTIFUL, tender, tormented, Alexander Blok dominated Russian poetry at the turn of the century. Blok was a Symbolist, and his work is at once extremely personal and typical of the Symbolist school. This is how D. S. Mirsky, one of the most knowledgeable Russian critics of the twenties, described the Symbolist movement in Russia: "Russian Symbolism is part of the general cultural upheaval that changed the face of Russian civilization between 1890 and 1910. It was at once an esthetic and a mystical movement: it raised the level of poetical craftsmanship, and it was united by a mystical attitude towards the world, which is expressed in the very name Symbolism. . . . The Symbolists actually saw the universe as a system of symbols. Everything was significant to them, not only by itself but as a reflection of something else. . . . The vision of the world as a 'forest of symbols' [cf. Baudelaire's 'Correspondences'] is an essential feature in the work of every Russian Symbolist and gives the whole school a distinctly metaphysical and mystic character. The only difference between the individual poets is the importance they attached to this mystical philosophy; to some, like Bryusov, Symbolism was primarily a form of art, and the 'forest of symbols' was only the material of which to build. But others, and among them the most original and characteristic poets of the schools—Ivanov, Blok, and Bely—wanted to make Symbolism above all a metaphysical and mystical philosophy, and poetry subservient to the higher ends of 'theurgy'. . . . Another feature common to all the Symbolist poets is the great stress laid on the emotional value of sounds."*

No one carried further than Blok the intense, bizarre mysticism of Russian Symbolism; no one had more influence on his contemporaries, notably on the young Revolutionary generation which followed his own by only a few years. The younger poets' love for Blok was profound and fraternal. All the doubts, all the fears, all the expectations which culminated in the Revolution had been deeply felt by Blok, and expressed by him.

In his youth the poet had been one of the founders of a new, neo-Platonic religion. He was twenty years old when his ethereal, musical verse was taken by some of his young poet-friends—and by himself—as an announcement of a new religious era. It was their belief that a "Beautiful Lady"—Wisdom, Sophia—was soon to descend upon the earth, bringing fresh metaphysical awareness to the world. But the poet lost his faith; the "Beautiful Lady" refused herself to him. After a traumatic break with his fellow Symbolists, Blok eventually elected for himself another "Beautiful Lady"—Russia. His love of Russia was that of a mystic, and he had a mystic's understanding of Russia's historical destiny. His gray-eyed handsomeness, his nobility of spirit, his sensitivity made him appear as an incarnation of the romantic poet, a knightlike figure. His visionary gifts were recognized by the Russian writers of that period. Pasternak saw an embodiment of the age in Blok:

. . . his style agreed with the spirit of the time, secretive, hiding, subterranean, barely emerging from the cellars, expressing himself in the language of conspirators—a spirit whose principal hero was the city, the main event, the street.

* D. S. Mirsky, *A History of Russian Literature*, Alfred Knopf, 1949.

In 1918 in a state of near trance, Blok wrote "The Twelve," and the poem was acclaimed at once as a masterpiece of the Revolution. No one expressed better than Blok the unleashing of elemental, yet specifically Russian forces which took place at that time:

Our sons have gone
to serve the Reds
to serve the Reds
to risk their heads!

O bitter, bitter pain,
Sweet living!
A torn overcoat
an Austrian gun!

— To get the bourgeois
We'll start a fire
a worldwide fire, and drench it in blood —
The good Lord bless us!

— O you bitter bitterness,
boring boredom,
deadly boredom.

This is how I will
spend my time.

This is how I will
scratch my head,

munch on seeds,
some sunflower seeds,

play with my knife
play with my knife.

You bourgeois, fly as a sparrow!
I'll drink your blood,

your warm blood, for love,
for dark-eyed love.

God, let this soul, your servant, rest in peace.

Such boredom!

Blok had been a socialist—the nonorthodox, nondogmatic kind. He himself was a victim of the Revolution. In 1921, while still a young man, he died. He had been deeply depressed; a poet who may be considered Russia's greatest after Pushkin was crushed less by the hardships of the Civil War than by his own premonitions of a terrifying future.

Blok's prophecies still haunt us today. His poem "The Scythians," which describes the position of Russia and the West in regard to Asia, has a prophetic ring. The Scythians, the ancient inhabitants of the south of Russia, who symbolize Russia in this poem, are addressing the West:

> You are but millions — we are an infinite number.
> Measure yourselves against us, try.
> We are the Scythians, we are the Asians
> With slanted and greedy eye.
>
> Centuries of your days are but an hour to us,
> Yet like obedient slaves,
> We've held a shield between two hostile races —
> Europe, and the Mongol hordes. . . .
>
> But time has come to term and the evil hour
> Flaps its wings. Each day multiplies
> Offenses: soon of your very Paestum
> There will be no trace. . . .
>
> From war and horror come to our open arms,
> The embrace of kin,
> Put the old sword away while there's time,
> Hail us as brothers. . . .
>
> Ah, Old World, before you have perished, join
> Our fraternal banquet. Hear,

Perhaps for the last time summoning you,
The barbaric lyre.

—ADAPTED BY ROSE STYRON

Blok's view of the poet's role in life was stated before a
solemn audience, in January, 1921, in his last, impas-
sioned public speech. He was commemorating the anniversary of Pushkin's death, and his homage to Pushkin
was a last call for freedom:

In the memory of our childhood, a joyful name lives on,
that of Pushkin. It is a proud sound, this name, enough to
fulfill many a day in our lifetime. Dark are the names of
emperors, great captains, inventors of assassinating instru-
ments, of hangmen and the martyrs of life. A brighter name
stands aside from these: Pushkin.

Pushkin bore his solemn burden with lightness and gaiety,
and yet the role of a poet is neither easy nor gay; it is tragic.
Pushkin played the role as a grand master, sure, free, and
with a broad control; and yet our heart is often torn at the
thought of Pushkin: the poet's joyful march of triumph,
which touched on nothing of the outer world—this march
was too often hindered by those heavy men who hold that a
kettle is more precious than God. . . .

On a day devoted to the memory of Pushkin, we shall not
argue whether he drew a careful distinction between what
we call "personal" and "political" liberty. We know that he
called for another "mysterious" liberty. For us it is "personal," but for the poet it isn't only that:

To reckon with no one else,
Serving and pleasing oneself.
To hold, among lackeys and kings,
Both head and conscience erect.
To walk about at one's ease,
Delighting in holy nature
And works of inspired art.
To sink in tender silence:
There is my justice, and joy.

—ADAPTED BY RICHARD RAND

34

Pushkin wrote this on the eve of his death. He had said the same thing in his youth:

> Love and mysterious liberty
> Raise in my heart a simple hymn.

Blok knew that Russia and her poets were coming into an age of trial. But this age was also to be a great age for poetry. A century before, Feydor Tyutchev had celebrated in his "Cicero" the exhilaration which may be experienced in "moments of destiny":

> When the state tore at itself in agony
> Rome's orator said, "I got up
> too late and the night of Rome overtook me
> on the way." Maybe,
> but as you bade farewell to Rome's glory
> you beheld from the Capitoline Hill
> her bloody star
> setting in full majesty.

> Blessèd is he
> whose visit to the world has fallen
> in its moments of destiny.
> The kind powers have welcomed him
> to their banquet, to converse as an equal. He
> sees the striding glories that they see,
> he has a place at their councils, he drinks
> from their own cup immortality,
> in his time he lives as they do in heaven.

> —ADAPTED BY W. S. MERWIN

Художник

В жаркое лето и в зиму мятельную,
В дни наших свадеб, торжеств, похорон,
Жду, чтоб спугнул мою скуку смертельную
Легкий, доселе неслышанный звон.

Вот он—возник. С холодным вниманием
Жду, что понять, закрепить и убить.
И перед зорким моим ожиданием
Тянет он еле приметную нить.

С моря ли вихрь? Или сирины райские
В листьях поют? Или время стоит?
Или осыпали яблони майские
Снежный свой цвет? Или ангел летит?

Длятся часы, мировое несущие.
Ширятся звуки, движенье и свет.
Прошлое страстно глядится в грядущее.
Нет настоящего. Жалкого—нет.

И, наконец, у предела зачатия
Новой души, неизведанных сил,—
Душу сражает, как громом, проклятие:
Творческий разум осилил—убил.

И замыкаю я в клетку холодную
Легкую, добрую птицу свободную,
Птицу, хотевшую смерть унести,
Птицу, летевшую душу спасти.

Вот моя клетка—стальная, тяжелая,
Как золотая в вечернем огне.
Вот моя птица, когда-то веселая,
Обруч качает, поет на окне.

Крылья подрезаны, песни заучены.
Любите вы под окном постоять?
Песни вам нравятся. Я же, измученный,
Нового жду—и скучаю опять.

1913

THE ARTIST

Torpid summers, snow-choked winters,
at all your weddings, birthdays, funerals,
always I listen for a dim, unheard chime
to drive away my deadly boredom.

There . . . ! Now, with cold concentration, I wait
—to understand, to pin it down, to kill it.
And as I wait intently, a thread begins
to spin itself, half perceptibly, before me.

Is that a whirlwind blown from the sea? Or legendary birds
in chorus among the leaves? Does Time exist?
Was that an explosion of white petals, or light
springing in plumes from a divine shoulder?

Hours pass, bearing the weight of the whole world.
Sound, motion, light, are bursting. The past
gazes deep in the eyes of the future. There is no present.
There's nothing left requiring pity.

And at last, as something new is thrusting toward birth,
some new soul, a mysterious energy,
creative reason strikes like a lightningbolt
and masters it, and kills it.

And I lock into a cold cage
the airy, wild, merciful feathers,
the bird that was flying to capture death,
the bird of salvation.

You see my cage, its thick steel bands
glittering coldly in the evening fires.
And here's my bird, my tamed gypsy,
pleased with its hoop, swinging and singing.

The wings are clipped, the song's by rote.
You like to listen, standing under the window.
But I, worn out with pain, am only waiting;
boredom sits on me like an aching scar.

—ADAPTED BY ADRIENNE RICH

37

З. Н. Гиппиус

Рожденные в года глухие
Пути не помнят своего.
Мы—дети страшных лет России—
Забыть не в силах ничего.

Испепеляющие годы!
Безумья ль в вас, надежды ль весть?
От дней войны, от дней свободы—
Кровавый отсвет в лицах есть.

Есть немота — то гул набата
Заставил заградить уста.
В сердцах, восторженных когда-то,
Есть роковая пустота.

И пусть над нашим смертным ложем
Взовьется с криком воронье,—
Те, кто достойней, боже, боже,
Да у́зрят царствие твое!

1914

TO ZINAIDA GIPPIUS

Those born in backwater years
forget their own way. Russia
gave birth to us in her years of anguish
and we can forget nothing.

Years of holocaust, do you
herald madness, or the advent of hope?
Days of war, days of freedom,
have stained our faces with bloody light.

We are speechless. The bells'
alarms sealed our lips. Where there was
a burning in our hearts once
there is nothing now, fixed, like a death.

Over the bed where we are dying
let the hoarse ravens sail—
may others, more worthy, O God, O God,
gaze on Thy kingdom!

—ADAPTED BY W. S. MERWIN

ANNA ANDREYEVNA AKHMATOVA
(1889–1966)

I did not look in moments of blossoming,
Cassandra, for your lips, Cassandra, for your eyes.
But now December, somber, watches
And in remembrance, torture lies.

Osip Mandelstam, "To Anna Akhmatova," 1917
—ADAPTED BY ROSE STYRON

ANNA ANDREYEVNA AKHMATOVA was essentially a St. Petersburg poetess; the refined sobriety of her verse is representative of that most orderly, most European of Russian cities. She became a famous St. Petersburg literary figure in 1912, when her first book of poems was published there. Her early verse was intensely feminine, sensitive, uncannily exact in capturing delicate shadings of emotion. Breaking as it did with literary conventions, and more specifically with Symbolist mannerisms, it created a fashion in pre-Revolutionary literary circles and was widely, though unsuccessfully, imitated. Today's reader may find this early work not altogether free of Victorian conceits.

Until her death in 1966, Akhmatova grew steadily as an artist, never ceasing to write, even in difficult times. Her biography, like that of many Russians of her age, is a succession of tragedies. Her former husband, the well-known St. Petersburg poet Nikolai Gumilev, was shot by the Bolsheviks in the early twenties; her son was sent to a labor camp in Siberia. She herself lived through part of the Leningrad siege, later to undergo many years of anguish and hardships during the Zhdanovshchina, an era of postwar Stalinist cultural repression known for its enforcer, Zhdanov. In her later work, perhaps as the result of her suffering, the universality of her themes sometimes evokes Pushkin himself, the greatest of all the St. Petersburg poets.

Despite her age and failing health—she suffered a heart attack in 1961—Akhmatova's last poems, of a very classical turn, are superb. She also found energy during those final years for occasional stays in Moscow, where literary life is more active than in Leningard. She went abroad twice in 1965—to Italy and England.

With an introduction from my father, the poet Vadim Andreyev, I called on Akhmatova at the home of friends with whom she was staying during one of her Moscow visits. It was in the early spring of 1962, and the weather was unusually mild. De-Stalinization in the U.S.S.R. was then at its most uninhibited; politically it was an exceptionally liberal, optimistic time. Throughout the capital the atmosphere was carefree, as the sun grew hotter and Orthodox Easter and the May First parade neared.

The apartment where Akhmatova stayed was near the Kremlin, in an old section full of ancient half-ruined churches, narrow streets, and muddy little squares where children played. An inner court which was a sea of melting snow, and then a flight of dark drafty stairs, scarcely prepared me for the modest but pleasant, well-lit apartment, full of comfortable old-fashioned furniture, its walls lined with books, paintings, and framed theatrical posters. Trees stood close to the tall double windows of the living-dining room. Their branches, which almost touched the windowpanes, were barely dusted with pale green.

Akhmatova intimidated me at first; her movements were slow and noble. She was portly and tall, and held her head high. She had a magnificent Bourbon profile softened by wings of gray hair; her profile, her expressive carriage, had been famous since youth. (Modigliani captured them in a beautiful drawing made in Paris in 1912, which was still in Akhmatova's possession. In it, the poetess, her head bowed, looks like a thoughtful slim muse.)

43

Akhmatova received me agreeably, yet without warmth, as a queen entertains foreign ambassadors, with benevolent tolerance and the suggestion that homage was due her. She unquestionably deserved homage, for she was not only a great poet, she was also an embodiment of Russian vitality and artistic conscience. She was a writer who had survived and developed in difficult, often horrifying, times without losing her courage and her sense of honor. I was happy to be able to tell her that all those interested in Russian letters outside of the U.S.S.R. knew and admired her work, both her early verse and her later poems, such as "Poem Without a Hero" and "Requiem," which is dedicated to those who perished in the purges of the late thirties and to their relatives who stood in the prison lines of Leningrad.

As she receivd her guests, for an hour or so at a time, Akhmatova sat on a half-moon red velvet couch that stood between the windows of the living room. During that time her hosts—the well-known Moscow playwright Ardov and his family—usually retired to another part of the apartment. On the round dining table near her there was a telephone that rang frequently. Most of the calls were for Akhmatova, from friends wishing to see her, from editors, from anonymous admirers. The news that she was in Moscow had spread throughout the capital. She answered the phone in an even, rather distant tone, making appointments with the editors, exchanging news with friends. Often she invoked her health in order to turn down social commitments and discourage new admirers from visiting.

I called on Akhmatova several times that spring. She always had a kind of majestic graciousness, in harmony with her whole person, massive but elegant. In the mornings she wore a silk robe edged in purple (purple was her favorite color, an inheritance perhaps from the fashions of the turn of the century) and sometimes an embroidered ivory silk Chinese shawl. In the afternoons she wore a dark suit.

After exchanging formal greetings and a few stiff comments on daily topics, our conversation turned to literature and became more free-flowing. Akhmatova was interested in French literature, but deplored the sterility of its recent trends. "There is no French poetry any more . . ." As usual, she quickly moved on to other literary matters. I was continually struck by the breadth of her interests. She discussed the fine points of Shakespearean translation into Russian and then took up the problems of interpreting certain events which led to Pushkin's death (she was one of the U.S.S.R.'s most passionate "Pushkinists").

Her conversation often centered on her contemporaries in pre-Revolutionary St. Petersburg, which was then the leading center of Russian literary life. Conflicting poetic movements competed there, and she explained at length the intricate relationships which existed between various rival groups — Symbolists, Decadents, and Acmeists like herself. In one of these discussions she touched upon the enmity she had sensed in those distant years in certain of her elders who were jealous of her fame; she had become a celebrated poetess when she was barely twenty. She also talked with intense admiration about another St. Petersburg poet, Osip Mandelstam, who was an intimate till his death in Siberia in 1938.

I was engrossed by Akhmatova's whole presence, by her enormous yet utterly unpedantic erudition, but I found her forbidding; she had a kind of dignified narcissism. She was always strained, as if her equanimity and her poetic achievements were the result of some hard-won daily battle with herself. Once she spoke to me about another woman poet, Marina Tsvetayeva, whom I had known in Paris as a child. Her tone was reserved, and it was clear that she had treated Tsvetayeva coldly when they had met shortly after Tsvetayeva's return from France. Of course the times were terrifying — it was the aftermath of the great purges — and suspicion was everywhere. Nonetheless, knowing how ardently Tsvetayeva had worshiped her as a poet and admired her as a person — above all, how soon after this visit she had committed suicide — I was saddened.*

The feeling of discomfort I felt with Akhmatova was dispelled whenever, at my request, she recited some of her poems to me. I had the impression of partaking in a poetic rite when I followed her into a back room of the apartment. She shut the door so as not to be disturbed even by the discreet household activities of her hosts, and sat at a tiny writing table, placing me across from her. Reciting from memory, her eyes half closed, her head slightly bowed, she seemed to listen deeply to the music of her own verse. She usually recited three or four poems in succession. Her voice was muffled yet melodious, and her reading had the incantatory quality of many Russian poets' reading; it emphasized the sounds rather than the meaning of the poem. The sound was slightly monotonous; yet paradoxically, the poems took on a marvelous life as she said them. Sitting close to her, I could see her profile against the light, and her arms, still rounded and youthful, resting on the desk. Once she recited her "Muse," an early poem, and it had a strange immediacy:

> Sometimes at night I wait for her coming
> And life seems to hang by a frail strand.
> Ah, what are glory and youth and freedom
> Beside the fair muse, a flute in her hand!
> Now she comes in, throwing back her mantle,
> And waits for my look: the attentive guest.

* Sometime after our conversation, Akhmatova dedicated a short, sympathetic poem to Tsvetayeva's memory.

"Was it you who came to play for Dante
The Inferno?" I ask, and she answers, "Yes."

1914
—ADAPTED BY ROSE STYRON

On another occasion she chose poems about the imperial, park-graced Tsarskoe Selo, where she had lived as a young woman. She urged me to go there on a pilgrimage to see the famous lycée that Pushkin attended as an adolescent. "I of course will never return to Tsarskoe," she said. "The place has been rather well restored after the war—but for me, too much has changed, too much of myself has lived and died there. . . ."

One sunny midday in late April we went for a walk. I helped Akhmatova across the muddy inner court of the apartment house, and we sat for a while in a little square next to an abandoned church. It was an eighteenth-century building with a cluster of cupolas and finely sculptured white stucco walls. I remember recalling to myself a poem addressed by Mandelstam to Tsvetayeva just before the Revolution:

The cupoled churches of Moscow
    With their Italian-Russian souls,
Are like Aurora's apparition
    —But with a Russian name, and wrapped in furs.*

The sky was a deep blue with round white clouds floating past the verdigris cupolas of the church. Akhmatova was speaking about the Russian language, how it was losing its purity under the influence of a technological culture. Near us a young mother called to her child: "Vikenty, Vikenty!" Vikenty is Vincent in Russian, and Akhmatova was dismayed by such a foreign sounding name given to a blond, round-cheeked Russian toddler.

When asked about her work, she regained her com-

* Many Moscow churches were built by Italian architects in the sixteenth and seventeenth centuries.

posure and said, "I have never stopped writing. I wrote my first poem when I was eleven. My poetry is my link with our times. When I write, I live with the very pulse of Russian life. . . ."

She recalled the heroic twenties. When she mentioned Pasternak, I had the feeling that nothing, not even the admiration now bestowed on her by her Russian contemporaries could make up for the fleeing years: "Boris Leonidovich was lyricism personified. He would have said, 'Anna Andreyevna in Moscow—but it is a real Akhmatovka!' It sounds like the name of a railroad station—it evokes a great deal of noise and confusion. It is the stream of friendly and literary visits, of phone calls that I cannot resist when I come to Moscow. Today a young poet is calling at five, then a delegation of physicists is coming to record some poems."

We came to the subject which interested me particularly, the immense popularity of poetry in contemporary U.S.S.R. "No, let us not make hasty comparisons," Akhmatova said when I inquired whether the present atmosphere reminded her of her youth. "The twenties were years of poetic blossoming, but interest in poetry was limited to the literary milieu. Our printings, even those of Mayakovsky, the most popular among us, were of the order of a couple of thousand copies. Now, since 1940, my books of poems have totaled a hundred thousand copies in print. On the other hand, this is an age of facility. I do not share your admiration for the fashionable poets of the younger generation. It is all *epigonstvo* —derivativeness. Not without vulgarity. It seems to me that the vogue for poetry which characterizes this era is altogether a new happening in Russia. It is by no means limited to a small group of people. In my experience, scientists are the most sophisticated, sensitive readers of poetry—much more refined in their perceptions than most young writers today.

48

"Because I was persecuted in Stalinist times, foreign scholars seem unaware that in what is an entirely new, freer atmosphere, I continue to write. The scientists rediscovered me first. Now Soviet editors compete for my new verse; I am asked to make records of my readings; people come from all over to see me."

It occurred to me that in spite of her age and of the very real lack of physical comforts (for example, she could not have her own apartment in Moscow, since she had a residence in Komarovo, a suburb of Leningrad), Akhmatova's fate might be envied by Western poets. A life of suffering, dedicated to an esoteric art, was suddenly meeting with an immense human echo.

Читая Гамлета

У кладбища направо пылил пустырь,
А за ним голубела река.
Ты сказал мне: «Ну что ж, иди в монастырь
Или замуж за дурака...»

Принцы только такое всегда говорят,
Но я эту запомнила речь,—
Пусть струится она сто веков подряд
Горностаевой мантией с плеч.

1909

Память о солнце в сердце слабеет,
Желтей трава,
Ветер снежинками ранними веет
Едва-едва.

В узких каналах уже не струится—
Стынет вода,
Здесь никогда ничего не случится,—
О, никогда!

Ива на небе пустом распластала
Веер сквозной.
Может быть лучше, что я не стала
Вашей женой.

Память о солнце в сердце слабеет.
Что это?—Тьма?
Может быть! За ночь прийти успеет
Зима.

1911

Вечером

Звенела музыка в саду
Таким невыразимым горем.
Свежо и остро пахли морем
На блюде устрицы во льду.

READING HAMLET

A barren patch to the right of the cemetery,
Behind it a river flashing blue.
You said: "All right then, get thee to a nunnery,
Or go get married to a fool . . ."

It was the sort of thing that princes always say,
But these are words that one remembers.
May they flow a hundred centuries in a row
Like an ermine mantle from his shoulders.

—ADAPTED BY STANLEY KUNITZ

Heart's memory of sun grows fainter,
Sallow is the grass,
A few flakes toss in the wind
Scarcely, scarcely.

The narrow canals no longer flow,
They are frozen over.
Nothing will ever happen here,
Oh, never!

In the bleak sky the willow spreads
Its bare-boned fan.
Maybe I'm better off as I am,
Not as your wife.

Heart's memory of sun grows fainter.
What's this? Darkness?
Perhaps! This very night will bring
The winter.

—ADAPTED BY STANLEY KUNITZ

IN THE EVENING

On the terrace, violins played
the most heartbreaking songs.
A sharp, fresh smell of the sea
came from oysters on a dish of ice.

Он мне сказал: «Я верный друг!»
И моего коснулся платья.
Как не похожи на объятья
Прикосновенья этих рук.

Так гладят кошек или птиц,
Так на наездниц смотрят стройных.
Лишь смех в глазах его спокойных
Под легким золотом ресниц.

А скорбных скрипок голоса
Поют за стелющимся дымом:
«Благослови же небеса:
Ты первый раз одна с любимым».

1913

Есть в близости людей заветная черта,
Ее не перейти влюбленности и страсти,—
Пусть в жуткой тишине сливаются уста,
И сердце рвется от любви на части.

И дружба здесь бессильна, и года
Высокого и огненного счастья,
Когда душа свободна и чужда
Медлительной истоме сладострастья.

Стремящиеся к ней безумны, а ее
Достигшие—поражены тоскою...
Теперь ты понял, отчего мое
Не бьется сердце под твоей рукою.

1915

Александру Блоку

Я пришла к поэту в гости.
Ровно полдень. Воскресенье.
Тихо в комнате просторной,
А за окнами мороз

He said: *I'm a faithful friend,*
touching my dress.
How far from a caress,
the touch of that hand!

The way you stroke a cat, a bird,
the look you give a shapely bareback rider.
In his calm eyes, only laughter
under the light-gold lashes.

And the violins mourn on
behind drifting smoke:
Thank your stars, you're at last alone
with the man you love.

—ADAPTED BY ADRIENNE RICH

There's a secret boundary hidden in the waving grasses:
neither the lover nor the expert sensualist
passes it, though mouths press silently together
and the heart is bursting.

And friends—they too lose their nerve there,
and so with years of fire and joy,
whole histories of high freedom
unburdened by sensual languor.

The crazy ones push on to that frontier,
while those who have found it are sick with grief . . .
And now you know
why my heart doesn't beat beneath your hand.

—ADAPTED BY ADRIENNE RICH

TO ALEXANDER BLOK

I have come to call on the poet.
It is Sunday, exactly midday.
The wide room is filled with quiet
and through the casements now I see

И малиновое солнце
Над лохматым сизым дымом...
Как хозяин молчаливый
Ясно смотрит на меня!

У него глаза такие,
Что запомнить каждый должен,
Мне же лучше, осторожной,
В них и вовсе не глядеть.

Но запомнится беседа,
Дымный полдень, воскресенье,
В доме сером и высоком
У морских ворот Невы.

1914

Борис Пастернак

Он, сам себя сравнивший с конским глазом,
Косится, смотрит, видит, узнает,
И вот уже расплавленным алмазом
Сияют лужи, изнывает лед.

В лиловой мгле покоятся задворки,
Платформы, бревна, листья, облака.
Свист паровоза, хруст арбузной корки,
В душистой лайке робкая рука.

Звенит, гремит, скрежещет, бьет прибоем
И вдруг притихнет,—это значит, он
Пугливо пробирается по хвоям,
Чтоб не спугнуть пространства чуткий сон.

И это значит, он считает зерна
В пустых колосьях, это значит, он
К плите дарьяльской, проклятой и черной,
Опять пришел с каких-то похорон.

И снова жжет московская истома,
Звенит вдали смертельный бубенец—
Кто заблудился в двух шагах от дома,
Где снег по пояс и всему конец...

a purple sun suspended in frost
over the winding disheveled gray
smoke. My silent host
(how clearly) looks at me.

Luminous, clairvoyant eyes—
Who could forget their gaze? I,
Being prudent, make a choice:
not to look into them. I turn away.

But I shall remember always
that smoky noon, Sunday
in a quiet high gray house
where the Neva courts the sea.

—ADAPTED BY ROSE STYRON

BORIS PASTERNAK

"The eye of a horse," he called his vision,
and now with his sidelong sight records
the puddles like liquid diamonds glistening,
the ice seized with a sudden longing,

lilac shadows in drugged backyards
and logs and leaves and clouds and the rind
of a melon cracking, the train's whistle,
and gloved in fragrant kid a shy hand.

His world goes roaring, scraping, banging,
beats as the tide beats . . . hush!
he runs with care over dry pine needles
not to startle the light sleep of space.

Or, look, he's picking out all the seeds
from empty pods; to a black Caucasian
monument in the cursed ravine
after a long funeral he's come.

And Moscow glows in sensuous languor;
a distant sleigh bell, augur, mourns
someone who's lost forever near home
in a drift of waist-deep snow.

За то, что дым сравнил с Лаокооном,
Кладбищенский воспел чертополох,
За то, что мир наполнил новым звоном
В пространстве новом отраженных строф,

Он награжден каким-то вечным детством,
Той щедростью и зоркостью светил,
И вся земля была его наследством,
А он ее со всеми разделил.

1936

Лотова жена

И праведник шел за посланником Бога,
Огромный и светлый, по черной горе.
Но громко жене говорила тревога—
Не поздно, ты можешь еще посмотреть

На красные башни родного Содома,
На площадь, где пела, на двор, где пряла,
На окна пустые высокого дома,
Где милому мужу детей родила.

Взглянула, и, скованы смертною болью,
Глаза ее больше смотреть не могли;
И сделалось тело прозрачною солью,
И быстрые ноги к земле приросли.

Кто женщину эту оплакивать будет?
Не меньшей ли мнится она из утрат?
Лишь сердце мое никогда не забудет
Отдавшую жизнь за единственный взгляд.

1922–1924

Н. В. Рыковой-Гуковской

Все расхищено, предано, продано,
Черной смерти мелькало крыло,
Все голодной тоскою изглодано,—
Отчего же нам стало светло?

Smoke he compared to Laocoön
and sang the cemetery thistle
and filled the air with a carillon
of stanzas ringing in new air

and so perceived, the generous stars
gave him the soul of a child to keep
and a heritage of earth and sky
he shares with us though we sleep.

—ADAPTED BY ROSE STYRON

Lot's Wife

The just man followed then his angel guide
Where he strode on the black highway, hulking and bright;
But a wild grief in his wife's bosom cried,
Look back, it is not too late for a last sight

Of the red towers of your native Sodom, the square
Where once you sang, the gardens you shall mourn,
And the tall house with empty windows where
You loved your husband and your babes were born.

She turned, and looking on the bitter view
Her eyes were welded shut by mortal pain;
Into transparent salt her body grew,
And her quick feet were rooted in the plain.

Who would waste tears upon her? Is she not
The least of our losses, this unhappy wife?
Yet in my heart she will not be forgot
Who, for a single glance, gave up her life.

—ADAPTED BY RICHARD WILBUR

To N. V. Rikov-Gukovski

All is despoiled, abandoned, sold;
Death's wing has swept the sky of color;
All's eaten by a hungry dolor.
What is this light which we behold?

Днем дыханьями веет вишневыми
Небывалый под городом лес,
Ночью блещет созвездьями новыми
Глубь прозрачных июльских небес.

И так близко подходит чудесное
К развалившимся грязным домам,
Никому, никому неизвестное,
Но от века желанное нам.

1922

Реквием

Нет, и не под чуждым небосводом,
И не под защитой чуждых крыл,—
Я была тогда с моим народом,
Там, где мой народ, к несчастью, был.

1961

ВМЕСТО ПРЕДИСЛОВИЯ

В страшные годы ежовщины я провела семнадцать месяцев в тюремных очередях в Ленинграде. Как-то раз кто-то «опознал» меня. Тогда стоящая за мной женщина с голубыми губами, которая, конечно, никогда не слыхала моего имени, очнулась от свойственного нам всем оцепенения и спросила меня на ухо (там все говорили шепотом):

— А это вы можете описать?

И я сказала:

— Могу.

Тогда что-то вроде улыбки скользнуло по тому, что некогда было ее лицом.

1 апреля 1957

Odors of cherry blossom sigh
From the rumored forest beyond the town.
At night, new constellations crown
The high, clear heavens of July.

Closer it comes, and closer still,
To houses ruinous and blind:
Some marvelous thing still undivined,
Some fiat of the century's will.

—ADAPTED BY RICHARD WILBUR

THE REQUIEM

Dedicated to the victims of the Stalinist repression in the late thirties, the Yezhovshchina, named after Yezhov, who was head of the secret police at the time. The *streltsi* were Peter the Great's musketeers whom he suspected of treason and had executed, with all sorts of refinements in cruelty, at the gates of the Kremlin in the presence of their families.

I wasn't under a new sky,
its birds were the old familiar birds.
They still spoke Russian. Misery
spoke familiar Russian words.

BY WAY OF INTRODUCTION

In the terrible years of the Yezhovshchina, I spent seventeen months in the prison lines at Leningrad. Once, someone somehow recognized me. Then a woman standing behind me, her lips blue with cold, who had of course never heard of me, woke up from the stupor that enveloped us, and asked me, whispering in my ear (for we only spoke in whispers):
"Could you describe this?"
I said, "I can."
Then something like a smile glided over what was once her face.

59

ПОСВЯЩЕНИЕ

Перед этим горем гнутся горы,
Не течет великая река,
Но крепки тюремные затворы,
А за ними «каторжные норы»
И смертельная тоска.
Для кого-то веет ветер свежий,
Для кого-то нежится закат—
Мы не знаем, мы повсюду те же,
Слышим лишь ключей постылый скрежет
Да шаги тяжелые солдат.
Подымались как к обедне ранней,
По столице одичалой шли,
Там встречались, мертвых бездыханней,
Солнце ниже и Нева туманней,
А надежда все поет вдали.
Приговор... И сразу слезы хлынут,
Ото всех уже отделена,
Словно с болью жизнь из сердца вынут,
Словно грубо навзничь опрокинут,
Но идет... Шатается... Одна...
Где теперь невольные подруги
Двух моих осатанелых лет?
Что им чудится в сибирской вьюге,
Что мерещится им в лунном круге?
Им я шлю прощальный свой привет.

Март, 1940

ВСТУПЛЕНИЕ

Это было, когда улыбался
Только мертвый, спокойствию рад.
И ненужным привеском качался
Возле тюрем своих Ленинград.
И когда, обезумев от муки,
Шли уже осужденных полки,
И короткую песню разлуки
Паровозные пели гудки.

DEDICATION

Grief turns the Neva to green glass,
soon the abiding hills are dust,
and yet the prison locks stand fast,
the convict, kicking in his lair,
breathes the consuming air.

For someone somewhere, a fresh wind;
for someone the low sun is a live coal,
but we know nothing. Blind and small,
we hear the keys clang through wards,
the sleepwalk of the guards.

Up, out, as if for early Mass—
when we prowled through wild Leningrad,
we were more breathless than the dead,
and lower than the sun. Low fog,
soon leveled out to fog.

We hoped! The verdict? . . . only tears,
each one cut off from everyone,
rudely cut off, tripped up, thrown down,
blood siphoned from the heart. Dead stone,
she walks still, sways . . . alone.

Oh two years' hell-black, line-up nights,
cry, cry, for your imprisoned friend,
clothe him from the Siberian wind,
shine in the haloed moon's snow eye . . .
I say good-bye, good-bye.

INTRODUCTION

Then only the hollow, smiling dead
dared to draw breath and sing;
by blocks and prisons, Leningrad
throbbed like a useless wing.

There convict regiments, miles long,
and mad with suffering,
heard engines hiss their marching song,
the cattle cars' wheel-ring.

Звезды смерти стояли над нами,
И безвинная корчилась Русь
Под кровавыми сапогами
И под шинами черных марусь.

1

Уводили тебя на рассвете,
За тобой, как на выносе, шла,
В темной горнице плакали дети,
У божницы свеча оплыла.
На губах твоих холод иконки.
Смертный пот на челе не забыть.
Буду я, как стрелецкие женки,
Под кремлевскими башнями выть.

1935

2

Тихо льется тихий Дон,
Желтый месяц входит в дом,

Входит в шапке набекрень,
Видит желтый месяц тень.

Эта женщина больна,
Эта женщина одна,

Муж в могиле, сын в тюрьме,
Помолитесь обо мне.

3

Нет, это не я, это кто-то другой страдает.
Я бы так не могла, а то, что случилось,
Пусть черные сукна покроют,
И пусть унесут фонари...
            Ночь.

4

Показать бы тебе, насмешнице
И любимице всех друзей,
Царскосельской веселой грешнице,
Что случится с жизнью твоей—

The star of death stood over us;
Russia convulsed, as ominous
removal trucks and black
police boots broke her back.

I

They led you off at dawn. I followed,
as if I walked behind your bier.
In the dark rooms, the children bellowed,
wax melted in the icon's glare.

Cold the small icon's final kiss,
cold the lined forehead's greenish sweat—
like the wives of the Streltsis,
I'll howl beneath the Kremlin's gate.

2

The dragging Don flows slow, so slow,
the orange moon climbs through a window.

Its hat is slanted on its brow,
the yellow moon has met a shadow.

This woman is alone,
no one will give the dog a bone.

Her husband's killed, her son's in prison;
Kyrie eleison!

3

Myself! No, she is someone else,
I couldn't take it. Light
no lanterns in these death cells—
black cloths for windows . . . night!

4

Think back on Tsarskoe's play world, soon
outgrown, soon dated, show-off child—
the tree house built to reach the moon . . .
Oh what has happened to that child?

Как трехсотая, с передачею,
Под Крестами будешь стоять
И своей слезою горячею
Новогодний лед прожигать.
Там тюремный тополь качается,
И ни звука—а сколько там
Неповинных жизней кончается . . .

5

Семнадцать месяцев кричу,
Зову тебя домой.
Кидалась в ноги палачу,
Ты сын и ужас мой.
Все перепуталось навек,
И мне не разобрать
Теперь, кто зверь, кто человек,
И долго ль казни ждать.
И только пыльные цветы,
И звон кадильный, и следы
Куда-то в никуда.
И прямо мне в глаза глядит
И скорой гибелью грозит
Огромная звезда.

6

Легкие летят недели,
Что случилось, не пойму.
Как тебе, сынок, в тюрьму
Ночи белые глядели,
Как они опять глядят
Ястребиным жарким оком,
О твоем кресте высоком
И о смерти говорят.

1939

Number 300 in the queues
of women lugging food and news
for felons. . . . Will your scalding tear
burn an ice hole in the new year?

No sound. A prison poplar waves
over the deadly closeness, waves
of white leaves whiten in the wind—
what innocent lives have reached the end!

5

For one month, five months, seventeen,
I called you back. I screamed
at the foot of the executioner.
You are my son, my fear.

Thoughts rush in circles through my head;
I can't distinguish white from red,
who is a man, and who a beast,
or when your firing squad will rest.

Here there are only musty flowers,
old clock hands tramping out the hours,
old incense drifting from a censer,
and somewhere, boot steps leading nowhere.

See, see, it pins us down from far;
now looking straight into my eye,
"Move quickly, be prepared to die,"
says the huge star.

6

These weeks are lightweight runners. Light
of foot, they skin the oblivious snow.
Son, tell me how the white-capped night
looks through your prison window.

"It watches with the owl's hard eye,
or chokes the air with its white snow.
It speaks to us of Calvary,
it speaks of death."

7

ПРИГОВОР

И упало каменное слово
На мою еще живую грудь.
Ничего, ведь я была готова,
Справлюсь с этим как-нибудь.

У меня сегодня много дела:
Надо память до конца убить,
Надо, чтоб душа окаменела,
Надо снова научиться жить.

А не то... Горячий шелест лета,
Словно праздник за моим окном.
Я давно предчувствовала этот
Светлый день и опустелый дом.

Лето, 1939

8

К СМЕРТИ

Ты все равно придешь—зачем же не теперь?
Я жду тебя—мне очень трудно.
Я потушила свет и отворила дверь
Тебе, такой простой и чудной.
Прими для этого какой угодно вид,
Ворвись отравленным снарядом
Иль с гирькой подкрадись, как опытный бандит,
Иль отрави тифозным чадом.
Иль сказочкой, придуманной тобой
И всем до тошноты знакомой,—
Чтоб я увидела верх шапки голубой
И бледного от страха управдома.
Мне все равно теперь. Клубится Енисей,
Звезда полярная сияет.
И синий блеск возлюбленных очей
Последний ужас застилает.

19 августа 1939
Фонтанный Дом
Ленинград

7

THE VERDICT

At last the silent judge spoke out,
and struck us with his stony word—
but never mind, I will make out,
I was prepared.

Stones, chores . . . I'll manage. Splitting rock
stops the split mind from looking back.
I can forget you now and then,
turn stone, and learn to live again—

or else? The woods' hot rustle, boughs
bursting, a window flying open . . .
I had long had a premonition
of this clear day and empty house.

8

TO DEATH

You will come anyway, so why not now?
I wait for you. Now truly miserable,
I've turned my lights off and unlocked the door.
You are so simple and so wonderful.

Come to me in whatever shape you will:
a poison-bomb shell, or the typhus mist—
housebreaker, coming from behind to kill,
lifting a clubbed revolver in your fist.

Come to me as your own invention, Fate,
familiar to the point of nausea here—
I want to see the top of the blue hat,
the cringing stupor of the janitor.

All's one now. In Siberia,
rivers are ice, the pole star shines from far,
and the blue rays of my beloved's eye
burn through the daily torture. Let me die.

9

Уже безумие крылом
Души закрыло половину,
И поит огненным вином
И манит в черную долину,

И поняла я, что ему
Должна я уступить победу,
Прислушиваясь к своему
Уже как бы чужому бреду.

И не позволит ничего
Оно мне унести с собою
(Как ни упрашивай его
И как ни докучай мольбою):

Ни сына страшные глаза —
Окаменелое страданье,
Ни день, когда пришла гроза,
Ни час тюремного свиданья,

Ни милую прохладу рук,
Ни лип взволнованные тени,
Ни отдаленный легкий звук—
Слова последних утешений.

4 мая 1940
Фонтанный Дом

10

РАСПЯТИЕ

«Не рыдай Мене, Мати,
во гробе сущу».

I

Хор ангелов великий час восславил,
И небеса расплавились в огне.
Отцу сказал: «Почто Меня оставил!»
А Матери: «О, не рыдай Мене ...»

9

MADNESS

Already madness — on my breast
are three black moles. I see a fox:
two ears, black muzzle. Let me rest,
this bed I lie on is a pine box.

So simple and so wonderful!
Careful to stress each syllable
the allegoric voices hiss,
I lie decoding images.

I've breathed in red wine from the air!
Now sickness gathers up its gains,
and kicks me as I kneel in prayer,
and nothing of my own remains—

no, not my son's shy smile of wonder
that turned the bars to lines of shadow,
the woods' hot rustle, summer thunder,
our whispers at the prison window—

no, not the roughhouse of the boys,
birch boughs filled with the new birds,
light noises changing to a voice,
the ache of the last words.

10

THE CRUCIFIXION

"Mother, do not cry for me as I lie in my grave . . ."

I

When angel choirs proclaimed his agony,
and fire destroyed the April sky,
Christ questioned, "Why have you forsaken me?"
and told his Mother not to cry.

II

Магдалина билась и рыдала,
Ученик любимый каменел,
А туда, где молча Мать стояла,
Так никто взглянуть и не посмел.

1940–1943

ЭПИЛОГ

I

Узнала я, как опадают лица,
Как из-под век выглядывает страх,
Как клинописи жесткие страницы
Страдание выводит на щеках,
Как локоны из пепельных и черных
Серебряными делаются вдруг,
Улыбка вянет на губах покорных,
И в сухоньком смешке дрожит испуг.
И я молюсь не о себе одной,
А обо всех, кто там стоял со мною,
И в лютый холод, и в июльский зной,
Под красною ослепшею стеною.

II

Опять поминальный приблизился час.
Я вижу, я слышу, я чувствую вас:

И ту, что едва до конца довели,
И ту, что родимой не топчет земли,

И ту, что, красивой тряхнув головой,
Сказала: «Сюда прихожу, как домой».

Хотелось бы всех поименно назвать,
Да отняли список, и негде узнать.

Для них соткала я широкий покров
Из бедных, у них же подслушанных слов.

О них вспоминаю всегда и везде,
О них не забуду и в новой беде,

70

II

Magdalen fought and hit the officer,
the loved disciple stood like stone—
all this, God, but your Mother weeps alone;
none dares or cares to look at her.

EPILOGUE

I

An Assyrian sculptor carved your spear
and skewered flanks. Oh, lioness—
I've seen their faces die like grass,
the lowered eyelid's tick of fear.

I've seen the sick-blond curls grow rough,
snow rot the brown, smiles disappear
from soft, obedient mouths, as fear
suppressed its dry, embarrassed cough.

I pray for you, companions, all
who stood in lines with heavy feet,
come winter's cold or summer heat,
under the red and blinding wall.

II

And now the requiem hour has come,
I see you, hear you, feel you. Some
marched to their deaths in cheering ranks,
others have faded into blanks.

Some, coming to Siberia, said,
"Why worry, this is home at last."
Some lived. I'd write their names in red
forever, but the list is lost.

I've made a sort of elegy
drawn from the scattered words they spoke.
Braced for the terror's second stroke,
now and always, I hear their cry.

И если зажмут мой измученный рот,
Которым кричит стомильонный народ,

Пусть так же они поминают меня
В канун моего поминального дня.

А если когда-нибудь в этой стране
Воздвигнуть задумают памятник мне,

Согласье на это даю торжество,
Но только с условьем—не ставить его

Ни около моря, где я родилась:
Последняя с морем разорвана связь,

Ни в царском саду у заветного пня,
Где тень безутешная ищет меня,

А здесь, где стояла я триста часов
И где для меня не открыли засов.

Затем, что и в смерти блаженной боюсь
Забыть громыхание черных марусь,

Забыть, как постылая хлопала дверь
И выла старуха, как раненый зверь.

И пусть с неподвижных и бронзовых век
Как слезы струится подтаявший снег,

И голубь тюремный пусть гулит вдали,
И тихо идут по Неве корабли.

Март, 1940

Tomorrow's the memorial day,
a hundred million people pray
through my tired mouth and lethargy:
"Remember me, remember me."

Friends, if you want some monument
gravestone or cross to stand for me,
you have my blessing and consent,
but do not place it by the sea.

I was a sea-child, hardened by
the polar Baltic's grinding dark;
that tie is gone: I will not lie,
a Tsar's child in the Tsarist park.

Far from your ocean, Leningrad,
I leave my body where I stood
three hundred hours in lines with those
who watched unlifted prison windows.

Safe in death's arms, I lie awake,
and hear the mother's animal roar,
the black truck slamming on its brake,
the senseless hammering of the door.

Ah, the Bronze Horseman* wipes his eye
and melts, a prison pigeon coos,
the ice goes out, the Neva goes
with its slow barges to the sea.

—ADAPTED BY ROBERT LOWELL

* The statue of Peter the Great astride a horse, which stands in the
heart of Leningrad on the quays above the Neva River.

BORIS LEONIDOVICH PASTERNAK

(1890–1960)

It has cleared its way
And stares from the hill
Winter
Upon my life through the frightened yellow leaves.

> Boris Pasternak, "False Alarm," 1941

BORIS PASTERNAK was born in 1890 in Moscow, the eldest son of Leonid Pasternak, a noted painter, and Rosa Kaufman, a concert pianist. He grew up in an artistic, warm-hearted milieu. Leonid Pasternak was an admirer and follower of Leo Tolstoi; Anton Rubinstein, Scriabin, Rainer Maria Rilke, Verhaeren were friends of the family. The Pasternaks were an exceptional family, yet one representative of the vital, cultured pre-Revolutionary Moscow intelligentsia.

As a child Pasternak wanted to become a composer; Scriabin was his idol. However, at about twenty he gave up music altogether, and studied philosophy at Marburg, Germany, under Professor Herman Cohen, a famous neo-Kantian. An unhappy love affair (described in the "The Breakup") caused him to plunge into poetry, and soon philosophy became a secondary concern with him. "I think a little philosophy should be added to life and art by way of seasoning, but to make it one's specialty seems to me as strange as eating nothing but horseradish," Lara says in *Doctor Zhivago*.

In the twenties Pasternak became recognized as one of Russia's leading poets—one of six greats in the Revolutionary generation that included Mandelstam, Yesenin, Akhmatova, Tsvetayeva, and Mayakovsky. He never ceased to write poetry, and in years of political repression when his work was seldom published he earned his living with translations. His rendering of the

Georgian poets and of Shakespeare, Goethe, and Schiller
are among the finest in Russian. He also wrote two marvelous autobiographies (1931 and 1957).

In 1935 Pasternak came to Paris to attend an international writers' congress. He was under extreme pres-
sure, aware of the widening Stalinist purges and of the
oncoming war, suffering from chronic insomnia and
depression. He made only a brief speech at the congress:

> Poetry will always be too simple to serve as a subject mat-
> ter for discussion at public assemblies; it will remain the
> organic function of a happy human being, overflowing with
> all the felicity of language that thrills in a candid and gener-
> ous heart; and the greater number of happy men, the easier
> it will be to become an artist.

Thereafter, he led a secluded life in his small country
house in the writers' colony of Peredelkino. Miraculously
he escaped Stalinist persecutions, despite his Tolstoian
heritage, which committed him to complete truthfulness
at all times, as a writer and as a man.

In 1958 the publication outside Russia of his epic
novel *Doctor Zhivago* caused a hysterical reaction in
Soviet official circles. Pasternak was expelled from the
Writers' Union and was ostracized in the U.S.S.R., while
his international fame grew. After his death in 1960
came a slow official rehabilitation. His *Selected Works*
were published in Russia in 1965. The book, with a
preface by Andrei Sinyavsky, written shortly before his
arrest, includes most of the poems from *Doctor Zhivago*.
Pasternak is now the object of an ever-growing, popular
cult in Russia. Like Pushkin's grave at Mikhailovskoye
near Pskov, Pasternak's grave in the Peredelkino cemetery has become a national shrine.

In the winter of 1960, shortly before Pasternak's
death, I went to Moscow and was able to meet and to

interview the poet. I have described these meetings with him in *Voices in the Snow:**

We entered a village which was in complete contrast with the massive apartment projects growing on the outskirts of Moscow. There were low, ancient-looking log cottages bordering a straight, snowy main street. A horse-drawn sled went by; women in kerchiefs were grouped near a small wooden church. It turned out this was a settlement very close to Peredelkino called Pavlenko. A five-minute drive on a small winding road through dense evergreen trees, and I was in front of Pasternak's house. I suddenly recognized it on my right, a brown building, with bay windows overlooking the road. I had seen photographs of it in magazines.

Peredelkino is a loosely settled little town, hospitable-looking and cheerful in the sunny midday. I had been told that it was inhabited mostly by writers and artists, but most of it looked like a settlement of small artisans and peasants; there is nothing "arty" about it, although it is one of the most important writers' colonies near Moscow. The village has a large rest home for writers and journalists which is run by the Soviet Writers' Union. Kornei Chukovsky lives there in a cozy frame house, where he entertains his family and close friends on Sundays. Konstantin Fedin, one of the best known of living Russian novelists, has a house next door to Pasternak's. He was the First Secretary of the Writers' Union for a while — a post long occupied by Alexander Fadeyev, who also lived in Peredelkino until his suicide in 1956. A long time ago, Isaac Babel was arrested here. The house where he lived can be seen from Pasternak's house, lost in the snow beyond a deep ravine.

Pasternak's house is on a gently curving country road which leads down the hill to a brook. On that sunny after-

* Random House, 1963.

noon the hill was full of children on skis and sleds.
Across the road there is a large fenced field. It is a communal field cultivated in the good season; now, in winter,
it was a vast white expanse dominated by a little cemetery — like a bit of background out of a Chagall painting.
The tombs are surrounded by wooden fences painted a
bright blue, and the crosses are planted at odd angles.
There were brilliant pink and red paper flowers on the
tombs, half buried in snow. It is a cheerful cemetery.
Beyond it in the distance children skated on a frozen
pond — small, swift figures gliding in wide circles.

The veranda on Pasternak's house gives it a superficial
resemblance to an American house of forty years ago,
but the dense firs against which it stands mark it as
Russian. They grow very close to each other and give the
feeling of deep forest, although there are only small
groves of them around Peredelkino. Those trees behind
low scalloped fences lend a fairytale air to the lanes of
the settlement. I was to find out that while visiting in
Peredelkino one is always taken for walks on the snowy
lanes. Walks are an established part of life in Russia —
like drinking tea.

I paid the driver and with great trepidation pushed
open the gate at the fence separating the garden from the
road. I walked up to the dark house. At the small veranda
on the side of the house there was a door with a withered,
half-torn note pinned on it saying, "I am working now.
I cannot receive anybody. Please go away." After a moment's hesitation I chose to disregard it, mostly because
it was so old-looking and also because of the little pack-
ages in my hands [they were gifts to Pasternak from
friends in the West]. I knocked, and almost immediately
the door was opened — by Pasternak himself.

He was wearing an astrakhan hat. He was strikingly
handsome. With his high cheekbones and dark eyes and
fur hat he looked like someone out of a Russian folk tale.

He was in perfect keeping with the tall fir trees and the wooden houses and the horse-drawn sleds. After the building anxiety of the trip, I suddenly wondered why I had ever doubted that I would see Pasternak.

I introduced myself as Olga Vadimovna Andreyeva. Andreyev is a fairly common Russian name, however, and it took him a minute to realize that I was Vadim Leonidovich's daughter and that I had come from abroad to visit him. He greeted me with great warmth, taking my hand in both his hands, and asking about my mother's health and my father's writing, and when I was last in Paris. I felt he was looking closely into my face in search of family resemblances. He said he was just going out to pay some calls. Had I been a minute later I would have missed him. He asked me to walk part of the way with him — as far as his first stop, at the Writers' Club.

One walks into Pasternak's house through the kitchen, to be greeted by a tiny, smiling middle-aged cook, who helps to brush the snow off one's clothes with a little whiskbroom. Here one may take off one's overshoes and overcoat. Then comes the dining room, with a bay window where geraniums grow. On the walls hang charcoal and *sanguine* studies by Leonid Pasternak, the writer's father who was a well-known and talented academic Russian painter. There are life studies and portraits. One recognizes Tolstoi, Gorky, Scriabin, Rachmaninoff. There are sketches of Boris Pasternak and his brother and sisters as adolescents, of ladies in big hats with veils. . . . It's very much the world of Pasternak's early reminiscences and of his poems about adolescent love. It echoes the world of *War and Peace*.

While Pasternak was getting ready to go, I had a chance to look around the room. From the moment I had stepped inside the house, I was struck by its resemblance to Leo Tolstoi's house in Moscow, which I had visited a few days before. It had the same atmosphere of both austerity and hospitality. Pasternak's house retained what must have been characteristic of a Russian nineteenth-century intellectual's home. Both houses are furnished with comfortable but utterly unpretentious old furniture—both look like an ideal setting for a studious life or for informal entertaining. Needless to say, Tolstoi's house, although it was extremely simple for the times, is a great deal vaster and more elaborate than Pasternak's, but the lack of concern about elegance or display is the same. In Pasternak's own words, it was a house in which "simplicity argued with comfort."

Ten or fifteen minutes later Pasternak was ready to leave. We stepped out into the sunlight and walked through the evergreen grove behind the house in the rather deep snow which quickly managed to get into my citified Swiss-made boots. The sunlight had started to turn yellowish with the advancing afternoon, but it was still warm.

Soon we were on a country road where the snow was packed and much more comfortable to walk on, although it had treacherous, icy patches. Pasternak, quite tall, walked with long lanky steps. On particularly perilous spots—deep snow or snow slippery as ice—he would take my arm. Otherwise he gave all his attention to the conversation. He seemed to love walking. We took what was obviously a roundabout path to the Writers' Club. The stroll lasted for about forty minutes, during which I felt an increasing friendliness on Pasternak's part. He plunged right away into an absorbing discussion of the art of translating, but he digressed from time to time to ask about the political and literary situations in France and America. He said that he rarely read papers "except when I sharpen my pencil and happen to glance over the sheet of newspaper into which I collect the shavings. This is how I learned last fall that there was a near-revolution against de Gaulle in Algeria, and that Soustelle was ousted. *Soustelle* was *ousted*," he repeated with satisfaction, emphasizing both his approval of de Gaulle's decision and the similarity of the words in Russian. Actually he seemed well informed about literary life abroad, and American literature interested him particularly.

From the first moment I was charmed and impressed by how much Pasternak's speech was like his poetry—full of alliterations and unusual images. He related words to each other musically, without, however, sounding affected or sacrificing the exact meaning. His word-sense was so inventive and acute that one felt his conversation was but the continuation of a poem—waves of words and images following each other in a crescendo.

Later in our acquaintance, I remarked to him on the musical quality of his speech. "In writing as in speaking," he said, "the music of the word is never just a matter of sound. It does not result from the harmony of vowels and consonants. It results from the relation between the speech and its meaning. And meaning—content—must always come first."

Pasternak appeared young and in good health. It was hard to believe that I was walking next to a man of almost seventy. There was something a little strange and forbidding in this youthfulness, as if something—was it art?—had mixed itself with the very substance of the man to preserve it. Even his movements were completely youthful—the gestures of the hands, the manner in which he threw his head back. His friend the poetess Marina Tsvetayeva once wrote: "Pasternak looks at the same time like an Arab and like his horse." And indeed, with his dark complexion and archaic features Pasternak did have something of an Arabic face. At certain times he seemed suddenly to become aware of the impact of his own extraordinary looks, of his whole personality. Then he seemed to withdraw for an instant,

82

half closing his slanted brown eyes, turning his head away, vaguely reminiscent of a horse balking.

In Moscow, I had been told that Pasternak was a man in love with his own image—but then I had been told so many different things about Pasternak in the past few weeks! Pasternak was a living legend—a hero to some; to others a man who had sold out to the enemies of Russia. It was his character Doctor Zhivago who seemed most controversial; many young people arbitrarily identified Pasternak the man with the fictional Yuri Zhivago.

In any event, I found that there was no truth to the charge that Pasternak was an egocentric. On the contrary, he seemed intensely aware of the world around him and reacted to every change of mood in people near him. It is hard to imagine a more perceptive conversationalist. He grasped the most elusive thought at once. The conversation lost all heaviness. Although he had seen my parents only a few times in his life, he remembered everything about them—their background, their tastes, their opinions. He recalled with surprising exactness some of my father's poems which he had liked. I soon discovered that it was difficult to get him to talk about himself, which I had hoped he would do.

As we walked in the winter sunshine, I told him what attention and admiration *Doctor Zhivago* had aroused in the West and particularly in the United States, despite the fact that the translation into English does not do justice to his book.

"Yes," he said, "I am aware of this interest and I am immensely happy and proud of it. I get an enormous amount of mail from abroad about my work. In fact, it is quite a burden at times, all those inquiries that I have to answer, but then it is indispensable to keep up relations across boundaries. As for the translators of *Doctor Zhivago*, do not blame them too much. It's not their fault. Like translators everywhere, they tend to reproduce the literal sense rather than the tone of what is said: in translating, it is the tone that is important. Actually, the only challenging translations are those of classics. It is rarely rewarding to translate modern works, although it might be easy. You said you were a painter. Well, translation is very much like copying paintings. Imagine yourself copying a Malevich. Wouldn't it be boring? And that is precisely what I have to do with the Czech surrealist poet Nezval. He is not really bad, but all this writing of the twenties has aged terribly. The translation which I have promised to finish and my own correspondence take too much of my time.

"As you can imagine, some of the letters I get about *Doctor Zhivago* are quite absurd. Recently somebody writing about *Doctor Zhivago* in France was inquiring about the plan of the novel — I guess it baffles the French sense of order. But how silly, for the plan of the novel is outlined by the poems accompanying it. This is partly why I chose to publish them alongside the novel. They are there also to give the novel more body, more richness. For the same reason I used religious symbolism, to give warmth to the book. Now some critics have become so wrapped up in those symbols — which are put in the book the way stoves go into a house, to warm it up — that they would like me to commit myself and climb into the stove . . .

"Scholars interpret my novel in theological terms. Nothing is further removed from my understanding of the world. One must live and write restlessly, with the help of the new reserves that life offers. I am weary of this notion of faithfulness to a point of view at all cost. Life around us is ever changing and I believe that one should try to change one's slant accordingly — at least once every ten years," he added jokingly. "The great heroic devotion to one point of view is alien to me — it's a lack of humility. Mayakovsky killed himself because his pride would not be reconciled with something new happening within himself — or around him."

We had reached a long, low wooden fence, and Pasternak stopped at the gate. Our walk had already made him late. I said good-bye with regret. There were so many things that I still wanted to ask him. Pasternak showed me the way to the railroad station, very close by, downhill behind the little cemetery. A little electric train took me into Moscow in less than an hour.

My subsequent visits with Pasternak merge in my memory into one long conversation. Although he declined to give me a formal interview — "For this, you must come back when I am less busy, next fall perhaps" — he was interested in the questions which I outlined to him. Except for meals, we were alone, and there were no interruptions. Each time as I was about to leave, Pasternak kissed my hand in the old-fashioned Russian manner and asked me to come back the following Sunday, so that for a brief period — four or five weeks — there was a pattern to my visits.

I remember coming to Pasternak's house from the railroad station at dusk by taking a shortcut near the cemetery. Suddenly the wind grew very strong; it was the beginning of a snowstorm. I could see snow flying in great round waves in the distant lights along the railroad station. It grew dark very quickly; the wind was so strong that I had difficulty walking. I knew this to be fairly customary Russian winter weather, but it was my first actual blizzard — *metel*. It evoked Pasternak's early poems, and the snowstorms of *Doctor Zhivago*. It was strange to step into Pasternak's house a few moments later and hear his elliptic sentences so much like his verse.

I had arrived too late to attend the midafternoon dinner. The family had retired and the house seemed deserted. Pasternak insisted that I have something to eat, and the cook brought some venison and vodka into the dining room. It was only about four o'clock, but the room was dark and warm, shut off from the world with only the sound of snow and wind outside. Pasternak sat across the table from me.

Although I was hungry and the food delicious, I found myself regretting the fact that I had to eat instead of giving my full attention to what Pasternak was saying about my grandfather. He had recently reread some of Andreyev's stories and liked them a great deal. "They bear the stamp of those remarkable years in Russia, the first decade of this century. Those years are now receding in our memory, and yet they loom in the mind like great mountains seen in the distance, enormous. Andreyev was under a Nietzschean spell; he took from Nietzsche his taste for excesses. So did Scriabin. Nietzsche satisfied the Russians' longing for the extreme, the absolute, their taste for the grandiose. Music, writing—men had to have this enormous scope before they acquired specificity, became themselves."

Pasternak told me about a piece he had recently written for a German magazine on the theme of "What is man?" "How old-fashioned Nietzsche seems, he who was the most important thinker in the days of my youth! What enormous influence—on Wagner, on Gorky. Gorky was impregnated with his ideas. Actually, Nietzsche's principal function was to be the transmitter of the bad taste of his period. How quickly his aura faded! It is Kirkegaard, barely known in those years, who was destined to influence our own epoch. I would like to know the works of Berdyaev better; he is in the same line of thought, I believe—truly a writer of our time."

It grew quite dark in the dining room, and we moved to a small lighted sitting room on the same floor. Pasternak brought me tangerines for dessert. I ate them with a strange feeling of something already experienced: tangerines often appear in Pasternak's work—in the beginning of *Doctor Zhivago*, in early poems. They seem to stand for a sort of ritual thirst-quenching. And then there was another vivid evocation of a Pasternak poem —like the snowstorm which blew outside—an open grand piano, black and enormous, filling up most of the room:

> . . . how could we be closer
> Than in the twilight here, the score like a diary
> Page after page, year after year, tossed on the fire?

On the walls, as in the dining room, there were simply framed sketches by Leonid Pasternak. Half-familiar faces of writers of the turn of the century looked upon us.

I had heard from people who had seen him while he was working on *Doctor Zhivago* that Pasternak rejected most of his early verse as too tentative and dated. I had difficulty believing it. There is a classical perfection to *Themes and Variations* and *My Sister Life,* experimental though they were in the 1920's. I found that writers and poets in Russia knew them by heart and would recite them with fervor. Often one could detect the influence of Pasternak in the verse of young poets. Mayakovsky and Pasternak, each in his own manner, are the very symbol of the years of the Revolution. Then art and the revolutionary ideas seemed inseparable. It was enough to let oneself be carried by the wave of overwhelming events and ideas. There were fewer heartbreaking choices to make, and I sensed a longing for those years on the part of many young Russians. Was it true that Pasternak rejected those early works?

In Pasternak's reply there was a note of slight irritation. It might have been because he didn't like to be admired solely for those poems, or perhaps he unconsciously resented the thought that he could never write anything that could equal them. Or was it the more general weariness of the artist dissatisfied with past achievements, concerned only with an immediate artistic task? Eventually, as I felt Pasternak's detachment from *Doctor Zhivago* at the expense of his new play, I tended to believe the latter.

"I have the feeling of an immense debt towards my contemporaries. I wrote *Doctor Zhivago* in an attempt to repay it. This feeling of debt was overpowering as I slowly progressed with the novel. After so many years of writing only lyric poetry or translating, it seemed to me that it was my duty to make a statement about our epoch — about those years, remote and yet looming so closely over us. Time was pressing. I wanted to record the past and to honor the beautiful and refined aspects of the Russia of those years. There will be no return of those days, or those of our fathers and forefathers, but in the great blossoming of the future their values will revive, I know. In the meantime, I have tried to describe them. I don't know whether my novel is fully successful, but then with all its faults, I feel that it has more value than those early poems. It is richer, more humane than the works of my youth. Those poems were like rapid sketches — just compare them with the works of our elders. Dostoevsky and Tolstoi were not just novelists, Blok not just a poet. The voices of those writers sounded like thunder because they had something to say. As against the facile artists of the twenties — my father, for example. How much effort went into one of his paintings! Our success in the twenties was partly due to chance. My generation found itself naturally in the focal point of history. Our works were dictated by the times. They lack universality now that they have aged. Moreover, I believe that it is no longer possible for lyrical poetry to express the immensity of our experience. Life has grown too cumbersome, too complicated. We have acquired values which are best expressed in prose. I have tried to express them through my novel, I have them in mind as I write my play."

"Among your contemporaries' writings," I asked him, "whose do you think have best endured?"

"You know how I feel about Mayakovsky. I have told it at great length in my autobiography, *Safe Conduct*. I am indifferent to most of his later works, with the exception of his last unfinished poem, 'In Full Voice.' The falling apart of form, the poverty of thought, the unevenness which is characteristic of poetry in the late twenties are alien to me. But there are exceptions. I love all Yesenin, who captures so well the smell of Russian earth. I place Tsvetayeva highest; she was a formed poet from her very beginning. In an age of affectations she had her own voice—human, classical. She was a woman with a man's soul. Her struggle with everyday life was what gave her strength. She strived for and reached perfect clarity. She is a greater poet than Akhmatova, whose simplicity and lyricism I have always admired. Tsvetayeva's death was one of the great sadnesses of my life."

"What about Andrei Bely, who was so influential in those years?"

"Bely was too hermetic, too limited. His scope is comparable to that of chamber music — never greater. If he had really suffered, he might have written the major work of which he was capable. But he never came into contact with real life . . . Perhaps this fascination with new forms is the fate of writers like Bely who die young. I have never understood those dreams of a new language, of a completely original form of expression. Because of this dream, much of the work of the twenties was merely stylistic experimentation and has ceased to exist. The most extraordinary discoveries are made when the artist is overwhelmed by what he has to say. In his urgency he uses then the old language and the old language is transformed from within. Even in those years one felt a little sorry for Bely because he was so cut off from the immediate, which alone could have helped his genius to blossom."

"What about today's young poets?" I asked. "I am impressed by the extent that poetry seems a part of everyday life for Russians. Large printings of works by young poets are amazing to a Westerner. Poetry in Russia seems very alive."

"Well, perhaps not as much as you think. It is fairly limited to a group of intellectuals. And today's poetry is often rather ordinary. It is like the pattern on a wallpaper, pleasant enough but without real *raison d'être*. Of course some young people show talent. Yevtushenko, for example. However, as I was saying earlier, I believe that prose is today's medium, elaborate, rich prose like that of Faulkner. Today's work must re-create whole segments of life. This is what I am trying to do in my new play. But everyday life has grown very complicated for me. It must be so anywhere for a well-known writer, but I am unprepared for this role. I don't like a life deprived of secrecy and quiet. It seems to me that in my youth work was an integral part of life which illuminated everything else in it. Now it is something I have to fight for. All those demands by scholars, editors, readers cannot be ignored, but together with the translations they devour my time. . . . You must tell people abroad who are interested in me that this is my only serious problem — this terrible lack of time."

My last visit with Pasternak was longer than the others. He had asked me to come early, in order to have a talk before a mid-afternoon dinner with the family. It was again sunny. I arrived at the house shortly before Pasternak returned from his morning stroll. As I was shown into his study, the house echoed with cheerful voices. Somewhere in the back of it, members of his family were assembled.

Pasternak's study was a large, rather bare room on the second floor. Like the rest of the house it had little furniture: a large desk near the bay window, a couple of chairs, a sofa. The light coming from the window looking over the large snowy field was brilliant. Pinned on the light gray wooden walls was a multitude of art postcards. When he came in, Pasternak explained to me that those were all sent to him by readers, mostly from abroad. Many were reproductions of religious scenes — medieval Nativities, St. George killing the dragon, St. Magdalene — which were related to *Doctor Zhivago*'s themes.

After his walk, Pasternak looked especially well. He was wearing a collegiate-looking navy-blue blazer and was in a good mood. He sat at the desk by the window. I remember vividly feeling happy; Pasternak looked so gay and the sun through the window was almost spring-like. As we sat there I wished our talk could be prolonged somehow: I was leaving Moscow the next morning. But the three or four hours I spent across the desk from Pasternak vanished like an instant.

HAMLET

This English version of "Hamlet" is as much a poem *about* Boris Pasternak as an adaptation *from* Boris Pasternak. An extremely free adaptation—or rather "imitation," as Robert Lowell calls it—it is based on three poems by Pasternak. Two of the poems, written in 1917, are from *My Sister Life*. The third is titled "Hamlet" and is from *Poems from Doctor Zhivago*. It was written in 1946, according to a close and knowledgeable friend of Pasternak's. Robert Lowell points out that the new English "Hamlet" tells us of the Russian poet's life in a way that he himself might not have perceived it. It opens with a pastoral version of youth, a boating scene which could have been depicted by an Impressionist. The poem ends tragically with the poet's crucifixion by the mob. In the adapter's interpreta-

tion, the clapping of the river ripples and that of the audience which greets the poet about to enact his own tragic
ending merge with each other, providing a transition for
poems belonging to very different periods and moods.

"My heart throbbed like a boat on the water.
My oars rested. The willows swayed through the summer,
licking my shoulders, elbows and rowlocks—
wait! this might happen,

when the music brought me the beat,
and the ash-gray waterlilies dragged, and a couple of daisies
    blew,
and a hint of blue dotted a point offshore—
lips to lips, stars to stars!

My sister, life!
the world has too many people for us,
the sycophant, the spineless—
silently, like snakes in the grass, they sting.

My sister!
embrace the sky and Hercules
who holds the world up forever
at ease, perhaps, and sleeps at night

thrilled by the nightingales crying . . .

The boat stops throbbing on the water . . .

The clapping stops. I walk into the lights
as Hamlet, lounge like a student against the door frame,
and try to catch the far-off dissonance of life—
all that has happened, and must!

From the dark the audience leans its one hammering brow
    against me—
ten thousand opera glasses, each set on the tripod!
Abba, Father, all things are possible with thee—
take away this cup!

I love the mulishness of Providence,
I am content to play the one part I was born for . . .
quite another play is running now . . .
take me off the boards tonight!

The sequence of scenes was well thought out;
the last bow is in the cards, or the stars—
but I am alone, and there is none . . .
All's drowned in the sperm and spittle of the Pharisee—

To live a life is not to cross a field."

1917–1965

Разрыв

1

О ангел залгавшийся, сразу бы, сразу б,
И я б опоил тебя чистой печалью!
Но так—я не смею, но так—зуб за зуб!
О скорбь, зараженная ложью вначале,
О горе, о горе в проказе!

О ангел залгавшийся,—нет, не смертельно
Страданье, что сердце, что сердце в экземе!
Но что же ты душу болезнью нательной
Даришь на прощанье? Зачем же бесцельно
Целуешь, как капли дождя, и как время,
Смеясь, убиваешь, за всех, перед всеми!

2

О стыд, ты в тягость мне! О совесть, в этом раннем
Разрыве столько грез, настойчивых еще!
Когда бы, человек,—я был пустым собраньем
Висков и губ и глаз, ладоней, плеч и щек!

Тогда б по свисту строф, по крику их, по знаку,
По крепости тоски, по юности ее
Я б уступил им всем, я б их повел в атаку,
Я б штурмовал тебя, позорище мое!

3

От тебя все мысли отвлеку
Не в гостях, не за вином, так на небе.
У хозяев, рядом, по звонку
Отопрут кому-нибудь когда-нибудь.

Вырвусь к ним, к бряцанью декабря.
Только дверь—и вот я! Коридор один.
«Вы оттуда? Что там говорят?
Что слыхать? Какие сплетни в городе?

Ошибается ль еще тоска?
Шепчет ли потом: «Казалось—вылитая».
Приготовясь футов с сорока
Разлететься восклицаньем: «Вы ли это?»

THE BREAKUP

I

O two-tongued angel, on my grief a hundred
proof no less I should have got you drunk.
But I'm not one, whatever pain the lies encouraged
from the start, to claim a tooth for a tooth.
And now the clever, festering doom!

Oh, no, betraying angel, it's not fatal,
not this suffering, this rash of the heart.
But why at parting shower me with such a rain
of blows to the body? Why this pointless
hurricane of kisses? Why, your mockery
supreme, kill me in everybody's sight?

2

O shame, how overwhelming you can be!
Yet at this breaking-up how many dreams persist.
Were I no more than a jumbled heap
of brows and eyes and lips, cheeks, shoulders, wrists,

for my grief so strong, forever young,
at the order of my verse, its ruthless march,
I would submit to those and, leading them
in battle, storm your citadel, O monstrous shame.

3

All my thoughts I now distract from you,
if not at parties, drinking wine, then in heaven!
Surely one day, as the landlord's next door bell
is ringing, for someone that door will open.

I'll rush in on them in tinkling December, say,
the door pushed wide—and here I am, far as the hall!
"Where've you come from? What's being said?
Tell us the news, the latest scandal from the city."

Is all my grief mistaken?
Will it mutter later, "She mirrored her exactly,"
as, gathering myself for a leap past forty feet,
I burst out crying, "Is it really you?"

Пощадят ли площади меня?
Ах, когда б вы знали, как тоскуется,
Когда вас раз сто в теченье дня
На ходу на сходствах ловит улица!»

4

Помешай мне, попробуй. Приди, покусись потушить
Этот приступ печали, гремящей сегодня, как ртуть
      в пустоте Торичелли.
Воспрети, помешательство, мне,—о, приди, посягни!
Помешай мне шуметь о тебе! Не стыдись, мы—одни.
О, туши ж, о, туши! Горячее!

5

Заплети этот ливень, как волны, холодных локтей
И как лилий, атласных и властных бессильем ладоней!
Отбивай, ликованье! На волю! Лови их,—ведь в бешеной
        этой лапте—
Голошенье лесов, захлебнувшихся эхом охот в Калидоне,
Где, как лань, обеспамятев, гнал Аталанту к поляне
        Актей,
Где любили бездонной лазурью, свистевшей в ушах
        лошадей.

Целовались заливистым лаем погони
И ласкались раскатами рога и треском деревьев, копыт
        и когтей.

— О, на волю! На волю—как те!

6

Разочаровалась? Ты думала—в мире нам
Расстаться за реквиемом лебединым?
В расчете на горе, зрачками расширенными,
В слезах, примеряла их непобедимость?

На мессе б со сводов посыпалась стенопись,
Потрясшись игрой на губах Себастьяна.
Но с нынешней ночи во всем моя ненависть
Растянутость видит, и жаль, что хлыста нет.

And the public squares, will they spare me?
Ah, if you could only know what pain I feel
when, at least a hundred times a day, the streets,
amazed, confront me with their counterfeits of you.

4

Go ahead, try to stop me, try to put out
this fiery fit of sorrow, soaring
like mercury in a barometer.
Stop me from raving about you. Don't be ashamed,
we are alone. Turn out the lights, turn them
out, and douse my fire with fire.

5

Like combers twine this cloudburst of cold elbows,
like lilies, silken-stalwart, helpless palms.
Sound the triumph! Break loose! Set to! In this wild race
the woods are roaring, choked on the echo of Calydonian
    hunts,
where Acteon pursued Atalanta like a doe to the clearing,
where in endless azure, hissing past the horses' ears,
they kissed and kissed to the uproarious baying of the chase,
caressed among the shrillest horns and crackling trees,
the clattering hoofs and claws.
Like those break loose, break loose, rush into the woods!

6

So you're disappointed? You think we should
part with a swan song for requiem,
with a show of sorrow, tears showering
from your eyes dilated, trying their victorious power?

As if during mass the frescoes, shaken by what's playing
on Johann Sebastian's lips, were to tumble from the arches!
From this night on in everything my hatred discovers
a dragging on and on that ought to have a whip.

97

Впотьмах, моментально опомнясь, без медлящего
Раздумья, решила, что всё перепашет.
Что—время. Что самоубийство ей не для чего.
Что даже и это есть шаг черепаший.

7

Мой друг, мой нежный, о, точь-в-точь как ночью,
                    в перелете с Бергена на полюс,
Валящим снегом с ног гагар сносимый жаркий пух,
Клянусь, о нежный мой, клянусь, я не неволюсь,
Когда я говорю тебе—забудь, усни, мой друг.

Когда, как труп затертого до самых труб норвежца,
В виденьи зим, не движущих заиндевелых мачт,
Ношусь в сполохах глаз твоих шутливым—спи,
                             утешься,
До свадьбы заживет, мой друг, угомонись, не плачь.

Когда совсем как север вне последних поселений,
Украдкой от арктических и неусыпных льдин,
Полночным куполом полощущий глаза слепых
                             тюленей,
Я говорю—не три их, спи, забудь: всё вздор один.

8

Мой стол не столь широк, чтоб грудью всею
Налечь на борт и локоть завести
За край тоски, за этот перешеек
Сквозь столько верст прорытого прости.

(Сейчас там ночь.) За душный свой затылок.
(И спать легли.) Под царства плеч твоих.
(И тушат свет.) Я б утром возвратил их.
Крыльцо б коснулось сонной ветвью их.

Не хлопьями! Руками крой!—Достанет!
О, десять пальцев муки, с бороздой
Крещенских звезд, как знаков опозданья
В пургу на север шедших поездов!

In the dark, instantly, without a thought
my hatred decides that it is time
to plough it all up, that suicide's folly
slow, too slow, the speed of a snail.

7

My love, my angel, just as in that night
flying from Bergen to the Pole, the wild geese
swooping, a snowstorm of warmest down, I swear,
O Sweet, my will's not crossed when I urge you,
Dearest, please forget and go to sleep.

When like a Norwegian whaler's wreck, to its stock ice-
    jammed,
a winter's apparition, rigid past its masts, I soar,
fluttered in your eyes' aurora borealis, sleep, don't cry:
all before your wedding day will heal, my dear.

When like the North itself beyond the outmost settlements,
hidden from the arctic and its ice floe wide awake,
rinsing the eyes of blinded seals with midnight's rim,
I say—don't rub your eyes, sleep, forget—it's all nonsense.

8

My table's not so wide that, pressing my chest
against its board, I cannot crook my elbow
round the edge of anguish, those straits
of countless miles, quarried by "Farewell."

(It's night there now) Ah, to have your cloudy hair
(They've gone to sleep) the kingdom of your shoulders!
(All lights are out) I'd return them in the morning,
and the porch would greet them with a nodding branch.

O shield me, not with flakes, but with your hands,
pain's ten sufficient fingers, the spikes
of winter stars, like the placards of delay
posted on trains northbound into blizzards!

99

9

Рояль дрожащий пену с губ оближет.
Тебя сорвет, подкосит этот бред.
Ты скажешь:—милый!—Нет,—вскричу я,—нет!
При музыке?!—Но можно ли быть ближе,

Чем в полутьме, аккорды, как дневник,
Меча в камин комплектами, погодно?
О пониманье дивное, кивни,
Кивни, и изумишься!—ты свободна.

Я не держу. Иди, благотвори.
Ступай к другим. Уже написан Вертер,
А в наши дни и воздух пахнет смертью:
Открыть окно, что жилы отворить.

1918

Болезнь

Мне в сумерки ты всё—пансионеркою,
Всё—школьницей. Зима. Закат лесничим
В лесу часов. Лежу и жду, чтоб смерклося,
И вот—айда! Аукаемся кличем.

А ночь, а ночь! Да это ж ад, дом ужасов!
Проведай ты, тебя б сюда пригнало!
Она—твой шаг, твой брак, твое замужество,
И тяжелей дознаний трибунала.

Ты помнишь жизнь? Ты помнишь, стаей горлинок
Летели хлопья грудью против гула.
Их вихрь крутил, кутя, валясь прожорливо
С лотков на снег, их до панелей гнуло!

Перебегала ты! Ведь он подсовывал
Ковром под нас салазки и кристаллы!
Ведь жизнь, как кровь, до облака пунцового
Пожаром вьюги озарясь, хлестала!

Движенье помнишь? Помнишь время? Лавочниц?
Палатки? Давку? За разменом денег
Холодных, звонких,—помнишь, помнишь давешних
Колоколов предпраздничных гуденье?

100

9

The trembling piano licks foam from its lips.
This delirium, tossing, will strike you down.
You murmur, "Dearest!" "No!" I cry back. "Never
in the midst of music!" And yet how could we be closer

than in the twilight here, the score like a diary,
page after page, year after year, tossed on the fire.
O wondrous memories that, luring us still,
astonish the spirit! But you are free.

I shan't keep you. Go on. Give yourself to others.
Leave at once. Werther's already had his day.
But now the air itself reeks death:
opening a window is like opening a vein.

—ADAPTED BY THEODORE WEISS

ILLNESS

At dusk you appear, a schoolgirl still,
a schoolgirl. Winter. The sunset a woodsman hacking
in the forest of hours. I lie back to wait for dusk.
At once we're hallooing; back and forth we call.

But the night! A torture chamber, bustling hell.
Come—if anything could bring you!—see for yourself.
Night's your flitting away, your engagement, wedding,
last proceedings of a hangman's court against me.

Do you remember that life, the flakes like doves
in flock thrusting their breasts against the howling
and, the tempest swirling them, fiendishly
dashed to the pavements?

You ran across the street, winds billowing under us,
a flying carpet—sleds, cries, crystals headlong!
For life, inspired by the blizzard, gushed
like blood into a crimson cloud.

Do you remember that moment, the hawkers,
the tents, the jostling crowd, the coins a puppy's
moist nose? Those bells, encumbered by snow,
do you remember their grumbling before the holidays?

101

Увы, любовь! Да, это надо высказать!
Чем заменить тебя? Жирами? Бромом?
Как конский глаз, с подушек, жаркий, искоса
Гляжу, страшась бессонницы огромной.

Мне в сумерки ты будто всё с экзамена,
Всё—с выпуска. Чижи, мигрень, учебник.
Но по ночам! Как просят пить, как пламенны
Глаза капсюль и пузырьков лечебных!

1918—1919

Воробьевы горы

Грудь под поцелуи, как под рукомойник!
Ведь не век, не сряду, лето бьет ключом.
Ведь не ночь за ночью низкий рев гармоник
Подымаем с пыли, топчем и влечем.

Я слыхал про старость. Страшны прорицанья!
Рук к звездам не вскинет ни один бурун.
Говорят—не веришь. На лугах лица нет,
У прудов нет сердца, бога нет в бору.

Расколышь же душу! Всю сегодня выпень.
Это полдень мира. Где глаза твои?
Видишь, в высях мысли сбились в белый кипень
Дятлов, туч и шишек, жара и хвои.

Здесь пресеклись рельсы городских трамваев.
Дальше служат сосны. Дальше им нельзя.
Дальше—воскресенье. Ветки отрывая,
Разбежится просек, по траве скользя.

Просевая полдень, Тройцын день, гулянье,
Просит роща верить: мир всегда таков.
Так задуман чащей, так внушен поляне,
Так на нас, на ситцы пролит с облаков.

1917

102

Alas, love, I must summon it all.
What can replace you? Pills? Patent medicines?
Frightened by my bottomless insomnia, sweat-soaked,
I look sideways from my pillow as with a horse's eye.

At dusk you appear, still taking exams.
It's recess: robins flutter, headaches, textbooks.
But at night how they clamor for thirst, how glaring
their eyes, the aspirins, the medicine bottles.

—ADAPTED BY THEODORE WEISS

SPARROW HILLS

Like water pouring from a pitcher, my mouth on your
  nipples!
Not always. The summer well runs dry. .
Not for long the dust of our stamping feet, encore on encore
from the saxes on the casino's midnight bandstand.

I've heard of age—its obese warbling!
When no wave will clap hands to the stars.
If they speak, you doubt it. No face in the meadows,
no heart in the pools, no god among the pines.

Split your soul like wood. Let today froth to your mouth.
It's the world's noontide. Have you no eyes for it?
Look, conception bubbles from the bleached fallows;
fir cones, woodpeckers, clouds, pine needles, heat.

Here the city's trolley tracks give out.
Further, you must put up with peeled pine. The trolley poles
  are detached.
Further, it's Sunday. Boughs screwed loose for the picnic
  bonfire,
playing tag in your bra.

"The world is always like this," say the woods,
as they mix the midday glare. Whitsunday and walking.
All's planned with checkerberry couches, inspired with
  clearings—
the piebalds clouds spill down on us, a country woman's
  house-dress.

—ADAPTED BY ROBERT LOWELL

103

В лесу

Луга мутило жаром лиловатым,
В лесу клубился кафедральный мрак.
Что оставалось в мире целовать им?
Он весь был их, как воск на пальцах мяк.

Есть сон такой,—не спишь, а только снится,
Что жаждешь сна; что дремлет человек,
Которому сквозь сон палят ресницы
Два черных солнца, бьющих из-под век.

Текли лучи. Текли жуки с отливом,
Стекло стрекоз сновало по щекам.
Был полон лес мерцаньем кропотливым,
Как под щипцами у часовщика.

Казалось, он уснул под стук цифири,
Меж тем как выше, в терпком янтаре,
Испытаннейшие часы в эфире
Переставляют, сверив по жаре.

Их переводят, сотрясают иглы
И сеют тень, и мают, и сверлят
Мачтовый мрак, который ввысь воздвигло,
В истому дня, на синий циферблат.

Казалось, древность счастья облетает.
Казалось, лес закатом снов объят.
Счастливые часов не наблюдают,
Но те, вдвоем, казалось, только спят.

1917

Мефистофель

Из массы пыли за заставы
По воскресеньям высыпали,
Меж тем как, дома не застав их,
Ломились ливни в окна спален.

IN THE WOODS

A lilac heat sickened the meadow;
high in the wood, a cathedral's sharp, nicked groins.
No skeleton obstructed the bodies—
all was ours, obsequious wax in our fingers . . .

Such, the dream: you do not sleep,
you only dream you thirst for sleep,
that someone elsewhere thirsts for sleep—
two black suns singe his eyelashes.

Sunbeams shower and ebb to the flow of iridescent beetles.
The dragonfly's mica whirs on your cheek.
The wood fills with meticulous scintillations—
a dial under the clockmaker's tweezers.

It seemed we slept to the tick of figures;
in the acid, amber ether,
they set up nicely tested clocks,
shifted, regulated them to a soprano hair for the heat.

They shifted them here and there, and snipped at the
    wheels.
Day declined on the blue clock-face;
they scattered shadows, drilled a void—
the darkness was a mast derricked upright.

It seems a green and brown happiness flits beyond us;
sleep smothers the woods;
no elegiacs on the clock's ticking—
sleep, it seems, is all this couple is up to.

—ADAPTED BY ROBERT LOWELL

MEPHISTOPHELES

Every Sunday they left a circus of dust behind them,
as they poured out on the turnpike in stately, overcrowded
    carriages,
and the showers found nobody at home,
and trampled through the bedroom windows.

Велось у всех, чтоб за обедом
Хотя б на третье дождь был подан,
Меж тем как вихрь—велосипедом
Летал по комнатным комодам.

Меж тем как там до потолков их
Взлетали шелковые шторы,
Расталкивали бестолковых
Пруды, природа и просторы.

Длиннейшим поездом линеек
Позднее стягивались к валу,
Где тень, пугавшая коней их,
Ежевечерне оживала.

В чулках как кровь, при паре бантов,
По залитой зарей дороге,
Упав как лямки с барабана,
Пылили дьяволовы ноги.

Казалось, захлестав из низкой
Листвы струей высокомерья,
Снесла б весь мир надменность диска
И терпит только эти перья.

Считая ехавших, как вехи,
Едва прикладываясь к шляпе,
Он шел, откидываясь в смехе,
Шагал, приятеля облапя.

1919

Анне Ахматовой

Мне кажется, я подберу слова,
Похожие на вашу первозданность.
А ошибусь,—мне это трын-трава,
Я всё равно с ошибкой не расстанусь.

Я слышу мокрых кровель говорок,
Торцовых плит заглохшие эклоги.
Какой-то город, явный с первых строк,
Растет и отдается в каждом слоге.

It was a custom at these staid Sunday dinners
to serve courses of rain instead of roastbeef;
on the baroque sideboard, by the Sunday silver,
the wind cut corners like a boy on a new bicycle.

Upstairs, the curtain rods whirled, untouched;
the curtains roared in salvos to the ceiling.
Outside the burghers kept losing themselves,
they showed up chewing straws by cowponds.

Earlier, when a long cortege of carriages
approached the city wall,
the horses would shy
from the shadows of the Weimar gallows.

The devil in blood-red stockings with rose rosettes
danced along the sunset-watered road—
he was as red
as a boiling lobster.

One snort of indignation
would have ripped the lid of heaven
from the skyline's low vegetation;
the devil's ribbons fluttered and danced.

The carriages swam through his eyes like road signs;
he scarcely lifted a finger in greeting.
He rolled on his heels, he trembled with laughter,
he sidled off hugging Faust, his pupil.

—ADAPTED BY ROBERT LOWELL

For Anna Akhmatova

It seems I am choosing words that will stand,
and you are in them,
but if I blunder, it doesn't matter—
I must persist in my errors.

I hear the soiled, dripping small talk of the roofs;
the students' black boots drum eclogues on the boardwalks,
the undefined city takes on personality,
is alive in each sound.

Кругом весна, но за город нельзя.
Еще строга заказчица скупая.
Глаза шитьем за лампою слезя,
Горит заря, спины не разгибая.

Вдыхая дали ладожскую гладь,
Спешит к воде, смиряя сил упадок.
С таких гулянок ничего не взять.
Каналы пахнут затхлостью укладок.

По ним ныряет, как пустой орех,
Горячий ветер и колышет веки
Ветвей и звезд, и фонарей, и вех,
И с моста вдаль глядящей белошвейки.

Бывает глаз по-разному остер,
По-разному бывает образ точен.
Но самой страшной крепости раствор—
Ночная даль под взглядом белой ночи.

Таким я вижу облик ваш и взгляд.
Он мне внушен не тем столбом из соли,
Которым вы пять лет тому назад
Испуг оглядки к рифме прикололи.

Но, исходив из ваших первых книг,
Где крепли прозы пристальной крупицы,
Он и во всех, как искры проводник,
Событья былью заставляет биться.

1928

Хмель

Под ракитой, обвитой плющем,
От ненастья мы ищем защиты.
Наши плечи покрыты плащом,
Вкруг тебя мои руки обвиты.

Я ошибся. Кусты этих чащ
Не плющом перевиты, а хмелем.
Ну, так лучше давай этот плащ
В ширину под собою расстелим.

1946–1953

Although it's spring, there's no leaving the city.
The sharp customers overlook nothing.
Day bends to its sewing until it weeps;
sunrise and sunset redden the same red eye.

You ache for the calm reaches of Ladoga,
then hurry off to the lake for a change
of fatigue. You gain nothing,
the shallows smell like closets full of last summer's clothes.

The dry wind dances like a dried-out walnut
across the waves, across your stung eyelids—
stars, branches, milestones, lamps. A white
seamstress on the bridge is always washing clothes.

I know that objects and eyesight vary greatly
in singleness and sharpness, but the iron
heart's vodka is the sky
under the northern lights.

That's how I see your face and expression.
This, not the pillar of salt, the "Lot's Wife" you pinned down
in rhyme five years ago to show up our fear,
limping forward in blinders, afraid of looking back.

How early your first dogged, unremitting idiom
took on life—no unassembled crumbs!
In all our affairs, your lines throb
with the high charge of the world. Each wire is a conductor.

—ADAPTED BY ROBERT LOWELL

WILD VINES

Beneath a willow entwined with ivy,
we look for shelter from the bad weather;
one raincoat covers both our shoulders—
my fingers rustle like the wild vine around your breasts.

I am wrong. The rain's stopped.
Not ivy, but the hair of Dionysus
hangs from these willows. What am I to do?
Throw the raincoat under us!

—ADAPTED BY ROBERT LOWELL

Свадьба

Пересекши край двора,
Гости на гулянку
В дом невесты до утра
Перешли с тальянкой.

За хозяйскими дверьми
В войлочной обивке
Стихли с часу до семи
Болтовни обрывки.

А зарею, в самый сон,
Только спать и спать бы,
Вновь запел аккордеон,
Уходя со свадьбы.

И рассыпал гармонист
Снова на баяне
Плеск ладоней, блеск монист,
Шум и гам гулянья.

И опять, опять, опять
Говорок частушки
Прямо к спящим на кровать
Ворвался с пирушки.

А одна, как снег бела,
В шуме, свисте, гаме
Снова павой поплыла,
Поводя боками.

Помавая головой
И рукою правой,
В плясовой по мостовой,
Павой, павой, павой.

Вдруг задор и шум игры,
Топот хоровода,
Провалясь в тартарары,
Канули, как в воду.

THE LANDLORD
(The Wedding)

Having crossed the curb in the courtyard,
the Landlord journeyed to the feast,
into the Bride's house—

with him departed the accordion player,
behind the bolted door of the Bride,
between one and seven.

The snatches of talk had quieted down,
but the sun rose blood red in the middle of the bed—
he wanted to sleep and sleep and sleep.

The accordion began to weep,
the accordion-player lay spread out on his instrument—
hearing the palms clapping, the shuffle of the shining serfs.

The feast's whole flourish jingled like silver in his hand,
again again again again,
the song of the broken accordion.

Rustling through the bed and the sleeper,
the noise, whistling and the cheering,
swam a white peahen.

She moved her hips,
and strutted out in the street,
this beautiful bird . . .

She shook her hair, she ruffled her breast feathers;
suddenly the noise of the game
is the stamping of a whole procession.

She dropped into the hole of the sun.

The sleepy courtyard grows businesslike,
horses stand up by the wooden well,
teamsters shout down the laughter of the feast.

Просыпался шумный двор.
Деловое эхо
Вмешивалось в разговор
И раскаты смеха.

В необъятность неба, ввысь
Вихрем сизых пятен
Стаей голуби неслись,
Снявшись с голубятен.

Точно их за свадьбой вслед,
Спохватясь спросонья,
С пожеланьем многих лет
Выслали в погоню.

Жизнь ведь тоже только миг,
Только растворенье
Нас самих во всех других
Как бы им в даренье.

Только свадьба, вглубь окон
Рвущаяся снизу,
Только песня, только сон,
Только голубь сизый.

1946—1953

A band of pigeons
blasts from the sky's blue bowl,
as if it were following the wedding party,

as if life were only an instant, of course,
the dissolution of ourselves into others,
like a wedding party approaching the window.

—ADAPTED BY ROBERT LOWELL

OSIP
EMILIEVICH
MANDELSTAM
(1891–1938)

I lie in the earth, moving my lips.
Every schoolboy will know what I say:

The earth is roundest in Red Square,
Its stubborn slant is growing sharp.

The earth is roundest in Red Square,
Slanting down open and wide,

Slanting down to the edge of rice fields
—until the last prisoner is dead.

Osip Mandelstam, 1935

OSIP MANDELSTAM was born in Warsaw in 1891; he died in 1938 in transit to a remote concentration camp in the north of Siberia. He grew up in a middle-class Jewish family in St. Petersburg, where he received a classic Russian education. *Kamen (Stone)* (1913) and *Tristia* (1922), his first collections of verse, were written and published in St. Petersburg. In these books, one of Mandelstam's sources of inspiration and his main theme was the city itself, with its opulent architecture and elegant, austere atmosphere.

Mandelstam's attitude towards his Jewish background is an important key to his sensibility. Judaism as he was acquainted with it through his relatives was a frightening ancient religion, an unknown language, a mercantile tradition. Russia, embodied by St. Petersburg, seemed to him by contrast to represent order and enlightenment. Mandelstam's rejection of the "chaos of Judaism," as it is expressed in his brief autobiography, *The Noise of Time* (1923),* throws light on middle-class Russian attitudes towards Jews in those years (and to some extent these attitudes are still to be found in the U.S.S.R.). Although Jews were mistreated in Russia, they were able to join the intellectual elite of the day, the intelligentsia, adopting its ideology and its language. This group, drawing on all classes of nineteenth-century

* Published in the U.S.A. in 1965 in *The Prose of Osip Mandelstam*, Princeton University Press.

Russian society, was embattled; as a whole it was poor and had little political power. But it had a sense of solidarity and of its own worth; it considered itself the elite of Russia. Mandelstam was a Russian intellectual and a completely Russian writer. Only his humor, which has a certain whimsy akin to Kafka's and differs from Russian humor, marks him as Jewish.

In his youth, Mandelstam, a man of remarkable culture, was linked with the Acmeists, a group of poets dedicated to freeing Russian verse from the encumbrances of the Victorian age. The Acmeists' inspiration came in part from the poet Innokenty Annensky (1856–1909), a teacher of Greek in a Tsarskoe Selo Gymnasium. Annensky, who was both a distinguished classical scholar and an esthete, wrote beautiful, ponderous, often strange poetry.

The Acmeists were rebelling against Russian Symbolism, the ill-defined, mystic creed which dominated St. Petersburg literary life at the turn of the century. Mandelstam, together with Anna Akhmatova and her husband, Nikolai Gumilev (whose verse is not unlike that of the French Parnassians), founded the Poets' Guild to emphasize the fact that poetry was a matter of craft. Mandelstam's lifelong intolerance of Alexander Blok may be traced to his anti-Symbolist, Acmeist days. Working at approximately the same time as the Imagists in England and America, the Acmeists endeavored, in Mandelstam's words, to reinstate "the power of the word itself," because "each word is a psyche, a live soul choosing its own sweet body."

Mandelstam's early verse is neoclassic, often hermetic and yet of crystalline clarity. While Pasternak's power is in the sweep of the whole poem, Mandelstam's poetic power may be felt at the level of the line, sometimes even of the word. *Tristia* is one of the most perfect and surely the most original collections of verse ever to appear in

117

Russian. In it the poet both welcomed the Revolution and dreaded it, as may be sensed in his famous "Twilight of Freedom."

A passage in Mandelstam's autobiography, *The Noise of Time*, reveals his approach to literary subject matter — and also his feelings about the Revolution:

I want to speak, not about myself but as an observer of the century, of the noise and germination of time. My memory is hostile to all that is personal. Were it up to me, I would merely wrinkle my brow remembering the past. I could never understand the Tolstois and the Aksakovs, the Bagrov grand-children in love with their family archives, so full of heroic household memoirs. Let me say it again—my memory is not amorous but hostile, working not on the re-creation of the past but on its removal. The *raznochinets* [commoner] needs no memory; all he must do is tell of the books he has read, and his biography is done. In the spot where for happy generations an epic poem unfolds in hexameter its chronicle, for me there is a blank space. Between myself and the century, in the place reserved for family archives, there is a gap, a ravine filled with clamorous time.

What did my family wish to say? I do not know. It had, from birth, a speech defect—nonetheless it did have things to impart. And we, my friends and I, suffer sadly from inarticulate births. We learn not to speak but to babble, and only by listening carefully to the ever increasing roar of the century, when the foam of the wave's crest bleaches us, do we acquire a tongue.

The revolution itself is both life and death, so it abhors our gossiping about life and death in its presence. Its throat is parched with thirst, yet it will not accept a single drop of moisture from strange hands. Nature—revolution—is eternal thirst, a state of inflammation. Perhaps it envies the centuries which quench their thirst in a quiet domestic manner at the sheep's watering hole. This sickness is characteristic of revolution, this fear of receiving something from alien hands. Nor does it dare to come close to the sources of being.

118

Mandelstam's genius was recognized in St. Petersburg literary circles when he was very young. At the same time, he had an ability to arouse animosity, as truly brilliant people tend to do. He had a complete intolerance of mediocrity in literature; moreover, he was very witty. His spontaneous, sharp sense of humor wounded the literary pundits of the times. This explains certain absurd episodes about Mandelstam's youth related in the memoirs of several émigré writers — notably Georgi Ivanov and Sergei Makovsky — who had known the poet in St. Petersburg. Makovsky was the editor of St. Petersburg's most influential literary journal, *Appollon*, in which Mandelstam's first poems were published. Ridiculing Makovsky's preciosity, Leonid Andreyev usually referred to him as The Moth Wearing Gloves. To the day she died, Akhmatova deplored these writers' tales which depicted Mandelstam as a hysterical weakling.

As for Soviet literary critics, after abusing Mandelstam in the Stalinist days, they are now silent. He is not yet rehabilitated as a writer in the U.S.S.R. A poet who is regarded by many as the greatest twentieth-century Russian poet is still unpublished in his own country. In May, 1965, an evening devoted to readings of Mandelstam's works and presided over by Ilya Ehrenburg took place in a hall of the mathematics department of Moscow University. It was followed by more readings held in various scientific institutions; in the Soviet Union, scientists are emancipated and knowledgeable in literary matters. A few poems have appeared in magazines, notably in the excellent Georgian journal, *Literaturnaya Gruzia*. This is the extent of Mandelstam's official recognition at this time in the U.S.S.R., although a volume of selected works has apparently been scheduled to be published in 1968.

It is not too surprising that Mandelstam's writings should not be promoted in the Soviet Union. Although he did not oppose the October Revolution, in the thirties the frail, urbane poet became an outspoken foe of Stalin's. In this respect he was the most lucid and the bravest of all Soviet writers. His complete works will be acceptable in the Soviet Union only when intellectual freedom is fully established there. In the meantime his work, circulated orally or in typescript, is becoming more popular in Russia each year. This is particularly true of his late poems, which are very tragic and more direct than either his early ones or his prose. In these late poems the classic themes recede. A bloody, terrifying everyday life takes over; a poetic St. Petersburg is replaced by torn flesh. Yet, even in these elemental works, in which Mandelstam succeeds in evoking terror more immediately than any other poet, tenderness remains at the core of his art.

The voice in Mandelstam's late poems is that of today's conscience-stricken Russians; dedicated to their country, they are at last releasing their feelings of horror in the face of the past, and Mandelstam's incantations both sharpen and heal their pain. In *Tristia*, Mandelstam wrote of Fate — of history's foreshadowing of doom. In his late poems he usually described reality in its fragmented immediate aspects, unlike Pasternak, for example, whose poems capture the present in its majestic, eternal, natural flow. For this reason Mandelstam is particularly meaningful for the alienated, disoriented Russians of today, and this also makes it difficult to incorporate him into a Social Realist literary framework.

Russia owes an extraordinary debt to Mandelstam's widow, Nadezhda Yakovlevna Mandelstam. An English scholar, she was brought up in a highly cultivated Jewish milieu in Kiev. In the twenties she studied art with one of Russia's best contemporary painters, Alexander Tishler. At the risk of her life, in time of persecutions and war, she managed to save Mandelstam's unpublished manuscripts — more than half of his life's work.

Preserve my words forever for their aftertaste of misfortune
and smoke,
for their tar of collective patience and conscientious work—
water in the wells of Novgorod must be black and sweetened
to reflect a star with seven fins at Christmas.

This poem, which I had never heard before, was recited to me one Easter in Moscow by a poet of the younger war generation, Alexander Mezhirov. On a warm holiday afternoon, we were visiting the flamboyant eighteenth-century Novodevichy monastery, all cupolas and
arabesques. The intensity with which Mezhirov recited
this strange, threatening poem as we walked among the
faithful crowding the monastery's enclosure, revealed to
me Mandelstam's total involvement with his country.

Excerpts from the Journal of Anna Akhmatova*

Mandelstam was one of the most brilliant conversa-
tionalists. In conversing he didn't listen to himself, nor
did he answer himself as almost everyone does today; he
was attentive, imaginative and infinitely varied. I have
never heard him repeat himself. Osip Emilievich could
learn foreign languages with extraordinary ease. He recited by heart in Italian whole pages out of *The Divine
Comedy*. Not long before his death, he had asked his wife
Nadia to teach him English, which he didn't know at all.
He spoke about poetry dazzlingly, often in a prejudiced
way, and sometimes he was monstrously unjust towards
other poets — towards Blok for example. About Pasternak he said: "I am thinking about him so much it even
makes me feel tired." And also, "I am sure he has never
read a single line of mine." About Marina Tsvetayeva:

* These are pages from a sketchy, carelessly edited journal which circulated in Moscow shortly before Akhmatova's death. A version of it
appeared in New York in a Russian-language magazine, *Aerial Ways*
(1965).

"I am an anti-Tsvetayevist." He was at home with music, and this for a poet is extremely rare. More than anything else, he feared the loss of his poetic voice. When this happened, he rushed around in a state of terror and invented all sorts of absurd reasons to explain this calamity. A second, frequent cause of distress was his readership. It always seemed to him that he was liked by the wrong readers. He knew well and remembered other poets' poems, sometimes falling in love with a single line. He could memorize with ease poems which were read to him.

I met Mandelstam in the spring of 1911, at Vyacheslav Ivanov's "Tower."* He was then a thin young boy with a sprig of lily of the valley in his buttonhole, his head thrown up and back, with eyelashes so long that they covered half his cheek.

Throughout the teens we frequently met at various literary occasions. These were very important years for Mandelstam as a writer. There is yet much thinking to be done, much to be said about these formative years. Mandelstam greeted the Revolution as a completely mature poet, and a well-known one, at least in a small circle.

I saw Mandelstam especially often in 1914–1917, in Petersburg. He would come by for me with a rented carriage, and we rode over the unbelievable holes of the revolutionary winter, among the famous bonfires which burned as late as May, listening to the sound of rifle-shooting coming towards us, from where we didn't know. Mandelstam was one of the first to write poems on civic themes. For him the Revolution was an enormous event, and it is not by chance that the words *the people* appears in his verse. In March, he disappeared. At that time people disappeared and reappeared and no one was surprised by it. In Moscow he was becoming a permanent

* A famous Symbolist literary salon in pre-Revolutionary St. Petersburg where an esoteric intellectual atmosphere prevailed.

collaborator of a magazine entitled *The Flag of Labor*.

In the summer of 1924 Osip Mandelstam introduced to me his young wife, Nadezhda. I was then living on Fontanka Street, No. 2. Nadia was what the French call *"laide mais délicieuse."* Our friendship started on that day, and it has lasted to this day. Osip loved Nadia extraordinarily, incredibly much. He didn't let her out of his sight, he didn't allow her to work, he was wildly jealous, he asked her for advice about every word of his poems. Altogether I have never seen anything like it in all my life.

In the fall of 1933, Mandelstam was finally allocated an apartment in Moscow, which he celebrated in his poems. It looked as if the vagabond life which took the couple back and forth between Leningrad and Moscow had ended. For the first time Osip started to collect books, mostly ancient editions of Italian poets; at that time he was translating Petrarch. But, in fact, things remained unsettled. He had to phone somewhere all the time; he waited and hoped and nothing ever came of it. There was no money at all, and only half-promises for reviewing and translating jobs. Although the times were relatively bloodless,* the shadow of disaster and doom hung over this house. About that time, Mandelstam changed physically a great deal: he became heavier, his hair turned gray, he had difficulty breathing. He looked like an old man (he was forty-two), but his eyes continued to sparkle. His poetry was becoming better all the time; so was his prose.

On May 30, 1934, he was arrested. On that very day, after a deluge of telegrams and telephone calls, I arrived at the Mandelstams from Leningrad. We were then all so poor that in order to be able to buy a return ticket, I took a statuette with me to sell, a 1924 Danko. The warrant

* Akhmatova writes "vegetarian." "Vegetarian" has the same literal meaning in Russian as in English.

for Mandelstam's arrest was signed by Yagoda* himself. All night the police searched the apartment. They were looking for poems. We all sat in one room. It was very quiet. Behind the wall, at Kirsanov's,** we could hear a Hawaiian guitar. The detective found "The Century of the Wolf"*** and showed it to Osip Emilievich, who nodded his head in silence. He was taken away at seven o'clock, when it was already daylight. He kissed me when we parted.

Fifteen days later, early in the morning, Nadia had a phone call and was told to be at the Kazan railroad station that night if she wanted to accompany her husband in exile. It was all over. Our friend X and I went around collecting money for the trip. People gave a lot. Mrs. B. burst into tears and stuffed into my hand, without counting it, a great deal of money.

I went to the Kazan station with Nadia, but my own train was leaving from the Leningrad station early that evening, and Osip was brought out only after I had left the Kazan station. No one was allowed to speak with him. It was too bad that I hadn't waited for him, and that he hadn't seen me, because later on, when he had fits of insanity (and these occurred from time to time thereafter), he was persuaded that I had surely been shot, and kept looking for my corpse.

In February of 1936 I went to visit Mandelstam in Voronezh and learned all the details of his "affair." It is striking that a sense of spaciousness and breadth appeared in Mandelstam's verse precisely in Voronezh, when he was not at all free.

It was there that he was forced, for ambiguous, treacherous reasons, to give a lecture about Acmeism. It

* The chief of the Soviet secret police at that time.

** A Soviet poet, younger than Mandelstam, who is still alive today.

*** Akhmatova refers to the untitled poem found here on bottom of page 143 in an adaptation by Robert Lowell.

mustn't be forgotten that he had said in 1937, "I do not disavow the living or the dead." *

There have been several gossipy, ill-informed books about Mandelstam published in Russian in recent years. One is Georgi Ivanov's *Petersburg Nights*. Even more shocking in its inaccuracies and trivialities is a book by Leonid Chatsky, published under the egis of the best, oldest American university, Harvard.

Mandelstam was a tragic figure. Even while in exile in Voronezh, he wrote works of untold beauty and power. And he had no poetic forerunners — wouldn't that be something worth thinking about for his biographers? In all of world poetry, I know of no other such case. We know the sources of Pushkin and Blok, but who will tell us where that new, divine harmony came from, Mandelstam's poetry?

I last saw Mandelstam in the fall of 1937. He and Nadia had come to Leningrad for a couple of days. The times were apocalyptic. Disaster was following in the footsteps of each of us. Mandelstam had no money whatever. He and his wife had no place to live. Osip breathed heavily; he was catching air with his lips. I came to meet him, I do not remember where. Everything was like a frightening dream. Someone who arrived after me said that Osip's father had no warm clothes. Osip took off the sweater he was wearing under his jacket and asked that it be given his father. At that time we were both reading Joyce's *Ulysses* — he in a good German translation, I in the original. Several times we started to talk about *Ulysses*, but we couldn't — it was not a time to talk about books.

Mandelstam was arrested for a second and last time on May 2, 1938. He died a few months later in Siberia.

* A reference to Akhmatova's first husband, Nikolai Gumilev, the leader of the Acmeists, who was accused of plotting against the Bolsheviks and was executed. According to Anna Akhmatova, this accusation was false.

Есть иволги в лесах, и гласных долгота
В тонических стихах единственная мера.
Но только раз в году бывает разлита
В природе длительность, как в метрике Гомера.

Как бы цезурою зияет этот день:
Уже с утра покой и трудные длинноты;
Волы на пастбище, и золотая лень
Из тростника извлечь богатство целой ноты.

1914

Тристия

Я изучил науку расставанья
В простоволосых жалобах ночных.
Жуют волы, и длится ожиданье,
Последний час вигилий городских,
И чту обряд той петушиной ночи,
Когда, подняв дорожной скорби груз,
Глядели вдаль заплаканные очи,
И женский плач мешался с пеньем муз.

Кто может знать при слове—расставанье,
Какая нам разлука предстоит,
Что нам сулит петушье восклицанье,
Когда огонь в акрополе горит,
И на заре какой-то новой жизни,
Когда в сенях лениво вол жует,
Зачем петух, глашатай новой жизни,
На городской стене крылами бьет?

Orioles live in the elms, and in classical verse
The length of the vowels alone determines the measure.
Once and once only a year nature knows quantity
Stretched to the limit as in Homer's meter.

O this is a day that yawns like a caesura:
Serene from the start, almost painfully slowed.
Oxen browse in the field, and a golden languor
Keeps me from drawing a rich, whole note from my reed.

—ADAPTED BY STANLEY KUNITZ

TRISTIA

This is the title poem in Mandelstam's second volume of
verse, published in 1922. The Latin name, meaning "Poems
of Sorrow," alludes to the elegiac epistles of Ovid, which the
Roman poet began to write on his journey into exile in
Tomis. In his *Tristia*, Ovid wrote of the sorrow of exile, of
his unconquerable will to survive and to write, and of his
hope that he might be allowed to return to Rome. The seven
following poems are part of the *Tristia* cycle, as well as the
poem on page 141, adapted by Robert Lowell.

I made myself an expert in farewells
By studying laments, the night-fall of a woman's hair.
Oxen chew their cud; anticipation lags;
It is the town's last restless hour;
And I praise that ritual night when the cocks crowed
And eyelids, heavy with the griefs that pass,
Opened to the light, while her weeping flowed
Into the sound of the Muses singing.

Who knows, when the time comes to say goodbye,
What separation we are meant to bear
And what for us cockcrow shall signify
When the acropolis burns like a flare,
And why, at the new daybreak of a life,
When the ox is ruminating in his stall,
The herald cock, prophetic of rebirth,
Should flap his wings on the town wall?

И я люблю обыкновенье пряжи:
Снует челнок, веретено жужжит,
Смотри, навстречу, словно пух лебяжий,
Уже босая Делия летит!
О, нашей жизни скудная основа,
Куда как беден радости язык!
Всё было встарь, всё повторится снова,
И сладок нам лишь узнаванья миг.

Да будет так: прозрачная фигурка
На чистом блюде глиняном лежит,
Как беличья распластанная шкурка,
Склонясь над воском, девушка глядит.
Не нам гадать о греческом Эребе,
Для женщин воск, что для мужчины медь.
Нам только в битвах выпадает жребий,
А им дано гадая умереть.

1918

Когда Психея-жизнь спускается к теням
В полупрозрачный лес, вослед за Персефоной,
Слепая ласточка бросается к ногам
С стигийской нежностью и веткою зеленой.

Навстречу беженке спешит толпа теней,
Товарку новую встречая причитаньем,
И руки слабые ломают перед ней
С недоумением и робким упованьем.

Кто держит зеркало, кто баночку духов—
Душа ведь женщина,—ей нравятся безделки,
И лес безлиственный прозрачных голосов
Сухие жалобы кропят, как дождик мелкий.

И в нежной сутолке не зная, что начать,
Душа не узнает прозрачные дубравы;
Дохнет на зеркало, и медлит передать
Лепешку медную с туманной переправы.

1920

I bless the craft of spinning: the to-and-fro
Action of the shuttle, the way the spindle hums.
Look! barefooted Delia, light as a feather,
Hurries to meet you, flying as she comes.
Oh, how scrawny is the language of joy,
That weak foundation of our mortal lot!
Everything happened before; it will happen again.
Only the flash of recognition brings delight.

Be it so: a small transparent puppet lies,
Like a dried squirrel skin
Extended on a plate,
While a girl crouches, staring, over the image.
Wax is for women what bronze is for men.
We, who cannot prophesy of Erebus,
Only in battle dare confront our fate—
But their gift is to die while telling fortunes.

—ADAPTED BY STANLEY KUNITZ

When Psyche, who is life, steps down into the shadows,
the translucent wood, following Persephone,
a blind swallow casts itself at her feet
with Stygian tenderness and a green branch.

The shades swarm to welcome the refugee,
their new little companion, and greet her with eager wailing,
wringing their frail arms before her
in awe and trouble and shy hope.

One of them holds out a mirror, and another, perfume,
because the soul is a woman and fond of trifles.
And the silence of the leafless forest is spotted
with transparent voices, dry laments, like a fine rain.

And in the fond confusion, uncertain where to begin,
the soul does not recognize the transparent woods.
She breathes on the mirror and she still clutches
the copper wafer, the fee for the misty crossing.

—ADAPTED BY W. S. MERWIN

Декабрист

—Тому свидетельство языческий сенат—
Сии дела не умирают!
Он раскурил чубук и запахнул халат,
А рядом в шахматы играют.

Честолюбивый сон он променял на сруб
В глухом урочище Сибири,
И вычурный чубук у ядовитых губ,
Сказавших правду в скорбном мире.

Шумели в первый раз германские дубы,
Европа плакала в тенетах.
Квадриги черные вставали на дыбы
На триумфальных поворотах.

Бывало, голубой в стаканах пунш горит.
С широким шумом самовара
Подруга рейнская тихонько говорит,
Вольнолюбивая гитара.

— Еще волнуются живые голоса
О сладкой вольности гражданства!
Но жертвы не хотят слепые небеса:
Вернее труд и постоянство.

Всё перепуталось, и некому сказать,
Что, постепенно холодея,
Всё перепуталось и сладко повторять:
Россия, Лета, Лорелея.

1917

На страшной высоте блуждающий огонь,
Но разве так звезда мерцает?
Прозрачная звезда, блуждающий огонь,
Твой брат, Петрополь, умирает.

На страшной высоте земные сны горят,
Зеленая звезда мерцает.
О если ты звезда—воды и неба брат,
Твой брат, Петрополь, умирает.

THE DECEMBRIST

"The arguments of freedom shall not die:
The Roman senate testifies to this . . ."
Lighting his clumsy pipe, he wraps his robe
About him, while the men continue playing chess.

He has exchanged his proud bedeviled dream
For a clearing in Siberia (deaf, lost)
And for this curved *chibouk* in his bitter lips
Which truth, in a world of sadness, dared to cross.

Remember when the German oaks first rustled
And Europe wept, wept in their spreading shade?
Black chariots with four wild horses reared
On each triumphant turn the procession made.

There was a time when blue punch flamed our glasses,
With wide and gracious sound the samovar
And the friend across the Rhine of freedom
And romance spoke softly. Ah, deceptive harp!

And the voices, lively still, are agitating
For the sweet liberty of citizenship,
But now blind skies do not demand their martyrs—
Toil, constancy, a surer harvest reaps.

The flame is dying fast, the night grows cold,
Reason and right have shifted, gone awry,
And it is sweet to whisper to oneself:
Russia, Lethe, Lorelei . . .

—ADAPTED BY ROSE STYRON

A radiance travels the terrifying height—
is it a star there, sighing?
Star of transparency, wandering light,
your twin, Petropolis, is dying.

The dreams of earth catch fire on high,
a green star shimmers, sighing—
O, if you are the star of water and sky,
your twin, Petropolis, is dying.

131

Чудовищный корабль на страшной высоте
Несется, крылья расправляет—
Зеленая звезда, в прекрасной нищете
Твой брат, Петрополь, умирает.

Прозрачная весна над черною Невой
Сломалась, воск бессмертья тает,
О если ты, звезда—Петрополь, город твой,
Твой брат, Петрополь, умирает.

1918

Сумерки свободы

Прославим, братья, сумерки свободы,—
Великий сумеречный год.
В кипящие ночные воды
Опущен грузный лес тенет.
Восходишь ты в глухие годы,
О солнце, судия, народ.

Прославим роковое бремя,
Которое в слезах народный вождь берет.
Прославим власти сумрачное бремя,
Ее невыносимый гнет.
В ком сердце есть, тот должен слышать, время,
Как твой корабль ко дну идет.

Мы в легионы боевые
Связали ласточек—и вот
Не видно солнца; вся стихия
Щебечет, движется, живет;
Сквозь сети—сумерки густые—
Не видно солнца и земля плывет.

Ну что ж, попробуем: огромный, неуклюжий,
Скрипучий поворот руля.
Земля плывет. Мужайтесь, мужи.
Как плугом, океан деля,
Мы будем помнить и в летейской стуже,
Что десяти небес нам стоила земля.

Москва, май, 1918

132

A monstrous ship on that terrifying height
spreads out its wings for flying;
in a beautiful poverty, green star of night,
your twin, Petropolis, is dying.

The glass of spring, the wax of immortality, melts down,
on the black Neva lying—
O, if you are a star, Petropolis, your town,
your twin, Petropolis, is dying.

—ADAPTED BY ROSE STYRON

TWILIGHT OF FREEDOM

Come celebrate, kinsmen, the twilight of freedom,
The darkening conscience, the great year obscured;
Into the boiling waters of nightfall
A heavy forest of nets is let down.
The days of your rising are numb,
O sun, judge, people!

Come glorify the deafening hour:
We take the helm in an age of tears.
Those who have courage know, O Time,
Your boat is sinking to the bottom.

Into battle legions we have tied the swallows.
Day is invisible, the whole element
Sings, whirrs, lives . . .
Between the nets clouded with twilight
The sun is dark and the land goes sailing.

Still, let us try a turn of the wheel—
Clumsy, rasping, enormous—
Dividing the ocean like a driven plow,
We will remember when Lethe is frozen
That life to us was worth ten heavens.

—ADAPTED BY ROSE STYRON

Сестры—тяжесть и нежность—одинаковы ваши приметы.
Медуницы и осы тяжелую розу сосут.
Человек умирает, песок остывает согретый,
И вчерашнее солнце на черных носилках несут.

Ах, тяжелые соты и нежные сети,
Легче камень поднять, чем имя твое повторить!
У меня остается одна забота на свете:
Золотая забота, как времени бремя избыть.

Словно темную воду я пью помутившийся воздух.
Время вспахано плугом, и роза землею была.
В медленном водовороте тяжелые нежные розы,
Розы тяжесть и нежность в двойные венки заплела.

1920

Возьми на радость из моих ладоней
Немного солнца и немного меда,
Как нам велели пчелы Персефоны.

Не отвязать неприкрепленной лодки,
Не услыхать в меха обутой тени,
Не превозмочь в дремучей жизни страха.

Нам остаются только поцелуи,
Мохнатые, как маленькие пчелы,
Что умирают, вылетев из улья.

Они шуршат в прозрачных дебрях ночи,
Их родина—дремучий лес Тайгета,
Их пища—время, медуница, мята.

Возьми ж на радость дикий мой подарок,
Невзрачное сухое ожерелье
Из мертвых пчел, мед превративших в солнце.

1920

Sisters—heaviness and tenderness—your signs are so alike!
Bees and wasps suck at a heavy rose.
A man dies, the heated sand cools down
And yesterday's sun is carried out on a black litter.

Ah! heavy honeycombs and tender nets,
To lift a stone is lighter than to repeat your name.
I have but one care left on earth, a golden care:
How to live out the yoke of time.

I drink the air, troubled, like a dark water,
And time is tilled with a plough, and the rose was earth.
In a slow whirlpool heavy tender roses,
Roses, heaviness and tenderness, twine into double
    wreaths.

—ADAPTED BY ROSE STYRON

Take for joy from my outstretched palms
A little honey and a little sun
As we were implored by the bees of Proserpine.

No one can loose a boat that is unmoored.
No one can hear the shadow shod in fur.
One cannot track down fear in the dense forest of life.

We are left only with kisses,
Prickling like tiny fuzzy bees
Which die, having left the hive.

In the translucent underbrush of night they rustle . . .
Their homeland: Taygeta's impenetrable wood,
Their nourishment: clover, and mint, and Time.

Take for joy, then, my wild present,
This simple necklace of dry dead
Bees who turned their honey into sun.

—ADAPTED BY ROSE STYRON

Я буду метаться по табору улицы темной
За веткой черемухи в черной рессорной карете,
За капором снега, за вечным, за мельничным шумом...

Я только запомнил каштановых прядей осечки,
Придымленных горечью, нет—с муравьиной кислинкой;
От них на губах остается янтарная сухость.

В такие минуты и воздух мне кажется карим,
И кольца зрачков одеваются выпушкой светлой,
И то, что я знаю о яблочной, розовой коже...

Но все же скрипели извозчичьих санок полозья,
В плетенку рогожи глядели колючие звезды,
И били в разрядку копыта по клавишам мерзлым.

И только и свету—что в звездной колючей неправде,
А жизнь проплывет театрального капора пеной,
И некому молвить: «из табора улицы темной»...

1925

Концерт на вокзале

Нельзя дышать, и твердь кишит червями,
И ни одна звезда не говорит,
Но, видит Бог, есть музыка над нами,
Дрожит вокзал от пенья аонид
И снова, паровозными свистками
Разорванный, скрипичный воздух слит.

Огромный парк. Вокзала шар стеклянный.
Железный мир опять заворожен.
На звучный пир в элизиум туманный
Торжественно уносится вагон.
Павлиний крик и рокот фортепьянный—
Я опоздал. Мне страшно. Это сон.

136

Through the dark gypsy camp, the streets of night, I shall
  be rushing
Seeking a blossoming alder branch in a black-springed
  sleigh,
For a bonnet of snow I shall be searching, for the endless
  mill-wheel noise.

I remember a chestnut strand of hair—as a misfired shot
Smoked through with bitterness, keeps that slight acidity of
  ants—
And on my lips remains a dryness like amber:

In these moments even the air seems to me brown.
The edge of my sight is dressed in a gown of softness
And all that I know of apple-pink skin.

And still the runners of the drawn sleigh scrape
And through its woven canvas shine the sharp rays of the
  sky
And hooves strike the pavement like frozen keys.

The only light is from the spiny untruth of the stars.
Life floats by, a foam-white bonnet, and there is no one
Left to listen: "through the dark gypsy camp, the streets of
  night . . ."

                      —ADAPTED BY ROSE STYRON

CONCERT AT THE STATION

I cannot breathe; the solid earth wriggles with worms
and not a star speaks out.
Yet the gods know there is music aloft,
for the station trembles, the Aonians sing,
and, soon to be rent by the engine's whistle,
the air sleeps like a violin.

A gleaming park. The glass dome of the station.
Again the iron world is stunned to charm.
Solemnly the railroad car is being drawn
toward a sonorous feast, some foggy Elysium,
the crying of peacocks, the banging of grand pianos . . .
I am late. Afraid. A dream.

137

И я вхожу в стеклянный лес вокзала,
Скрипичный строй в смятеньи и в слезах.
Ночного хора дикое начало,
И запах роз в гниющих парниках,
Где под стеклянным небом ночевала
Родная тень в кочующих толпах.

И мнится мне: весь в музыке и пене
Железный мир так нищенски дрожит,
В стеклянные я упираюсь сени;
Куда же ты? На тризне милой тени
В последний раз нам музыка звучит.

1921

Ленинград

Я вернулся в мой город, знакомый до слез,
До прожилок, до детских припухлых желез.
Ты вернулся сюда—так глотай же скорей
Рыбий жир ленинградских речных фонарей!
Узнавай же скорее декабрьский денек,
Где к зловещему дегтю подмешан желток.
Петербург! я еще не хочу умирать:
У тебя телефонов моих номера.
Петербург! у меня еще есть адреса,
По которым найду мертвецов голоса.
Я на лестнице черной живу, и в висок
Ударяет мне вырванный с мясом звонок,
И всю ночь напролет жду гостей дорогих,
Шевеля кандалами цепочек дверных.

Декабрь, 1930, Ленинград

Лишив меня морей, разбега и разлета
И дав стопе упор насильственной земли,
Чего добились вы? Блестящего расчета:
Губ шевелящихся отнять вы не могли.

Воронеж, 1935

138

I enter now the crystal forest of the station,
the court of violins is in disarray
and the chorus of darkness wildly beginning,
and fermenting in the greenhouse the roses smell.
Under a sky of glass the familiar shadow
hides all night in the crowd.

And to me it seems that in music and foam
the iron earth trembles like a beggar.
I push against the glass waiting room—
hot steam is blinding the violinist's bow.
Where are you going? At the feast in memory of a dear
    shadow
the music sounds for us a last time.

LENINGRAD

Return to my city, dearer to me than tears,
to its veins, the swollen glands of childhood nights,
return, remembering—swallow, O quickly then
the codliver oil of Leningrad's rivered lights.
Recognize swiftly that small day of December:
see, in the sinister asphalt, egg yolks run . . .
St. Petersburg, say that I need not die yet!
You still list the number of my telephone.
St. Petersburg! I have kept all your addresses
that I may find the voices of the dead.
I live on a back stairway; against my temple
a constant doorbell's striking, tearing my flesh.
And all night long I await the sound of guests
shifting the heavy handcuffs of the door.

—ADAPTED BY ROSE STYRON

Depriving me of sea, of a space to run and space to fly,
And giving my footsteps the brace of a forced land,
What have you gained? The calculation dazzles,
But you cannot seize the movement of my lips, their silent
    sound.

—ADAPTED BY ROSE STYRON

139

Надежде Яковлевне Мандельштам

Твоим узким плечам под бичами краснеть,
Под бичами краснеть, на морозе гореть.

Твоим детским рукам утюги поднимать,
Утюги поднимать да веревки свивать.

Твоим нежным ногам по стеклу босиком,
По стеклу босиком, да кровавым песком.

Ну а мне за тебя—черной свечкой гореть,
Черной свечкой гореть, да молиться не сметь.

1937

На розвальнях, уложенных соломой,
Едва прикрытые рогожей роковой,
От Воробьевых гор до церковки знакомой
Мы ехали огромною Москвой.

А в Угличе играют дети в бабки,
И пахнет хлеб, оставленный в печи.
По улицам меня везут без шапки,
И теплятся в часовне три свечи.

Не три свечи горели, а три встречи—
Одну из них сам Бог благословил,
Четвертой не бывать, а Рим далече,—
И никогда он Рима не любил.

Ныряли сани в черные ухабы,
И возвращался с гульбища народ.
Худые мужики и злые бабы
Переминались у ворот.

Сырая даль от птичьих стай чернела,
И связанные руки затекли;
Царевича везут, немеет страшно тело—
И рыжую солому подожгли.

1916

To N.Y.M.

Under such blows
your narrow shoulders will redden
and flame, even in the snow.

Your childlike hands
will lift up irons
and weave the heaviest ropes.

Barefoot on glass
your slight feet will go,
barefoot on glass in the blooded sand.

And I will burn for you
like a black candle
(a black candle). I shall not dare pray.

—ADAPTED BY ROSE STYRON

Somehow we got through the miles of Moscow,
left the Sparrow Hills, and found the small, familiar church.
Our open sled was filled with straw, and roughly hooded
with coarse, frozen cloth that hurt us.

Then in Uglitch the children played knucklebones.
When we drove through it, I reached for my lost hat,
the air smelled like bread left in the oven,
three candles were melting in the chapel.

They were not three candles but three meetings—
one of them had been blessed by the Lord Himself.
There couldn't be a fourth—Rome was so far away,
and the Lord had never really been Himself there.

Our sled stuck in a black rut,
and people shuffled by us to stare.
The men were all bones, the women were crows.
They gossiped and wasted time by the door.

Birds blackened the bare distance with spots—
his tied hands were icy. The Tsarevitch's
body was like a frozen sack when they drove him in,
and set fire to the reddish straw.

—ADAPTED BY ROBERT LOWELL

С миром державным я был лишь ребячески связан,
Устриц боялся и на гвардейцев смотрел исподлобья—
И ни крупицей души я ему не обязан,
Как я ни мучил себя по чужому подобью.

С важностью глупой, насупившись, в митре бобровой
Я не стоял под египетским портиком банка
И над лимонной Невою под хруст сторублевой
Мне никогда, никогда не плясала цыганка.

Чуя грядущие казни, от рева событий мятежных
Я убежал к нереидам на Черное море,
И от красавиц тогдашних,—от тех европеянок нежных—
Сколько я принял смущенья, надсады и горя!

Так отчего ж до сих пор этот город довлеет
Мыслям и чувствам моим по старинному праву?
Он от пожаров еще и морозов наглеет,
Самолюбивый, проклятый, пустой, моложавый!

Не потому ль, что я видел на детской картинке
Лэди Годиву с распущенной рыжей гривой,
Я повторяю еще про себя под сурдинку:
Лэди Годива, прощай... Я не помню, Годива...

                                                    1931

За гремучую доблесть грядущих веков,
За высокое племя людей
Я лишился и чаши на пире отцов,
И веселья и чести своей.

Мне на плечи кидается век-волкодав,
Но не волк я по крови своей,
Запихай меня лучше, как шапку, в рукав
Жаркой шубы сибирских степей,—

Чтоб не видеть ни труса, ни хлипкой грязцы,
Ни кровавых костей в колесе,
Чтоб сияли всю ночь голубые песцы
Мне в своей первобытной красе.

I spoke with a child's gibberish to authority,
I was afraid to eat oysters,
I looked at the guardsmen out of the corner of my eye.

Everyone tortured me about this,
but how could I sulk in the foolish beaver miter of a bishop
by the Egyptian porticoes of the banks?

No gypsy girl ever danced for me
under the crackle of hundred-ruble bills
in a café high over the lemon-yellow Neva.

Far from the sirens and the ominous crush of events,
I shivered at the oncoming wave of murders,
and fled to the nymphs of the Black Sea.

I had to put up with much pain and anguish
from the famous beauties of the day,
those delicate, continental ladies.

Why then does this city move me like an old Mass,
when its fires and ice storms only make it
more arrogant, self-loving, empty and youthful?

Is it because I saw the naked, red-haired
Lady Godiva in some old picture book?
Lady Godiva, I do not remember. Lady Godiva.

—ADAPTED BY ROBERT LOWELL

In the name of the higher tribes of the future,
in the name of their foreboding nobility,
I have had to give up my drinking cup at the family feast,
my joy too, then my honor.

This cutthroat wolf century has jumped on my shoulders,
but I don't wear the hide of a wolf—
no, tuck me like a cap in the sleeve
of a sheepskin shipped to the steppes.

I do not want to eat the small dirt of the coward,
or wait for the bones to crack on the wheel.
I want to run with the shiny blue foxes
moving like dancers in the night.

Уведи меня в ночь, где течет Енисей,
И сосна до звезды достает,
Потому что не волк я по крови своей
И неправдой искривлен мой рот.

1931

Сохрани мою речь навсегда за привкус несчастья и дыма,
За смолу кругового терпенья, за совестный деготь труда.
Так вода новгородских колодцев должна быть черна и
сладима,
Чтобы в ней к Рождеству отразилась семью плавниками
звезда.

И за это, отец мой, мой друг и помощник мой грубый,
Я—непризнанный брат, отщепенец в народной семье—
Обещаю построить такие дремучие срубы,
Чтобы в них татарва опускала князей на бадье.

Лишь бы только любили меня эти мерзлые плахи!
Как нацелясь на смерть городки зашибают в саду,
Я за это всю жизнь прохожу хоть в железной рубахе
И для казни петровской в лесах топорище найду.

3 мая 1931

Нет, не спрятаться мне от великой муры
За извозчичью спину-Москву—
Я трамвайная вишенка страшной поры
И не знаю—зачем я живу.

Ты со мною поедешь на «А» и на «Б»
Посмотреть, кто скорее умрет.
А она—то сжимается как воробей,
То растет, как воздушный пирог,

И едва успевает грозить из дупла—
Ты—как хочешь, а я не рискну,
У кого под перчаткой не хватит тепла,
Чтоб объехать всю курву-Москву.

1931

144

There the Siberian river is glass,
there the fir tree touches a star,
because I don't have the hide of a wolf
or slaver in the wolf trap's steel jaw.

—ADAPTED BY ROBERT LOWELL

Preserve my words forever for their aftertaste of misfortune
    and smoke,
for their tar of collective patience and conscientious work—
water in the wells of Novgorod must be black and sweetened
to reflect a star with seven fins at Christmas.

Oh my Fatherland, my friend, my rough helper,
remember your unrecognized brother, the apostate from the
    people's family—
I have promised to build you forests of log wells,
such as the Tartars built to lower the princes in wooden
    buckets.

If only your executioners, those frozen blocks, could love
    me,
as the Tsar Peter, a deadly marksman, loved the balls he
    bowled on the lawn—
for your love, I'll walk through life in an iron shirt,
for my execution, I'll walk the woods like Peter, and find a
    handle for the axe.

—ADAPTED BY ROBERT LOWELL

No, I will not hide from the great mess
behind the coachman's back of Moscow;
I am hanging on the outside of a terrifying time, a moving
    bus.
I do not know why I live.

You and I, we will go to Avenues "A" and "B,"
and see who is going to die first—
Oh Moscow, she huddles like a scared sparrow,
then she swells like a sponge cake.

She has just time to threaten from behind a corner.
You do as you wish, I am not afraid—
who has enough heat in his gloves to hold the reins and ride
around Moscow, the whore, her ribbon of boulevards?

—ADAPTED BY ROBERT LOWELL

145

Колют ресницы. В груди прикипела слеза.
Чую без страха, что будет и будет гроза.
Кто-то чудной меня что-то торопит забыть.—
Душно, и все-таки до смерти хочется жить.

С нар приподнявшись на первый раздавшийся звук,
Дико и сонно еще озираюсь вокруг,—
Так вот бушлатник шершавую песню поет
В час, как полоской заря над острогом встает.

1931

О, как мы любим лицемерить
И забываем без труда
То, что мы в детстве ближе к смерти,
Чем в наши зрелые года.

Еще обиду тянет с блюдца
Невыспавшееся дитя,

А мне уж не на кого дуться,
И я один на всех путях...

1932

Лазурь да глина, глина да лазурь,
Чего ж тебе еще? Скорей глаза сощурь,
Как близорукий шах над перстнем бирюзовым,
Над книгой звонких глин, над книжною землей,
Над гнойной книгою, над глиной дорогой,
Которой мучимся как музыкой и словом.

1930

Помоги, Господь, эту ночь прожить:
Я за жизнь боюсь—за Твою рабу—
В Петербурге жить—словно спать в гробу.

1931

Я больше не ребенок,
                    Ты, могила,
Не смей учить горбатого—молчи!
Я говорю за всех с такою силой,
Чтоб небо стало нёбом, чтобы губы
Потрескались, как розовая глина.

1931

My eyelash prickles—a tear boils up from my chest.
I'm not afraid. I know what's on the calendar—a storm.
Someone marvelous is hurrying me on to forget everything.
It's stuffy here. It's boring how much I want to live.

At the first noise I lift my head from the bunks.
I look around me wildly, half asleep.
I am like a convict singing his rough song,
when morning blues a gray strip above his prison.

—ADAPTED BY ROBERT LOWELL

FRAGMENTS

Now that I have learned to be discreet,
now that I am brown and brittle for my harvest,
shall I go on pretending
death was much closer in my childhood?

The children still grow drowsy with apprehension,
and hurt all over when they are forced to eat;
but I have lost my taste for sulking,
I am alone no matter where I look.

I look at sky and fields, sky and fields.
What more do I want? Suddenly I am squinting
like a nearsighted sultan at his turquoise ring.
The earth is just another book—so bookish.

I too am earth, this dear, dear earth
that tortures me like talk or music.
My God, help me to live through this night.
I fear for my life, my life, your slave. . . .

Living in Petersburg is to sleep in a coffin.
But I am no longer a child!
The grave can teach
the cripple to run in circles.

Look, my lips cake
and crack like red clay.
I am everyone speaking
for the sky to remain sky.

Мы с тобой на кухне посидим.
Сладко пахнет белый керосин.

Острый нож, да хлеба каравай...
Хочешь, примус туго накачай,

А не то веревок собери
Завязать корзину до зари,

Чтобы нам уехать на вокзал,
Где бы нас никто не отыскал.

1931, Ленинград

Турчанка

Мастерица виноватых взоров,
Маленьких держательница плеч—
Усмирен мужской опасный норов,
Не звучит утопленница-речь.

Ходят рыбы, рдея плавниками,
Раздувая жабры. На, возьми
Их—бесшумно окающих ртами,—
Полухлебом плоти накорми.

Мы не рыбы красно-золотые,
Наш обычай сестринский таков:
В теплом теле ребрышки худые
И напрасный влажный блеск зрачков.

Маком бровки мечен путь опасный.
Что же мне, как янычару, люб
Этот крошечный, летуче-красный,
Этот жалкий полумесяц губ?

Не серчай, турчанка дорогая,
Я с тобой в глухой мешок зашьюсь,
Твои речи темные глотая,
За тебя кривой воды напьюсь.

Ты, Мария—гибнущим подмога.
Надо смерть предупредить, уснуть.
Я стою у твоего порога.
Уходи. Уйди. Еще побудь...

1934, Москва

148

You and I will sit for a while in the kitchen.
The white kerosene smells sweetly.

A sharp knife, a loaf of bread.
Why don't you pump the petroleum stove tight?

You can collect some strings,
and tie up our basket before sunrise,

then we will escape to the railway station.
No one will find us.

—ADAPTED BY ROBERT LOWELL

THE TURKISH WOMAN

Everything rests on your small shoulders:
the sidelong glances of conscience,
our dangerous, wolfish simplicity—
my words, like a drowned woman, are dumb.

Red fins shining, red gills fanning,
their wondering mouths rounded in wordless
and famished O's, the fish fin here and there.
Take this, feed them the half-risen bread of your flesh!

But we are not goldfish swimming round the globe,
and bubbling when we meet by a water fern;
ours the heat of the warm-blooded body, little ribs
vain as wishbones, the wet, white glitter of the eyeball.

I am gathering poppies from the dangerous fields
of your eyebrows. I love
your tiny, fluttering fish-gill red lips,
as a janissary loves his pitiful, small crescent moon.

Dear Turkish woman, do not be angry,
we will be tied together in a strong sack
and thrown into the Black Sea. I'll do it myself,
while drinking your words, their black water.

Maria, comfort those who must die;
death must be frightened off, and put to sleep.
I stand on a steep cliff by the sea.
Go away from me, stand off—another minute!

—ADAPTED BY ROBERT LOWELL

Сталин

Мы живем, под собою не зная страны,
Наши речи за десять шагов не слышны,
А где хватит на полразговорца,—
Там помянут кремлевского горца.

Его толстые пальцы, как черви, жирны,
А слова, как пудовые гири, верны.
Тараканьи смеются усища,
И сияют его голенища.

А вокруг его сброд толстокожих вождей,
Он играет услугами полулюдей.
Как подковы кует за указом указ—
Кому в лоб, кому в бровь, кому в пах, кому в глаз.

Что ни казнь у него,—то малина
И широкая грудь осетина.

1934

Чапаев

STALIN

This poem is said to have caused
Mandelstam's arrest in 1934

We live. We are not sure our land is under us.
Ten feet away, no one hears us.

But wherever there's even a half-conversation,
we remember the Kremlin's mountaineer.

His thick fingers are fat as worms,
his words reliable as ten-pound weights.

His boot tops shine,
his cockroach mustache is laughing.

About him, the great, his thin-necked, drained advisors.
He plays with them. He is happy with half-men around him.

They make touching and funny animal sounds.
He alone talks Russian.

One after another, his sentences hit like horseshoes! He
pounds them out. He always hits the nail, the balls.

After each death, he is like a Georgian tribesman,
putting a raspberry in his mouth.

—ADAPTED BY ROBERT LOWELL

CHAPAYEV

Vasily Chapayev was a famous partisan commander, a legendary figure of the Civil War, who drowned during a battle
against the Whites. Chapayev's story was made into a memorable Soviet movie in 1934. In one scene, White officers,
on foot, with cigarettes in their mouths, march into battle
"against the open loins of the steppes." In Part Two, images
out of Chapayev are mixed with Mandelstam's impressions
as he was taken eastward into exile after his first arrest. On
the train, the young soldiers who guarded him and Mme.
Mandelstam were reading Pushkin.

151

1

От сырой простыни говорящая,—
Знать, нашелся на рыб звукопас—
Надвигалась картина звучащая
На меня и на всех, и на вас.

Начихав на кривые убыточки,
С папироской смертельной в зубах
Офицеры последнейшей выточки
На равнины зияющий пах.

Было слышно гудение низкое
Самолетов, сгоревших до тла,
Лошадиная бритва английская
Адмиральские щеки скребла.

Изменяй меня, край, перекраивай—
Чуден жар прикрепленной земли!—
Захлебнулась винтовка Чапаева—
Помоги, развяжи, раздели!

1935

2

День стоял о пяти головах. Сплошные пять суток
Я, сжимаясь, гордился пространством за то, что
                                        росло на дрожжах.
Сон был больше, чем слух, слух был старше, чем
                                        сон—слитен, чуток...
А за нами неслись большаки на ямщицких вожжах...

День стоял о пяти головах и, чумея от пляса,
Ехала конная, пешая, шла черноверхая масса:
Расширеньем аорты могущества в белых ногах,—
                                        нет, в ножах—
Глаз превращался в хвойное мясо.

На вершок бы мне синего моря, на игольное
                                        только ушко,
Чтобы двойка конвойного времени парусами неслась
                                        хорошо.
Сухомятная русская сказка! Деревянная ложка—ау!
Где вы, трое славных ребят из железных ворот ГПУ?

I

Unreeling, speaking from the wet film—
they must have had a shepherd of sounds for the fish—
the loud images were moving in
upon me—and upon all, upon you too . . .

They had given up their privileged smallness,
their teeth gripped the deadly last cigarettes.
The brand new White Russian officers
stood against the open loins of the steppes.

A low roaring was heard—airplanes
streaking in burning to the very end—
an English razor blade, large enough to shave a horse,
scraped Admiral Kolchak's cheek.

After me, Oh land, refit me—
the heat of the fixed earth is beautiful—
Chapayev's smoking rifle has jammed.
Help me, untie me, separate me . . .

2

Passing the dragon with five heads. For five whole days,
I shrank back, I was proud of our huge open spaces rising
    like dough.
Sleep had swallowed the sounds, but sound wore through
    my sleep.
Behind us, the harnessed highways rushed and ran us
    down.

A five-headed dragon. Our cavalry, drunk with dancing,
    riding on;
our infantry, a fur-capped, blacktopped mass, widening,
rushing like an aorta, power in the white night—no, knives!
They slashed our eyeballs to strips of flesh like pine needles.

If only I had an inch of blue sea, as little as a needle's eye,
enough for the lowest cardholders, convicts chained two
    and two, to hoist sail,
but this is a plain Russian tale without a drink to go with
    it, or a wooden spoon.
Hey, who are those three boys coming out of the iron gates
    of the GPU!

153

Чтобы Пушкина славный товар не пошел по рукам
дармоедов,
Грамотеет в шинелях с наганами племя пушкиноведов—
Молодые любители белозубых стишков,
На вершок бы мне синего моря, на угольное только
ушко!

Поезд шел на Урал. В раскрытые рты нам
Говорящий Чапаев с картины скакал звуковой—
За бревенчатым тыном, на ленте простынной
Утонуть и вскочить на коня своего!

1935

Памяти Ольги Ваксель

Возможна ли женщине мертвой хвала?
Она в отчужденьи и силе ...
Ее чужелюбая власть привела
К насильственной жаркой могиле.

И твердые ласточки круглых бровей
Из гроба ко мне прилетели
Сказать, что они отлежались в своей
Холодной стокгольмской постели.

И прадеда скрипкой гордился твой род,
От шейки ее хорошея,
И ты раскрывала свой маленький рот,
Смеясь, итальянясь, русея ...

Я тяжкую память твою берегу—
Дичок, медвежонок, Миньона—
Но мельниц колеса зимуют в снегу,
И стынет рожок почтальона.

1935

Не мучнистой бабочкою белой
В землю я заемный прах верну—
Я хочу, чтоб мыслящее тело

154

To keep Pushkin's wonderful goods from falling to parasites,
our youthful lovers of his white-toothed verse
were becoming learned, a tribe of Pushkin-specialists with
    pistols . . .
If only I had an inch of blue sea, as little as a needle's eye!

The train was going toward the Urals. Commander
    Chapayev spoke
from the sonorous screen into our open mouths—
Oh to clear the tall wooden fence, go through the screen,
    and drown . . .
Like Chapayev, to drown, to die on one's own horse!

—ADAPTED BY ROBERT LOWELL

TO THE MEMORY OF OLGA VAXEL

Is it possible to praise a dead woman?
She was an alien to her people and full of strength.
The power of her love for a stranger
brought her to a hot and violent grave.

The firm black swallows of her eyebrows
swoop down at me from the grave.
They tell me they've lain too long
In their cold bed at Stockholm.

Your people were proud of an ancestor's violin—
Your neck bending over its neck improved its looks.
When you opened your mouth to laugh,
you too looked more Italian, and better-looking.

I keep your heavy memory,
wild one, little bear, Mignon . . .
But the wheels of the mills are fast in winter,
the horn of the postman is thinly blowing.

—ADAPTED BY ROBERT LOWELL

My body, all I borrowed from the earth,
I do not want it to return here—
some flour-white butterfly.

Превратилось в улицу, в страну—
Позвоночное, обугленное тело,
Осознавшее свою длину.

Возгласы темнозеленой хвои—
С глубиной колодезной венки—
Тянут жизнь и время дорогое,
Опершись на смертные станки,
Обручи краснознаменной хвои—
Азбучные, круглые венки.

Шли товарищи последнего призыва
По работе в жестких небесах,
Пронесла пехота молчаливо
Восклицанья ружей на плечах.

И зенитных тысячи орудий—
Карих то зрачков иль голубых—
Шли нестройно—люди, люди, люди—
Кто же будет продолжать за них?

1935

Стихи о Неизвестном Солдате

1

Этот воздух пусть будет свидетелем—
Дальнобойное сердце его—
И в землянках всеядный и деятельный—
Океан без окна, вещество.

До чего эти звезды изветливы:
Все им нужно глядеть—для чего?—
В осужденье судьи и свидетеля,
В океан без окна вещество.

Помнит дождь, неприветливый сеятель,
Безымянная манна его,
Как лесистые крестики метили
Океан или клин боевой.

156

My body, scratched and chewed with thought,
I want it to become a street, a land—
it was too full of vertebrae.

The dark green pine needles howling in the wind
look like funeral wreaths thrown into the water . . .
how our pastimes and life were drained away!
when we sat like galley slaves at our gruelling benches—
bodies spread against a backdrop of green pine,
red flags colored like the A B C's of a child!

The comrades of the last contingent are on the move;
no conversation; on their shoulders,
the exclamation points of rifles.
From the heights of the sky, a thousand guns,
brown eyes, blue eyes; no one sets the step—men, men, men!
Who will follow after them?

—ADAPTED BY ROBERT LOWELL

THE UNKNOWN SOLDIER

I

Let this air here be a witness
to his distant, pounding heart
out in the trenches—all-seeing, hungry air:
ocean without a window, matter.

Those stars—how inquisitive
their looks at all times—but why inquire
into the downfall of the judge and witness,
into an ocean without a window, matter?

The heavy-booted sower aches in his joints
from the rain, the nameless manna,
the forest of crosses dotting
the ocean like a suicide battalion.

Будут люди холодные, хилые
Убивать, голодать, холодать,
И в своей знаменитой могиле
Неизвестный положен солдат.

Научи меня, ласточка хилая,
Разучившаяся летать,
Как мне с этой воздушной могилою
Без руля и крыла совладать,

И за Лермонтова Михаила
Я отдам тебе строгий отчет,
Как сутулого учит могила
И воздушная яма влечет.

2

Шевелящимися виноградинами
Угрожают нам эти миры,
И висят городами украденными,
Золотыми обмолвками, ябедами—
Ядовитого холода ягодами—
Растяжимых созвездий шатры—
Золотые созвездий миры.

3

Сквозь эфир десятичноозначенный
Свет размолотых в луч скоростей
Начинает число опрозраченный
Светлой болью и молью нулей,

А за полем полей поле новое
Треугольным летит журавлем—
Весть летит светопыльной дорогою—
И от битвы вчерашней светло.

Весть летит светопыльной дорогою—
Я не Лейпциг, не Ватерлоо,
Я не Битва Народов. Я—новое,—
От меня будет свету светло.

В глубине черномраморной устрицы
Аустерлица погас огонек—
Средиземная ласточка щурится,
Вязнет чумный Египта песок.

The thin, cold people will kill,
or they will starve, or they will freeze to the wires.
The unknown soldier expatiates on his rest
in the unknown graves.

Oh thin little swallow who has all
but forgotten how to fly, teach me
how to handle this airy grave,
without wings, without a rudder.

Ah, Michael Lermontov killed for sport!
I'll give you a strict accounting,
tell how huddled flesh is broken by the grave,
by an ocean without a window, matter.

2

These worlds go on proscribing us,
as they rustle through their frost-killed vineyards,
as they hover like a mirage of golden, stolen Meccas,
taletelling children,
wet, poisonous berries,
crashing pavilions or stars—
like the golden fat of the stars.

3

Through the ether measured in decimals,
light-time congeals to one beam,
the numbers grow transparent with pain,
a mothlike summation of zeros.

Beyond this battlefield, a field, then fields—
like a triangular flight of cranes,
the news flies ahead on its lighted beam of dust.
Everything is lit up by yesterday's casualties.

Napoleon, the small star of Austerlitz,
has wizened in his black oystershell;
the Mediterranean swallow squints,
the infected sand of Egypt sinks back to Nile.

The news flies ahead on its lighted beam of dust,
says, "I am not Waterloo, Leipzig,
the Battle of the Nations.
I am something novel that will light the world."

4

Аравийское месиво, крошево,
Свет размолотых в луч скоростей—
И своими косыми подошвами
Луч стоит на сетчатке моей.

Миллионы убитых задешево
Притоптали траву в пустоте,
Доброй ночи, всего им хорошего
От лица земляных крепостей.

Неподкупное небо окопное,
Небо крупных окопных смертей,
За тобой—от тебя—целокупное—
Я губами несусь в темноте.

За воронки, за насыпи, осыпи,
По которым он медлил и мглил,
Развороченный—пасмурный, оспенный
И приниженный гений могил.

5

Хорошо умирает пехота,
И поет хорошо хор ночной
Над улыбкой приплюснутой Швейка,
И над птичьим копьем Дон-Кихота,
И над рыцарской птичьей плюсной.
И дружит с человеком калека:
Им обоим найдется работа.
И стучит по околицам века
Костылей деревянных семейка—
Эй, товарищество—шар земной!

6

Для того ль должен череп развиться
Во весь лоб—от виска до виска,—
Чтоб в его дорогие глазницы
Не могли не вливаться войска.
Развивается череп от жизни
Во весь лоб—от виска до виска,—
Чистотой своих швов он дразнит себя,

4

The Arabian fireworks flutter like mixed horse food,
light-time congeals to one beam,
a single bayonet pushed by oblique footsteps,
stuck like a hair on my retina.

A million men killed at knockdown prices
have serviced the trail to nothingness—
good night to them, my best wishes
from these mass graves of mammoth molehills.

The sky over these trenches is the incorruptible
Robespierre fed on important deaths;
my lips kiss nothingness . . .
Out of you, after you, O high-priced sky!

Over the shell holes, the earth masses, and the trenches
where the unknown soldier lagged a little in the dark,
hunches the genius of nothingness,
frowning, infected, humiliated.

5

How beautifully the butchered infantry sings,
how beautifully the night sings,
over the thick smile of Good Soldier Schweik,
over Don Quixote's frail bird leg of a lance,
over the birdlike rushes of the robber barons.
The cripple makes friends with the runner,
both will have work enough on their hands,
and the crutches beat with the dry clatter
of rain against the century's caterpillar wheels—
this is friendship . . . all over the world.

6

Is this why the skull develops
such an imposing dome—a handbreadth and a hand-
    breadth?
Are the beloved eyes opened
as a breakthrough for the battalions?
The skull grows pompous with life—
a handbreadth and another handbreadth.

Понимающим куполом яснится,
Мыслью пенится, сам себе снится—
Чаша чаше, отчизна—отчизне,—
Звездным рубчиком шитый чепец—
Чепчик счастья—Шекспира отец.

7

Ясность ясеневая и зоркость яворовая
Чуть-чуть красная мчится в свой дом,
Словно обмороками затоваривая
Оба неба с их тусклым огнем.

Нам союзно лишь то, что избыточно,
Впереди—не провал, а промер,
И бороться за воздух прожиточный—
Это слава другим не в пример.

И сознанье свое затоваривая
Полуобморочным бытием,
Я ль без выбора пью это варево,
Свою голову ем под огнем?

Для того ль заготовлена тара
Обаянья в пространстве пустом,

Чтобы белые звезды обратно
Чуть-чуть красные мчались в свой дом?

Слышишь, мачеха, звездного табора—
Ночь, что будет сейчас и потом?

8

Наливаются кровью аорты
И звучит по рядам шепотком:
— Я рожден в девяносто четвертом,
Я рожден в девяносто втором...
И, в кулак зажимая истертый
Год рожденья с гурьбой и гуртом,
Я шепчу обескровленным ртом:
— Я рожден в ночь с второго на третье
Января в девяносто одном
Ненадежном году, и столетья
Окружают меня огнем.

1937, Воронеж

Its suture is as neat as a zipper.
It rises like Santa Sophia, the Dome,
rounded with thought, the self of its dream,
mosaic of the stars,
the cup of cups, the homeland of homelands,
the cap of joy, bald Shakespeare's father.

7

Clarity and its possibility of outline
are pricked with red. Things run home,
and the sky swarms with their disappearance
whitening with lazy afterlight.

The only shell hole ahead of us is miscalculation,
only the superfluous is close to us.
We fight for the everyday air,
this glory should not serve as an example.

We hold our consciousness in reserve,
day-by-day life is half dead—
is it really me finishing this drink,
eating my own head toasting on the grill?

The dress shirt of joy is starched with our blood,
the stars are pricked in red.
Night, stepmother of those herds of stars,
hear what is, what will be!

8

The aortas fill with blood,
and a dull grumble rises from the ranks:
"I was born in ninety-four."
"I was born in ninety-two."
Along with the others I too crumple
the used-up year of my birth in my fist.
My blood leaves my throat dry.
I murmur, "I was born on a January night
in the year ninety-one,
unenviable year, unenviable century,
my barbed wire of fire."

—ADAPTED BY ROBERT LOWELL

MARINA

IVANOVNA

TSVETAYEVA

(1892–1941)

Read on my stone, your arms bouqueted
  with poppy, primrose, rue,
that I was called Marina
  and how many years I grew.
    . . . . .
I can't accept eternity.
  Why was I buried? sealed?
I begged so not to go under the earth
  from my beloved field.

   Marina Tsvetayeva, 1931
   —ADAPTED BY ROSE STYRON

A PROUD WALK, high forehead under close-cropped bangs—is this a wild young lad or a proper young lady? Tsvetayeva does not read her verse, she chants it, accelerating the last words of each stanza. The wild young lad sings well, he likes wild songs, about the Kaluzhskaya Highway, about Stenka Razin* and his hell-raising. The proper young lady prefers the Comtesse de Noailles and the flags of Vendée.

In one of her poems Marina Tsvetayeva speaks of her two grandmothers. One is a simple Russian woman, very much her own kind; the other a Polish lady with white hands. Two grandmothers, one Marina. She did nothing but sing the praises of Stenka the Bandit, but in March of 1917 she saw the soldiers, and she slammed her shutters closed and started to cry. 'Oh, my noble, my royal sadness!'

That was the Polish lady—the nostalgia for bygone days, the *beau geste*, heraldry, and pompous, honest Chénier. But from her Russian grandmother, Tsvetayeva has inherited not words but a voice. How much wild independence of spirit in her nostalgia for the past! For some time, I have been more interested in the way people say things than in what they say. Listening to Tsvetayeva's verse, I hear the singing of free-ranging pioneers, not an orderly harmony. . . .

The best way to understand Tsvetayeva is to forget about the political content of her verse, to look at her stubborn face and listen to the proud, haughty accents in her poetry. Somewhere in a poem she admits that she loves to laugh when it is forbidden to laugh. I must add that she loves to do all sorts

* A seventeenth-century Cossack chief who was a celebrated bandit.

of things that are forbidden. Defiance of taboo is the hidden force in the poetry of freedom.

As soon as she entered the sedate society of Russian poets, Tsvetayeva discovered what was forbidden and she proceeded immediately to attack the infallibility of Bryusov, who was then the dean of Russian poets, in just the same way as Rimbaud had attacked the indignant Parnassians. I am convinced that she doesn't care whom she is rebelling against—like Vesuvius she doesn't care whom it happens to be that she is engulfing. At the present time there is no place for heraldry, but she celebrates it with an insolent defiance worthy of the great heretics and rebels. However, in the verse of Tsvetayeva, beyond the provoking mannerisms, beyond the technical prowess, there is tenderness and love. The love is not addressed to God or man but to the black Russian earth moistened with spring dew. One does not choose one's mother, nor can one give her up. Marina Tsvetayeva knows this and she will never betray her country.

Russia is too often conceived as a medieval monk or a highway robber with a knife in his boot. Tsvetayeva resembles neither. She is a candid and sweet pagan, not from Greece but from Moscow, where warm, living flesh lurks underneath the gilded vestments of the Byzantine icons. . . .

Needless to say, all the romantic trappings will be forgotten—the beautiful verse of Marina Tsvetayeva will remain. In it will be preserved her thirst for life, the gallant fighting of one against all, and love, full of solemnity in the face of approaching death.

—ILYA EHRENBURG, 1920*

Thus Ilya Ehrenburg celebrated Marina Tsvetayeva shortly after the Revolution. She was then young and beautiful, at the peak of her short-lived literary fame. The following years were bitter for one of the most brilliant poets of the Revolutionary generation. Tsvetayeva's verse was banned in the U.S.S.R. from about 1925 until 1961. The story of her life is like a grim tale of our times.

* *An anthology of Russian Poetry*, Berlin, 1920.

It is as if Russia had deliberately destroyed one of her most gifted, most loving children.

Marina Ivanovna Tsvetayeva was born in 1892 in Moscow, the daughter of a man of modest origin who had become a distinguished professor of art history in Moscow University; he was the founder of what is now the capital's Pushkin Museum of Fine Arts. Her mother was a musician, and music played an important role in the young girl's education. Like Pasternak's, her poetry stemmed from music — in her case, less from Scriabin and Chopin than from Russian folk ballads and gypsy songs.

Part of Tsvetayeva's childhood was spent in the town of Tarusa, her father's birthplace. On the Oka River, some one hundred and fifty miles from Moscow, Tarusa was then, as it is now, an intellectuals' colony. However, at the turn of the century, the peasants of the country-side surrounding it were still imbued with the ways of ancient Russia. Tsvetayeva considered Tarusa as her home. In 1934 in Paris she wrote:

> I would like to be buried in the flagellants' graveyard in Tarusa, under an elderberry bush, in one of those graves with a silver dove on it, where the reddest, biggest strawberries grow.
>
> But if this cannot be, if I will not come to rest there, and the graveyard is gone, then on one of those hills where the Kirillovas* walked to our house, and we went to Tarusa to see them, I would like a stone from the town quarry to be placed: *Marina Tsvetayeva wanted to rest here.*

A world of birch forests and of folk tales nurtured Tsvetayeva — and a Russian language spoken by the people of Tarusa with breathtaking purity. During my visit there in 1964, my most memorable encounter was

---

* The Kirillovas were peasant women belonging to a local flagellants' sect. In the summer they sold berries to Tsvetayeva's family.

with an old peasant woman who sold milk and vege-
tables to my hosts, a progressive Moscow literary critic
and his wife. For the first time in my life I had some
understanding of the sources of the strange melodic
sweetness, direct and strong, which is at the core of
Pushkin's poetry. I understood the almost unbearable
longing for Russia and the sound of Russian which has
tortured many Russian poets in exile, notably Tsvetayeva. Never in my life have I heard a nobler, more musical
language spoken with more natural grace.

The musical richness and complexity of Tsvetayeva's
poetry is unsurpassed in Russian literature. Her masterpieces are lengthy poems. She has full opportunity to
demonstrate her inventiveness with sounds and rhythms
in the epic "The Pied Piper," "The Poem of the End," "The
Poem of the Mountain," and *Molodets,* her masterpiece.
Molodets [*The Young Man*] is an abstract yet extraordinarily vivid poetic version of a folk epic about a vampire.

Alas, Tsvetayeva is particularly hard to translate into
English, precisely because of her melodic richness.
Stripped of their sound patterns, her poems, especially
the early ones, reveal at times an excessive romanticism.
Tsvetayeva can be overly assertive in a feminine, annoying way. However, she was first to create a new approach
to the Russian language, to reveal its contrapuntal possibilities. Her technical mastery was instinctive — she
maintained that she knew nothing about metrics. Yet
she created many new rhythms that are commonly used
by Soviet poets today. While Bella Akhmadulina sometimes imitates her less fortunate, self-centered attitudes,
Voznesensky is greatly indebted to Tsvetayeva for his
strongest asset — technical virtuosity. His "Goya" might
not have been written without Tsvetayeva's forceful melodic pioneering.

Modern poets evolve through mutations. If Tsvetayeva
had survived World War II, she would have surely grown

169

emotionally and philosophically, catching up with her own extraordinary poetic gifts. But she was the victim of a passionate nature and of her love for Russia. During the Revolution she took a strong anti-Bolshevik stand; she wrote a collection of poems to the glory of the White Army, *The White Flock*. However, she did not publish it; nor did she ever engage in any anti-Soviet literary activity. She emigrated to Prague and then to Paris, but found exile unbearable. In 1938 she went back to the U.S.S.R. Her husband, Sergei Efron, once a White officer, by then a dedicated Communist, had returned earlier. However, because of his past as a White cavalryman, he was a compromised man in the eyes of the Soviet authorities. In the thirties he was assigned unsavory secret missions by the Stalinist secret police. When the war broke out and the Russians started retreating before the Germans in the summer of 1941, he was shot, along with others who were "politically unsafe" in the eyes of the police. On August 31, 1941, Tsvetayeva killed herself in the provincial town of Elabuga. She was living there in circumstances of utter isolation and despair, a refugee from invasion-threatened Moscow. None of her old literary comrades, like the Poet Aseyev and Ilya Ehrenburg—not even Pasternak—went out of their way to help her after her return from France. More concerned was a younger poet, Arseni Tarkovsky, who left for the front in June, 1941. (Recently Tarkovsky has published several beautiful poems dedicated to Tsvetayeva's memory.)

In his *Autobiography* (1957), some of Pasternak's most moving pages are dedicated to Tsvetayeva. Nothing would have been more precious to her than this homage, for she had adored Pasternak both as a man and as a poet:

One had to immerse oneself into Tsvetayeva's writings. When I did this [in the early twenties] I was astounded by the depths of purity and strength which opened before me. There was nothing like it around at the time. I won't be far from the mark if I say quite simply that, with the exception of Annensky, Blok, and to some degree Andrei Bely, the early Tsvetayeva was everything the other Symbolists wanted and could not be.

While their writings splashed around helplessly in a sea of planned doctrine and of lifeless, deliberate anachronisms, Tsvetayeva gracefully soared over the difficulties of creation, overcoming its hazards as if it was a game, with unequaled technical brilliance.

In the spring of 1922, Tsvetayeva was already outside of Russia when I bought in Moscow her small volume of poems, *Versti* [*Miles*]. I was struck by the power of Tsvetayeva's forms. They were felt in the blood, never weak-kneed; concentrated, tightly knit, they never ran out of breath from line to line; consecutive stanzas were bound together without rhythmic breaks. I felt a kind of kinship to Tsvetayeva quite beyond the peculiarities of her verse, based on the similarity of early influences and experience, the outcome perhaps of a similar role played by family and music—we had the same background and the same goals and tastes.

I wrote to Tsvetayeva in Prague, full of enthusiasm and astonishment over the fact that I had gone so long without knowing her. She replied. We began a correspondence that grew more intensive in the midtwenties, when her *Remeslo* [*Craft*] was published; at that time, copies of her poems— "Poem of the Mountain," "Poem of the End," "The Pied Piper"—circulated in typescript in Moscow. They were grand in scope and thought, vivid, striking in their originality.

We became friends. In the summer of 1935, scarcely myself and on the verge of a mental breakdown following almost a full year of insomnia, I found myself in Paris on the occasion of an antifacist congress. There I became acquainted with the son and daughter of Tsvetayeva, and with her husband, and I came to love as a brother this charming, refined, solid man.

Tsvetayeva's family urged her return to Russia, partly out of nostalgia for their country and their sympathies for Communism and the Soviet regime, and partly because they felt that Tsvetayeva had no life in Paris; she would perish there as a poet without the echo of her readers. Tsvetayeva asked me what I thought about this. I had no clear opinion on the subject. I had no idea what to suggest to her, although I felt strongly that she and her remarkable family might find the going difficult and uncertain among us. The eventual tragedy which befell this family immeasurably exceeded any forebodings that I might have had at that time.

Tsvetayeva was a woman with an active, masculine spirit, determined, warring, indomitable. In her life and her work she strove avidly, recklessly, almost rapaciously for clarity and finality, and in this pursuit she far outdistanced everyone in her generation. I think that the most far-reaching reappraisal of her work and the greatest recognition still awaits Tsvetayeva.

Although I was eight years old in 1938, I remember clearly the day when Marina Ivanovna came to say goodbye to my family in Paris; she was leaving for the U.S.S.R. the following week. We did not know then that a long, bloody war was about to engulf Europe; that the Soviet Union was just then in the process of destroying millions of Russians, including many writers, some of whom had fought for the Revolution, like Babel; that we would never see Tsvetayeva again.

Tsvetayeva was an important part of my Parisian childhood. Her angular presence, her hypnotic, rhythmic reading, are part of many of my early memories. When I knew her she was nearing middle age; she looked like a gypsy, with her hair turning white against her very dark skin, her many silver rings, her electric laughter. My family was devoted to her; they had helped her during the hardest, post-Depression emigration years. They put up with her notoriously difficult disposition for the sake of her talent and of her sense of honor. Once, one of my uncles challenged to a duel an émigré critic who had written insultingly about Tsvetayeva.

172

Отрок

Виноградины тщетно в садах ржавели,
И наложница, тщетно прождав, уснула.
Палестинские жилы!—Смолы тяжеле
Протекает в вас древняя грусть Саула.

Пятидневною раною рот запекся.
Тяжек ход твой, о кровь, приближаясь к сроку!
Так давно уж Саулу-царю не пьется,
Так давно уже землю пытает око.

Иерихонские розы горят на скулах,
И работает грудь наподобье горна.
И влачат, и влачат этот вздох Саулов
Палестинские отроки с кровью черной.

1917

Косматая звезда,
Спешащая в никуда,
Из странного ниоткуда.
Между прочих овец приблуда,
В златорунные те стада.
Налетающая, как ревность—
Волосатая звезда древних!

1921

Душа, не знающая меры,
Душа хлыста и изувера,
Тоскующая по бичу.
Душа—навстречу палачу,
Как бабочка из хризалиды!
Душа, не съевшая обиды,
Что больше колдунов не жгут.
Как смоляной высокий жгут
Дымящая под власяницей...
Скрежещущая еретица,
— Савонароловой сестра—
Душа, достойная костра!

1921

THE ADOLESCENT

The grapes in the royal garden have rusted;
the concubine, waiting, sleeps by the wall.
Veins of Palestine, heavy with sap,
in you flows the ancient sadness of Saul.

Like a five-day-old wound his mouth crusts over:
thick is the blood with its term at hand.
How long it has been since King Saul felt like drinking!
How long his eye has been probing the land.

The roses of Jericho burn on his temples,
like bellows his chest heaves, working its load,
and they drag, and they drag, their souls all sighing,
the young men of Palestine with their black blood.

—ADAPTED BY ROSE STYRON

Tousle-haired star
hurrying into nothing
out of a crazy nowhere,
a lone sheep among the starry horde,
into those golden flocks rushing
like jealousy you overwhelm me,
star of the ancients, shaggy star!

—ADAPTED BY ROSE STYRON

Soul, scorning all measure
Singer of heresy, martyr
longing for the whip's lashing.
Soul, you greet your assassin
like a butterfly fresh from its chrysalis,
nor can you brook this offense:
that wizards are not still burnt.
Smoking under your hair shirt
like a resinate high wick
screeching heretic
sister of Savonarola,
Soul,
You deserve the stake!

—ADAPTED BY ROSE STYRON

175

Как разгораются—каким валежником!
На площадях ночных—святыни кровные!
Пред самозванческим указом Нежности—
Что наши доблести и родословные!

С какой торжественной постепенностью
Спадают выспренные обветшалости!
О наши прадедовы драгоценности
Под самозванческим ударом Жалости!

А проще: лоб склонивши в глубь ладонную,
В сознаньи низости и неизбежности—
Вниз по отлогому—по неуклонному—
Неумолимому наклону Нежности...

1921

Хвала Афродите

1

Уже богов—не те уже щедроты
На берегах—не той уже реки.
В широкие закатные ворота
Венерины, летите, голубки!

Я-ж на песках похолодевших лежа
В день отойду, в котором нет числа...
Как змей на старую взирает кожу—
Я молодость свою переросла.

1921

Разлука

1

Башенный бой
Где-то в Кремле
Где на земле,
Где—

Крепость моя,
Кротость моя,
Доблесть моя,
Святость моя.

How they flare up, a tinder bonfire
on the plaza of night, our holy convictions!
Before the usurping edict of tenderness
what are our heroes, our marble traditions?

How solemnly fall the lofty antiques
one by one, and the modes of nobility,
and, oh, our ancestral jewels under
the blow of that king-pretender: pity.

The simpler gesture: to bend our heads
aware that lowliness has us in harness
down along the precipitous slope,
the irresistible incline of tenderness

—ADAPTED BY ROSE STYRON

PRAISE TO APHRODITE

I

No more so rich are the gifts of the Gods;
even the river is different now.
Through wide and widening sunset gates
the doves of Venus fly away.

And I, stretched out on the cooling sand,
soon into numberless days go forth.
Like a snake, looking back at his old bright skin—
I have outgrown my youth.

—ADAPTED BY ROSE STYRON

SEPARATION
(for S. Ephron)

I

The bell towers are ringing
somewhere in the Kremlin
somewhere in my homeland
somewhere

Towers are ringing
abandoned, ringing
where on this earth?

Башенный бой.
Брошенный бой.
Где на земле

Мой
Дом,
Мой—сон,
Мой—смех,
Мой свет,
Узких подошв—след.

Точно рукой
Сброшенный в ночь—
Бой
— Брошенный мой.

2

Уроненные так давно
Вздымаю руки.
В пустое черное окно
Пустые руки
Бросают в полуночный бой
Часов—домой
Хочу!—Вот так: вниз головой:
В шопот и шелест...
Мне некий Воин молодой
Крыло подстелет.

3

Всё круче, всё круче
Заламывать руки!
Меж нами не версты
Земные. Разлуки,
Небесные реки, лазурные земли,
Где друг мой навеки уже—
Неотъемлем.

178

My fortress
my laughter
my dream
my light
of narrow feet, the footsteps

deftly flung out
into the night
my abandoned one,
ringing

2

I shall lift my arms
my empty hands
through the black window
and fling myself
down the midnight clanging
of the clock tower
home. I would go home
like this: head down
from the noisy tower. Home,
not against the cobblestoned square
but into the rustling
whispering
wings of My Warrior.

3

Tighter and tighter wringing my hands
till they be riven—
Between us are not the miles of earth
but the rivers of heaven,
of separation, the azure lands
where my friend is forever
inalienable.

Стремит столбовая
В серебряных сбруях.
Я рук не ломаю!
Я только тяну их—
Без звука!—
Как дерево машет рябина—
В разлуку.
Вослед журавлиному клину.

Стремит журавлиный,
Стремит безоглядно.
Я спеси не сбавлю!
Я в смерти—нарядной
Пребуду! твоей быстроте златоперой
Последней опорой
В потерях простора!

1921

8

Я знаю, я знаю,
Что прелесть земная,
Что эта резная
Прелестная чаша—
Не более наша,
Чем воздух,
Чем звезды,
Чем гнезда,
Повисшие в зорях.

Я знаю, я знаю,
Кто чаше—хозяин!
Но легкую ногу вперед—башней
В орлиную высь!
И крылом—чашу
От грозных и розовых уст—
Бога!

1921

The highway dashes
in silvery harness;
my hands are not wrung now
but open, reaching
soundlessly,
like the ash tree climbing
after a flight of cranes.

To fly like the cranes and not look back!
Haughtiness
would be mine, and in death's country
in costly dress
I would arrive, to your fleet gold feathers
a last buttress
in the airy losses of space.

8

I know, I know
that earth's enchantment—
this carved
charmed cup—
is no more ours
than air is ours
than stars
than nests
suspended in the dawn.

I know, I know
it has a master.
Still, like a towering
eagle rising
high
with your wing
purloin this cup
from the cold pink lips
of God.

—ADAPTED BY ROSE STYRON

Маяковскому

Превыше крестов и труб,
Крещенный в огне и дыме,
Архангел-тяжелоступ—
Здорово, в веках Владимир!

Он возчик и он же конь,
Он прихоть и он же право.
Вздохнул, поплевал в ладонь:
— Держись, ломовая слава!

Певец площадных чудес—
Здорово, гордец чумазый,
Что камнем—тяжеловес
Избрал, не прельстясь алмазом.

Здорово, булыжный гром!
Зевнул, козырнул—и снова
Оглоблей гребет—крылом
Архангела ломового.

1921

Эренбургу

Небо катило сугробы
Валом в полночную муть.
Как из единой утробы—
Небо—и глыбы—и грудь

Над пустотой переулка,
По сталактитам пещер
Как раскатилося гулко
Вашего имени Эр!

Так, между небом и нёбом,
— Радуйся же, маловер!—
По сновиденным сугробам
Вашего имени Эр...

1921

TO MAYAKOVSKY '

Louder than crosses and trumpets,
long christened by fire and grime,
Archangel, your clumsy footsteps
resound on the quay of time.

Vladimir! steed and still horseman,
by law and caprice both drawn,
how you'd tease, spitting into the palms of your hands,
"Here I come, heavy glory—hold on!"

Singer of street-corner miracles,
proud boy with the sooty clothes,
diamonds by firelight were nothing to you:
how weighted the stones you chose.

A toast through the years, then, clatterer!
You yawn, tip your cap like no king
and again row away, with a noisy oar
like a cobblestoned archangel's wing.

—ADAPTED BY ROSE STYRON

TO EHRENBURG

The sky rolled snowdrifts,
Masses of troubled midnight.
You and the mountainous sky
Were of one essence.

Through the deserted side streets
The stalactites of caverns
The R of your name
Proudly rolls and resounds....

Caught between sky and palate
Ehrenburg, doubter, rejoice!
In the snowdrifts of winter,
Your name rolls and resounds....

—ADAPTED BY OLGA CARLISLE

Письмо

Так писем не ждут,
Так ждут—письма.
Тряпичный лоскут,
Вокруг тесьма
Из клея. Внутри—словцо.
И счастье.—И это—всё.

Так счастья не ждут,
Так ждут—конца:
Солдатский салют
И в грудь — свинца
Три дольки. В глазах красно́.
И только.—И это—всё.

Не счастья—стара!
Цвет—ветер сдул!
Квадрата двора
И черных дул.

(Квадрата письма:
Чернил и чар!)
Для смертного сна
Никто не стар!

Квадрата письма.

11 августа, 1923

A LETTER

So they don't expect
letters. So they wait for—
a letter.

A ragged scrap
circled
by sticky tape. Inside—

a scribble,
and happiness.
And that's all.

So, they don't expect
happiness. So they expect—
the end.

A soldierly
salute, and
three slugs of lead in the breast.

They see a flash
of red. And
that's all.

It's not happiness, old girl!
The wildflower color—
the wind blew it away.

A square courtyard
and black gun-muzzles.
A square letter,

ink, sorcery.
When it comes to
death, the

last dream, no one's
old.
A square letter.

—ADAPTED BY DENISE LEVERTOV

Осень в Тарусе

Ясное утро не жарко,
Лугом бежишь налегке.
Медленно тянется барка
Вниз по Оке.

Несколько слов поневоле
Все повторяешь подряд.
Где-то бубенчики в поле
Слабо звенят.

В поле звенят? На лугу ли?
Едут ли на молотьбу?
Глазки на миг заглянули
В чью-то судьбу.

Синяя даль между сосен,
Говор и гул на гумне...
И улыбается осень
Нашей весне.

Жизнь распахнулась, но все же...
Ах, золотые деньки:
Как далеки они, Боже!
Господи, как далеки!

1909

Со мной не надо говорить.
Вот губы: дайте пить.
Вот волосы мои: погладь.
Вот руки: можно целовать.
— А лучше дайте спать.

1920

AUTUMN IN TARUSA

A clear morning, the air is
cool. Lightly you cross
the meadow. And there
on the Oka, a barge
slowly draws by.
Unwilled, a word is
speaking itself, over and over, and
others follow. A bell can be heard
somewhere, faintly
rung in a field.
A wheat field? A field of hay?
Are they going to be threshing?
My eyes looked away
for an instant, straight into
someone's fate,
between pine trees the deep
rifts of blue, the voices
across the noise and the heaps of
chaff and grain . . . And autumn
smiles at our springtime.
Life has thrown open its coat
and yet—
oh golden days, how remote,
how remote they are, Lord,
oh God, how far-off.

—ADAPTED BY DENISE LEVERTOV

No need for talk:
my lips are for you to
drink from,
the thick of my hair
hangs heavy for you to
stroke. Please.
And my hands.
For you to kiss.
Or let me
go down into
black sleep.

—ADAPTED BY DENISE LEVERTOV

Стихи к Блоку

1

Имя твое—птица в руке,
Имя твое—льдинка на языке.
Одно-единственное движенье губ.
Имя твое—пять букв.
Мячик, пойманный на лету,
Серебряный бубенец во рту.

Камень, кинутый в тихий пруд,
Всхлипнет та́к, как тебя зовут.

В легком щелканьи ночных копыт
Громкое имя твое гремит.
И назовет его нам в висок
Звонко щелкающий курок.

Имя твое—ах, нельзя!—
Имя твое—поцелуй в глаза,
В нежную стужу недвижных век.
Имя твое—поцелуй в снег.
Ключевой, ледяной, голубой глоток.
С именем твоим—сон глубок.

15 апреля, 1916

2

У меня в Москве—купола горят,
У меня в Москве—колокола звонят,
И гробницы, в ряд, у меня стоят,—
В них царицы спят и цари.

И не знаешь ты, что зарей в Кремле
Легче дышится—чем на всей земле!
И не знаешь ты, что зарей в Кремле
Я молюсь тебе—до зари.

И проходишь ты над своей Невой
О ту пору, как над рекой-Москвой
Я стою с опущенной головой,
И слипаются фонари.

POEMS FOR BLOK

I

Your name a bird in my hand.
Your name ice on my tongue.
The lips make a single gesture—
Your name:
A ball caught in mid-air,
a silver bell in my mouth.

A stone tossed into a pond
claps your name.
Horsehooves at night
dryly thud out your name.
The loud click of a gun's trigger
inscribes that name in our temple.

Your name—
         But no,
it is a kiss on the eyelids.
Mute, cold, unblinking lids—
your name kissing the snow.
Your name in my mouth an icy
gulp of blue brook water.
With your name,
a depth of sleep.

2

In my home in Moscow cupolas glow,
in my home in Moscow bells clang,
tombs stand in my home in rows,
queens sleep there, and kings.

Didn't you know that in the Kremlin at dawn
it's easier to breathe than anywhere else?
Didn't you know that in the Kremlin at dawn
I pray for you—from dawn to dusk?

While you walk by your proud Neva,
I am standing here by the Moskva.
I stand still and I bow my head.
In the streets the lights run together.

Всей бессонницей я тебя люблю,
Всей бессонницей я тебе внемлю—
О ту пору, как по всему Кремлю
Просыпаются звонари.
Но моя река—да с твоей рекой,
Но моя рука—да с твоей рукой
Не сойдутся, Радость моя, доколь
Не догонит заря—зари.

7 мая, 1916

3

И тучи оводов вокруг равнодушных кляч,
И ветром вздутый калужский родной кумач,
И посвист перепелов, и большое небо,
И волны колоколов над волнами хлеба,
И толк о немце, доколе не надоест,
И желтый-желтый—за синею рощей—крест,
И сладкий жар, и такое на всем сиянье,
И имя твое, звучащее словно: ангел.

18 мая, 1916

4

Без зова, без слова,—
Как кровельщик падает с крыш.
А может быть, снова
Пришел,—в колыбели лежишь?

Горишь и не меркнешь,
Светильник немногих недель…
Какая из смертных
Качает твою колыбель?

Блаженная тяжесть!
Пророческий певчий камыш!
О, кто мне расскажет,
В какой колыбели лежишь?

«Покамест не продан!»
Лишь с ревностью этой в уме,
Великим обходом
Пойду по российской земле.

190

With my insomnia, all of it, I love you.
With my insomnia, all of it, I listen
to you,
   while the vast caverns of the Kremlin
stir with the waking of the ringers of bells.

But never will my river and your river,
never will my hand and your hand
meet, O my joy, never,
unless daybreak overtakes daybreak.

3

And flies swarming round the indifferent mares,
and the familiar grass lifting in the wind,
and whistled tunes and the immense sky,
and waves of bells breaking over waves of wheat,
and endless boring tales about the Germans,
and the yellow, yellow cross beyond the blue grove,
and the sweet heat and such a light overhead,
and your name which sounds like the word *angel*.

4

Without a call, without a word,
like snow softly sliding off the roof,
can it be you've come back?
Are you asleep in a cradle?

Brightly you burn,
icon lamp only a few weeks old . . .
Who among mortal women
is rocking your cradle?

Blissful burden,
prophetic reed,
who will tell me
in what crib you are sleeping?

Let me be worthy,
no other thought in mind,
trudging the Russian earth,
walking the whole country—

Полночные страны
Пройду из конца в конец.
Где рот-его-рана,
Очей синеватый свинец?

Схватить его! Крепче!
Любить и любить его лишь!
О, кто мне нашепчет,
В какой колыбели лежишь?

Жемчужные зерна,
Кисейная сонная сень.
Не лавром, а тёрном—
Чепца острозубая тень.

Не полог, а птица
Раскрыла два белых крыла!
— И снова родиться,
Чтоб снова метель замела?!

Рвануть его! Выше!
Держать! Не отдать его лишь!
О, кто мне надышит,
В какой колыбели лежишь?

А может быть, ложен
Мой подвиг, и даром—труды.
Как в землю положен,
Быть может,—проспишь до трубы.

Огромную впалость
Висков твоих—вижу опять.
Такую усталость—
Ее и трубой не поднять !

Державная пажить,
Надежная, ржавая тишь.
Мне сторож покажет,
В какой колыбели лежишь.

1921

Yes, I'll walk
from end to end of the midnight earth
(Where is his mouth—a wound—
and the leaden blue of his eyes?)

To find and hold him, to love
no one but him . . .
Who will whisper to me
where he is sleeping?

Seed pearls upon the foam-white
cradle curtains, the sleepy
gauze that enfolds him.
                         Not laurels but sharp
thorns, the shadows cast by his pleated bonnet.

It is not the curtains that part,
it is the wings of a bird,
white, outstretched! . . .
To be born again, only to be
caught in the blizzard again.

To find him . . . To lift him
over the storm wind . . . To hold him
and not let go!
O, who will whisper to me
telling me where he is cradled?

But perhaps
all that I do is useless.
You lie in the earth
perhaps, till those trumpets blow . . .

I see the curve
of your temples. Such
fatigue! The trumpets
might not awake you!

Powerful silence,
a hopeful, a rusted silence.
Ah, if the watchman would show me
the cradle where you are sleeping . . .

—ADAPTED BY DENISE LEVERTOV

Vladimir Vladimirovich Mayakovsky
(1893–1930)

I have no gray hairs in my soul
No old-age meekness!
My thundering voice shakes the world.
I walk,
Handsome
Twenty-two years old.

Vladimir Mayakovsky, "Cloud in Trousers," 1916

TWO OVERSIZED STATUES stand in the middle of Moscow, off the city's main artery, Gorky Street. One is a ponderous 1880 effigy of Pushkin. Not far from it there is a huge Social Realist Mayakovsky. It is hard to realize, looking at this heavy giant, that Maykovsky was one of the most magnificent poets of the Russian Revolution.

Nor does the Victorian Pushkin do justice to the poet of the Golden Age. He stands with a melancholy expression on his downcast face, clutching a big bronze top hat. Across a few city blocks, Mayakovsky reaches out to Pushkin; in the middle of noisy, modern Moscow, slightly embarrassed by their attire, two heroes of Russian letters who lived almost a century apart seem to find comfort in each other's presence.

These two statues are beloved Moscow landmarks. Muscovites keep their pedestals surrounded with fresh flowers all year round. One very cold spring morning, in the company of the poet Andrei Voznesensky, I deposited some African violets at the foot of Mayakovsky's statue. It was April 14, 1964, the thirty-fourth anniversary of the poet's death. Never having garlanded any public monument before, I felt quite self-conscious, but I was carried along by Voznesensky's fervor. We had spent a long time in a small, steamy flower shop nearby, deciding which flowers to buy. Not that the florist's choice is great in Moscow in April, but there was a great variety of African violets in rich velvety colors — purple, dark red,

196

dark blue. We finally chose two big pots of blue ones, which looked beautiful against the snowdrifts edging the black statue. Dozens of other offerings stood around the monument, some half buried in light snow, but the square surrounding Mayakovsky's statue was deserted. Imprisoned in his awkward bronze disguise, one of the most complex figures of Russian poetry might have been proclaiming:

> My verse will reach you
> > across sierras of time,
> over heads of poets and governments.

Vladimir Mayakovsky was born in 1893 in a small village in Transcaucasia. His father worked as a forest ranger in that remote mountainous region; while belonging to the gentry, he was impoverished. As a child Mayakovsky hated living in the Caucasus, and he also disliked school. He was a provincial youth dreaming of great cities. When he was fifteen, he moved at last to Moscow with his family; his father had died in 1906. He joined the Bolshevik party in 1908, and was active as an underground propagandist among the working class. He was soon arrested and spent eleven months in prison. There for the first time he wrote poetry. After his release he gave up revolutionary activity for a time and studied painting — he had had a talent for drawing since his childhood — but he also continued to write poetry.

The very first poem Mayakovsky ever read to anyone was acclaimed as the work of a genius. After hearing the work (which Mayakovsky said was someone else's), David Burliuk, a Futurist painter in the bohemia of the day, who guessed the poem's true author, began introducing the young man to the Muscovite avant-garde as "my friend the genius — the poet Vladimir Mayakovsky." This was in 1911. The young poet became a literary celebrity overnight. In his *Autobiography*, Pasternak gives us a portrait of Mayakovsky at that time, and re-creates the atmosphere of the heroic pre-Revolutionary years:

And thus, in the summer of 1914 there was to be a fight between two rival literary groups in a coffee shop on the Arbat. On our side there were Bobrov and myself. Tretyakov and Shershenevich were to represent the opposite side, and they brought along Mayakovsky.

It turned out, quite unexpectedly, that I recognized this young man, having seen him in the halls of the Fifth Gymnasium, where he had studied two classes below me, and in the corridors of symphony halls where I had noticed him during intermissions.

Shortly before the impending clash, one of the people who was to be one of Mayakovsky's blind followers showed me a poem of his which had just been published. At that time this man not only did not understand his future god, but he was showing this novelty with derisive laughter and indignation, as obviously talentless nonsense. I, however, liked the poem enormously. It was part of Mayakosky's first, most brilliant, experiment, later to be included in the collection *Easy as Mooing.*

Now in that coffee shop I liked the author no less than his work. A beautiful young man of somber appearance with the bass voice of a first deacon and the fist of a boxer was sitting before me—relentlessly, murderously witty, a character half-way between Alexander Grin's mythical hero and a Spanish toreador.*

At once one guessed that although he was handsome and witty and talented—perhaps even super-talented—this was not the main thing about him. The main thing was the steely, inner hold he had of himself, a code of law in regard to true nobility; because of it, Mayakovsky could not allow himself to be less striking looking, less witty, less talented than he was.

At once his resoluteness, and his mane which he rumpled

* Alexander Grin was a turn-of-the-century Russian writer, the author of romantic sea stories in the English manner.

198

with all five fingers, reminded me of a composite underground figure, of a young terrorist from Dostoevsky—one of
his junior, provincial characters.

Mayakovsky was in love with revolution, with everything modern and gigantic, with machinery and architecture. Unlike most Russian poets, he was unmoved by
nature—he was the Fernand Léger of Russian poetry.
His poems are a crescendo of sweeping abstractions, an
accumulation of oversized symbols, of huge figures
evolving in a vast urban landscape. In the middle of it
looms the biggest figure of all—Mayakovsky himself.
He created a completely new, somehow coarse poetic
texture which was an outcome of his taste for bigness—
a language made of colloquialisms, of puns, of hyper-
bolic metaphors. Yet underneath the clanging exterior,
there is a poignant lyricism in the best of Mayakovsky,
particularly in the early poems and in the very late ones.
Paradoxically, Mayakovsky's self-proclamation sometimes verges on self-pity; one can detect this even in his
most heroic-sounding works. In this sense, his poems
often sound like those of a contemporary American poet.

Mayakovsky's tour de force was to make his continual
loud use of "I" in his poems acceptable, and in fact irresistible, to the Russian intelligentsia of his time, and
eventually to the whole Russian people. His personality
and his poetry matched each other perfectly—both were
the creations of a virtuoso. Mayakovsky might have
learned from Walt Whitman about the use of the "I" in
poetry; from the *estradnik* (stage poet) Igor Severianin
about stage performance.* However, he was profoundly
original. His self-proclaiming as well as his versification
(based on the number of stress accents in a line disre-

---

* Severianin was the rage of pre-Revolutionary Russian salons and
concert halls. A Decadent poet who was an accomplished showman,
he had an eccentric way of chanting his poems, which were filled with
fin de siècle exoticism.

199

garding all unstressed syllables, and on punning of rhymes) created a new Russian poetic style. Yevtushenko, for example, is sometimes derivative of Mayakovsky, who has, however, proven inimitable.

The poet was like a thunderstorm descending on the calm of the Russian literary scene dominated by the middle-aged sedate Symbolists. With the exception of Alexander Blok and Andrei Bely, these poets were pondering extremely esoteric religious and philosophical problems. For the most part they lived in St. Petersburg, the capital of Russian Symbolism and a formal, aloof city. The Acmeists, Mayakovsky's exact contemporaries, also worked there. (Certain Acmeists, such as Mandelstam, were as revolutionary as Mayakovsky in terms of literary craft, but through the years they remained unconcerned about shocking the middle class, an endeavor which was extremely important to Mayakovsky.)

People who knew Mayakovsky personally often speak of his extraordinary gentleness in private life, of his tenderness and vulnerability. But his public presence was quite the opposite — self-assertive and full of defiance, all the more so perhaps because of this insecurity.

Mayakovsky was a Byronic figure; his powers to charm and astound exceeded even his considerable poetic gifts. His friends were under his spell. The two other important Moscow poets, Pasternak and Tsvetayeva, worshiped him, and so did the Futurists, whose ranks he joined in 1912. (They were a shrill, Dada-like group of poets and painters bent on disrupting the decorum of pre-Revolutionary Russian artistic life.* Their

* In his *Autobiography* Pasternak described the literary life of that time, as well as literary life in general: "What is literature in the generally accepted and most widely understood meaning of the word? It is a world of eloquence, platitudes, well-rounded sentences, and venerable names of people who, when young, had observed life and who, on becoming famous, had passed on to abstractions, reiterations, and reasoning. And when in this realm of accepted, and only because of that unnoticed, artificiality, someone opens his mouth, not because of

theoretician was the poet, Khlebnikov, who wrote beautiful, obscure poems.) Mayakovsky's modernism, his roaring voice, his uninhibited manners struck his contemporaries as an intimation of oncoming political and social changes. In the decade preceding the Revolution, Russian intellectuals were discovering modern art; they longed for a revolution, and Mayakovsky was an incarnation of their aspirations. His roughness and his pseudoproletarian pose were both exciting and reassuring.

The poet, who never became a Party member, was a dedicated Bolshevik all his life. But the Revolution was cruel to him. As it succeeded and became institutionalized, the rebel *par excellence* found himself trapped in the role of an official poet at the service of the state. At first this appealed to him and flattered his outsized ego. However, temperamentally he was unsuited for such functions. The quality of his verse became uneven in the middle twenties as he felt compelled to write *agit-prop* (propaganda) verse. Stalin grew more tyrannical, and Mayakovsky's situation became more and more untenable, although there is no evidence that he ever admitted to himself the failings of the Revolution, or his own inability to conform to the role assigned to him. Ostensibly he was at the peak of literary recognition, in full possession of his creative powers. His *Bedbug* (1928) is a satiric masterpiece; his unfinished "In Full Voice" is one of his best poems. But hostile critics were hounding him; he was hated by literary officials. The poet wanted to lead a life of inner nobility and outward *éclat* and he couldn't bear the atmosphere of suspicion which prevailed. The great Stalinist purges were nearing. On April

---

any inherent bent for literature, but because he knows something and wants to say it, this creates the impression of a revolution, just as though a door were flung open and the noise of the life going on outside came through it, just as though it were not a man explaining what was going on in the town, but the town itself announcing its presence through the lips of a man."

14, 1930, at 10:15 A.M. in his studio on Lubiansky Way in the center of Moscow, Mayakovsky shot himself.

The reactions to Mayakovsky's death in Russia and abroad were divergent and extreme, in keeping with his own complicated personality and the passionate political divisions of the times. Thus, French leftist writers mourned him as one of their own: Aragon bodily attacked a detractor of the poet. But a committee of émigré writers in Paris, which included Ivan Bunin and Vladimir Nabokov, declared:

No matter what nuances of appreciation one might apply to Mayakovsky's poetic talent, we who as Russian writers are better informed of the present situation of our literature—we assert that Mayakovsky was never a great Russian poet, but only a composer of verse attached to the Communist Party and to the government of the U.S.S.R.

Pasternak described the dead Mayakovsky in his *Safe Conduct,* in what is one of the most moving chapters in all of Russian biography:

He lay on his side, his face to the wall, brooding and big, a sheet pulled up to his chin, his mouth half open. Proudly turning his back on everyone, even though lying down, even in this sleep, he was insistently breaking away, leaving. His face took one back to the times when he was calling himself "handsome, twenty-two years old." Death had petrified an expression which it almost never succeeds in catching, that with which one beings life rather than ends it. He was both brooding and indignant.

Stalin was cunning; he chose to ignore the protest implicit in Mayakovsky's death. In 1935, at the start of the terror, he declared: "Mayakovsky was and remains the best and the most talented poet of our Soviet epoch. Indifference to his memory and to his work is a crime." Thus, Mayakovsky was canonized throughout the Stalinist years. The cult left its marks; countless portraits and statues of the poet are still to be seen everywhere in the U.S.S.R. — oversized, offensive effigies in which the poet's energetic but sensitive face takes on a cast of threatening brutality. But Mayakovsky was good enough to survive this misfortune. He was one of a half dozen poets who created a second Golden Age of Russian poetry in the early years of this century. Today his statue in the center of Moscow has become a symbol of his country-men's thirst for more freedom, as well as their basic loyalty to the Soviet regime. In the middle fifties, the first "Days of Poetry" took place in that square. These public poetry readings were the first sign of the slow liberalization which took place in the U.S.S.R. after the death of Stalin.

Во весь голос

(Первое вступление в поэму)

Уважаемые
        товарищи потомки!
Роясь
    в сегодняшнем
                окаменевшем г......,
наших дней изучая потемки,
вы,
    возможно,
           спросите и обо мне.
И, возможно, скажет
              ваш ученый,
кроя эрудицией
            вопросов рой,
что жил-де такой
          певец кипяченой
и ярый враг воды сырой.
Профессор,
       снимите очки-велосипед!
Я сам расскажу
         о времени
             и о себе.
Я, ассенизатор
        и водовоз,
     революцией
           мобилизованный и призванный,
ушел на фронт
        из барских садоводств
поэзии—
      бабы капризной.
Засадила садик мило,
    дочка,
        дачка,
           водь
              и гладь—
сама садик я садила,
сама буду поливать.
Кто стихами льет из лейки,
кто кропит,
      набравши в рот—

IN FULL VOICE

(First Introduction)

Most respected comrade descendants!
Excavating in this day's petrified crap,
probing the darkness of our century,
you might, possibly, ask about me too.
And, possibly, your scholars will tell you,
smothering problems in their learned terms,
that once there lived a bard of boiled water,
and dedicated enemy of unboiled water.
Professor, remove those bicycle specs!
I'll tell you myself

                about my times

                        and me.

I, the sewer cleaner and waterboy,
drafted and mobilized by the Revolution
went off to the front from the baronial gardens
of poetry—capricious broad.
She planted a pretty garden,
kids,

      cottage,

            pond,

                 and lawn.
"Myself a garden I did sow
and watered it to make it grow."
Some pour poems from watering cans,
others spit water from their mouths—

кудреватые Митрейки,

мудреватые Кудрейки,—

кто их к черту разберет!

Нет на прорву карантина—

мандолинят из-под стен:

«Тара-тина, тара-тина,

т-эн-н...»

Неважная честь,

чтоб из этаких роз

мои изваяния высились

по скверам,

где харкает туберкулез,

где б.... с хулиганом

да сифилис.

И мне

агитпроп

в зубах навяз,

и мне бы

строчить

романсы на вас—

доходней оно

и прелестней.

Но я

себя

смирял,

становясь

на горло

собственной песне.

Слушайте,

товарищи потомки,

агитатора,

горлана-главаря.

Заглуша

поэзии потоки,

я шагну

через лирические томики,

как живой

с живыми говоря.

Я к вам приду

в коммунистическое далеко

не так,

как песенно-есененный провитязь.

curlyheaded Mitreky,

                clever-minded Kudreky—
but what in hell is it all about!
There's no end to this quarantine—
beneath the walls they mandolin:
"Tara-tina, tara-tina,
twang . . ."
It's no great honor that among such roses
my sculpture soars
over public squares where TB wheezes,
and whores stroll with their spivs and syphilis.

Agitprop sticks in my craw too,
I'd rather spin love songs for you—
There's more profit in it,

                it's more attractive.
But I have mastered myself,
standing on the throat

             of my own song.

Listen, comrade descendents,
to the agitator, the rabble-rouser.
Silencing torrents of poetry,
I'll skip the slim volumes;
alive, I'll speak to the living.
I'll come to you in the Communist hereafter
and not like a singsong Yesenin messiah.

Мой стих дойдет
                    через хребты веков
и через головы
                    поэтов и правительств.
Мой стих дойдет
                    но он дойдет не так,—
не как стрела
                    в амурно-лировой охоте,
не как доходит
                    к нумизмату стершийся пятак
и не как свет умерших звезд доходит.
Мой стих
          трудом
                    громаду лет прорвет
и явится
          весомо,
                    грубо,
                              зримо,
как в наши дни
                    вошел водопровод,
сработанный
                    еще рабами Рима.
В курганах книг,
                    похоронивших стих,
железки строк случайно обнаруживая,
вы
     с уважением
                    ощупывайте их,
как старое,
                    но грозное оружие.
Я
     ухо
          словом
                    не привык ласкать;

ушку девическому
                    в завиточках волоска
с полупохабщины
                    не разалеться тронуту.
Парадом развернув
                    моих страниц войска,
я прохожу
          по строчечному фронту.

My verse will reach you
                              across sierras of time,
over heads of poets and governments.
My verse will reach you, but not
like an arrow in a lyrical cupid hunt,
not as an old penny
                              reaches the coin man,
not as a dead star's light reaches you.
My verse by labor will break through the years
and appear,
                    ponderous,
                              crude,
                                        plain,
as an aqueduct built by slaves
of Rome enters our days.

When, in mounds of books,
                              where verse lies interred,
you discover the iron fragments of lines,
handle them with respect
like old but menacing weapons.
It is not my habit
                    to caress
                              the ear
                                        with words;

the maiden's ear, ringed with curls,
will never blush from my innuendoes.
Deploying on parade the armies of my pages,
I shall review the lines.

Стихи стоят
              свинцово-тяжело,
готовые и к смерти,
                    и к бессмертной славе.
Поэмы замерли,
              к жерлу прижав жерло
нацеленных
           зияющих заглавий.

Оружия
       любимейшего
                   род,
готовая
        рвануться в гике,
застыла
        кавалерия острот,
поднявши рифм
              отточенные пики.
И все
      поверх зубов вооруженные войска,
что двадцать лет в победах
                           пролетали,
до самого
          последнего листка
я отдаю тебе,
              планеты пролетарий.
Рабочего
         громады класса враг—
он враг и мой,
               отъявленный и давний.
Велели нам
           идти
                под красный флаг
года труда
           и дни недоеданий.
Мы открывали
             Маркса
                    каждый том,
как в доме
           собственном
                        мы открываем ставни,
но и без чтения
                мы разбирались в том,

The verses stand heavy as lead,
ready for death and immortal fame.

The poems are rigid,
                                    their gaping titles
aimed muzzle to muzzle.

The cavalry of witticisms aligned
to launch a shouting charge, stands steady,
leveling the pointed lances of its rhymes.

And all these troops armed to the teeth,
which have passed in victory
                                    for twenty years,
all these, to the very last page,
I present to you,
                        proletarian of this planet.
The enemy of the working-class masses
is my enemy too, sworn and long-standing.
Years of toil and days of hunger
ordered us under the red flag.
We opened each volume of Marx
as we would open the shutters of our own house,
but even without reading we could decide

в каком идти,

       в каком сражаться стане.

Мы

    диалектику

          учили не по Гегелю.

Бряцанием боев

         она врывалась в стих,

когда

      под пулями

            от нас буржуи бегали,

как мы

      когда-то

            бегали от них.

Пускай

     за гениями

           безутешною вдовой

плетется слава

          в похоронном марше—

умри, мой стих,

        умри, как рядовой,

как безымянные

         на штурмах мерли наши!

Мне наплевать

        на бронзы многопудье,

мне наплевать

        на мраморную слизь.

Сочтемся славою—

        ведь мы свои же люди,—

пускай нам

      общим памятником будет

построенный

      в боях

         социализм.

Потомки,

     словарей проверьте поплавки:

из Леты

     выплывут

        остатки слов таких,

как «проституция»,

      «туберкулез»,

         «блокада».

which side to join which side to fight on.
Our dialectics were not learned from Hegel.
In the clang of battle,

                      they burst forth in verse
when,

      under fire,

             the bourgeois turned back,
as we once

        turned back from them.

Let fame follow genius
as an inconsolable widow

               follows the hearse—
and so die, my verses,

           die like common soldiers,
die as our men died, nameless in attack.

I spit

      on the tons of bronze.
I spit

      on the slimy marble.
We'll settle our accounts with fame among ourselves;

let socialism built in battle
be our common monument.

Descendent fishermen, watch the bobs of dictionaries:
from Lethe will float up debris of words

like "prostitution,"

           "tuberculosis,"

                    "blockade."

213

Для вас,
　　　　которые
　　　　　　　　здоровы и ловки,
поэт
　　　вылизывал
　　　　　　　　чахоткины плевки
шершавым языком плаката.

С хвостом годов
　　　　　　　　я становлюсь подобием
чудовищ
　　　　ископаемо-хвостатых.

Товарищ жизнь,
　　　　　　давай
　　　　　　　　быстрей протопаем,
протопаем
　　　　по пятилетке
　　　　　　　　дней остаток.

Мне
　　и рубля
　　　　　　не накопили строчки,
краснодеревщики
　　　　　　　　не слали мебель на́ дом.

И кроме
　　　свежевымытой сорочки,
скажу по совести,
　　　　　　мне ничего не надо.

Явившись
　　　　в Це Ка Ка
　　　　　　　　идущих
　　　　　　　　　　　светлых лет,
над бандой
　　　　поэтических
　　　　　　　　рвачей и выжиг
я подыму,
　　　как большевистский партбилет,
все сто томов
　　　　моих
　　　　　　партийных книжек.

1930

214

POETS ON STREET CORNERS

For you who are healthy and nimble

the poet licked up consumptives' spittle
with the rough tongue of posters.
With the tail of my years behind me

I look like those big-tailed dug-up monsters.

Comrade life, let us beat our way
faster through the five-year-plan of remaining days.

Not a ruble have my verses brought me,
no mahogany furniture has been sent to my house.

In all conscience I need nothing,
except a freshly washed shirt.
When I appear before the C.C.C.* of clear bright years

ahead I'll raise—as my Bolshevik party card—
over the gang
                    of poet-profiteers,
the whole hundred volumes
                              of my party-committed books.

—ADAPTED BY HENRY CARLISLE

* The Central Control Commission (of the Communist Party).

Неоконченное: последняя запись Маяковского

1

Любит? не любит? Я руки ломаю
и пальцы
    разбрасываю разломавши
так рвут загадав и пускают
       по маю
венчики встречных ромашек
пускай седины обнаруживает стрижка и бритьё,
Пусть серебро годов вызванивает
        уймою,
надеюсь верую вовеки не придёт
ко мне позорное благоразумие.

2

Уже второй
    должно быть ты легла
А может быть
    и у тебя такое
Я не спешу.
    И молниями телеграмм
мне незачем
   тебя
     будить и беспокоить

THE LAST ENTRIES IN MAYAKOVSKY'S NOTEBOOK

Found in Mayakovsky's notebook after his suicide, this fragment is thought to have been part of a projected lyrical introduction to his long poem *In Full Voice*.

I

She loves me? She loves me not?

I wring
My hands and scatter the broken-off fingers.
Like petals you pluck from some
White little flower along your way.
You hold them up to the breeze,
They've told your fortune,
They drift off into May.

Though
Now a haircut
Lays bare thorns of gray,
Though my morning shave shows me
On the bib the salt of age,
I hope, I believe

I will never weaken.

Never be caught
Showing good sense.

2

Past one. You must have gone to sleep.
Or do

You feel, perhaps you feel the same as I?
I'm in no hurry.

Is
There no point

In a telegram that would only
Wake you? And disturb you.

3

море уходит вспять
море уходит спать
Как говорят инцидент исперчен
любовная лодка разбилась о быт
С тобой мы в расчёте
И не к чему перечень
взаимных болей бед и обид

4

Уже второй должно быть ты легла
В ночи Млечпуть серебряной Окою
Я не спешу и молниями телеграмм
Мне незачем тебя будить и беспокоить
как говорят инцидент исперчен
любовная лодка разбилась о быт
С тобой мы в расчете и не к чему перечень
взаимных болей бед и обид
Ты посмотри какая в мире тишь
Ночь обложила небо звёздной данью
в такие вот часы встаёшь и говоришь
векам истории и мирозданию

5

Я знаю силу слов я знаю слов набат
Они не те которым рукоплещут ложи
От слов таких срываются гроба
шагать с четверкою своих дубовых ножек
Бывает выбросят не напечатав не издав

3

The tide ebbs.
The sea too
Is going to sleep.
The incident as they say
Is closed.
Love's skiff
Has stove
In on the daily grind.
It would be useless
Making a list
Of who did what to whom.
We shared
Weapons
And wounds.

4

Past one. Like a

Silent moonlit Oká, the Milky Way
Streams into the night. I'm in no hurry.

As they say: the incident is closed.
A telegram would wake you.

How still it is!
Night, night sky, and stars.
What stillness there is in the world!
What stillness we are capable of!

In hours like these one rises
To address the Ages—History—the Universe!

5

I know
The power of words.

(Not the gas
The loges applaud.)

Но слово мчится подтянув подпруги
звенит века и подползают поезда
лизать поэзии мозолистые руки
Я знаю силу слов Глядится пустяком
Опавшим лепестком под каблуками танца
Но человек душой губами костяком . . .

1930

That make
Coffins rear up and break loose

And clomp off
Robotlike, rocked forward like a crate.

So we are rejected,
So we go unpublished

But the word gallops on, cinching the saddle tighter,
The word rings for centuries—a tocsin!

I know
The power of words.

It is nothing!
A fallen

Petal under
A dancer's heel.

But man
In his soul, his lips, in his bones . . .

—ADAPTED BY FREDERICK SEIDEL

Sergei Alexandrovich Yesenin

(1895–1925)

Already you've begun to fade
    to wither like a flower
And other young men soon
    will be singing other
Songs, and surely they will sound
    more interesting by far
For not this town alone
    but all earth is their mother.

Oh my country! What an absurdity
    I see that I've become—
My hollow cheeks are coloring;
    I blush, dry as a clown.
All at once, alien to me
    is the language of my countrymen
And I am as a foreign thing
    in my own town.

Sergei Yesenin, "Soviet Russia," 1924
—ADAPTED BY ROSE STYRON

SERGEI
ALEXANDROVICH

Today in the U.S.S.R., the masses of readers seem to prefer Sergei Yesenin to all other Russian poets. His poems are full of the genuine lore and imagery of the people. Many of them have even been set to music. Traveling through the U.S.S.R., one hears Yesenin's poems sung or recited everywhere one goes — and they have great lyric impact.

Yesenin was born into a peasant family in the heart of Great Russia, where the inhabitants had long been semi-nomadic. A certain anarchic streak, blended with a rare lyric gift, made him into the most profoundly Russian of all poets of the Revolution.

In the early twenties, Yesenin became extremely successful. He led a fashionable and at times dissolute life. He was married briefly to the American dancer Isadora Duncan. Pasternak, who felt a warm kinship to Yesenin despite their differences in background and in literary aspirations, said of him:

Yesenin treated his own life like a fairytale. He was Ivan the Prince who flew over the ocean on a gray wolf to catch the Firebird, Isadora Duncan, by the tail. His verse too he wrote with the help of fairly tale magic, sometimes arranging words like cards in a game of patience, and sometimes writing them out with his heart's blood. The most precious thing he conveys is an image of nature, of his own Ryazan countryside in the depth of wooded Great Russia. He was able to describe it with an overwhelming freshness as he saw it in childhood.

Yesenin himself spoke charmingly about his early years in an essay written in October, 1925, shortly before his death:

I was born on the twenty-first of September, 1895, in the Ryazan district, in the village of Constantinovo. At the age of two I was sent to live with my mother's father and his three unmarried sons, and among them, in the country, in rather well-to-do circumstances, I passed the greater part of my childhood. My uncles were tough, gay, wild. When I was three and a half they sat me bareback on a horse and set the horse to galloping. I remember I lost my head in panic, but held the mane tight. Later they taught me to swim. One uncle, Uncle Sasha, would take me out in a skiff, undress me, and throw me into the water like a puppy. Clumsy and frightened, I splashed till I choked. "Beast! What are you good for?" he'd shout. (In his language, "beast" was a tender word.) Still later, when I was about eight, I used to serve as a hunting dog for another of my uncles, swimming out into the lake to retrieve some duck that he had just shot. I was quite good at climbing trees; among the other boys I was the leader and a dedicated fighter—I was forever covered with scratches.

For my wild ways I was scolded only by my grandmother. My grandfather, always ready for a fist fight himself, said to her more than once, "Don't you touch him, you foolish woman! He'll grow up to be stronger this way."

My grandmother loved me with all her heart and there were no boundaries to her gentleness. On Saturdays I was bathed and my nails were clipped and my head was rubbed with oil in vain hopes of untangling my stubborn curls. I would fuss and holler, I remember, and even now a certain uneasiness descends on me on Saturdays.

Thus my childhood unfolded. When I was grown, they hoped I would be a country teacher. I was packed off to a school for priests and teachers, and was then supposed to go to the Moscow teacher's college. Luckily, this never came to pass.

I began to write poetry early, about the age of nine, creating it deliberately at sixteen or seventeen. A few of the poems written then were published in *Radunitza* [*Rainbow,* Yesenin's 1916 collection of poems]. At eighteen, then, having sent more poems to various magazines, I was surprised to find them rejected, and I set out for Petersburg. There I was received quite warmly. The first person I saw was Blok, the second Gorodyetsky. When I met Blok I was aware of sweating profusely because I was seeing a live poet for the first time. Gorodyetsky introduced me to Kluyev, about whom I knew nothing at the time.* For all our personal differences, a strong friendship grew between us. During that period I entered the Shanyavsky courses, where I stayed only for a year and a half before returning to my own village. Among my contemporaries, Blok, Bely, and Kluyev appealed to me most. Bely taught me much about poetic form, while Blok and Kluyev instructed me in lyricism.

In 1919 with a group of friends I published the manifesto of the Imagists. Imagism was a school of literature we hoped to establish, rather formally, but since it had no roots it died a natural death, reasserting thus the authenticity of organic imagery.

I would cheerfully throw out much of my religious verse now but I think it has significance in the mapping of my path as a poet before the Revolution. From the age of eight I was taken regularly by my grandmother to visit monasteries; she saw to it that we gave refuge to every sort of male and female wanderer; religious poetry was often chanted in our home. My grandfather was just the opposite: he liked to drink. For him there was always a wedding banquet laid— without, of course, the wedding.

Later, when I left my village for good, it took me a long time to sort out my background, my beliefs. In the years of the Revolution I was completely on the side of October. Yet I understood it only in my own way, with a peasant bent. As to formal development, I am drawn more and more to Push-

---

* Sergei Gorodyetsky was a minor poet. Nikolai Kluyev, a writer of peasant origin like Yesenin, was a remarkable poet who used ancient religious imagery in his verse glorifying new Russia.

kin. Other autobiographical information can be found in my poems.

For his compatriots, Yesenin will be forever a romantic figure whose star rose and burned out with the Revolution. Symbolically, this peasant-poet was destroyed as the Russian peasant class was then slowly being destroyed by Stalin; in a fit of depression, in a Leningrad hotel, he committed suicide. It was December 28, 1925. Soon afterwards, Mayakovsky, once a close friend of Yesenin's wrote a long sententious poem in which he showed disapproval for Yesenin's lack of civic responsibility. Mayakovsky had no more insight into his friend's destiny than into his own.

В том краю, где желтая крапива
И сухой плетень,
Приютились к вербам сиротливо
Избы деревень.

Там в полях, за синей гущей лога,
В зелени озер,
Пролегла песчаная дорога
До сибирских гор.

Затерялась Русь в Мордве и Чуди,
Нипочем ей страх.
И идут по той дороге люди,
Люди в кандалах.

Все они убийцы или воры,
Как судил им рок.
Полюбил я грустные их взоры
С впадинами щек.

Много зла от радости в убийцах,
Их сердца просты,
Но кривятся в почернелых лицах
Голубые рты.

Я одну мечту, скрывая, нежу,
Что я сердцем чист.
Но и я кого-нибудь зарежу
Под осенний свист.

И меня по ветряному свею,
По тому ль песку,
Поведут с веревкою на шее
Полюбить тоску.

И когда с улыбкой мимоходом
Распрямлю я грудь,
Языком залижет непогода
Прожитой мой путь.

1915

In the country of yellow nettles
    the twig fences are brittle
the log houses huddle like orphans
    into the pussy-willows

through fields over the hills' blue
    by the greenness of lakes
a road of sand leads to the mountains
    of Siberia

Between Mongols and Finns Russia
    is lost there before she is frightened
along the road men make their way
    in irons

Each one has robbed or killed
    as his fate would have it
I am in love with the grief of their eyes
    and the graves in their cheeks

many have killed from pure joy
    they are simple-hearted
but in their darkened faces
    the blue mouths are twisted

I cherish one secret dream
    that I am pure in heart
but I too will cut a throat
    to the whistling of autumn

I too on the blown road
    on these same sands
will go with a rope at the neck
    to make love to mourning

I will smile as I go by
    I will swell out my chest
and the storm will lick over
    the way I came

—ADAPTED BY W. S. MERWIN

Свищет ветер под крутым забором,
    Прячется в траву.
Знаю я, что пьяницей и вором
    Век свой доживу.
Тонет день за красными холмами,
    Кличет на межу.
Не один я в этом свете шляюсь,
    Не один брожу.
Размахнулось поле русских пашен,
    То трава, то снег,
Все равно, литвин я иль чувашин,
    Крест мой как у всех.
Верю я, как ликам чудотворным,
    В мой потайный час.
Он придет бродягой подзаборным,
    Нерушимый Спас.
Но, быть может, в синих клочьях дыма
    Тайноводных рек
Я пройду его с улыбкой пьяной мимо,
    Не узнав навек.
Не блеснет слеза в моих ресницах,
    Не вспугнет мечту.
Только радость синей голубицей
    Канет в темноту.
И опять, как раньше, с дикой злостью
    Запоет тоска ...
Пусть хоть ветер на моем погосте
    Пляшет трепака.

1917

Сорокоуст

3

Видели ли вы,
Как бежит по степям,
В туманах озерных кроясь,
Железной ноздрей храпя,
На лапах чугунных поезд?

Wind whistles through the steep fence
    hides in the grass
a drunk and a thief
    I'll end my days
the light sinking in red hills
    shows me the path
I'm not the only one on it
    not the only one
plowed Russia stretches away
    grass and then snow
no matter what part I'd come from
    our cross is the same
I believe in my secret hour
    as in icons not painted by hands
like a tramp who sleeps back of a fence
    it will rise my inviolate Saviour
but through the blue tattered fogs
    of unconfessed rivers
I may pass with a drunken smile
    never knowing Him
no tear lighting up on my lashes
    to break my dream
joy like a blue dove
    dropping into the dark
sadness resuming
    its vindictive song
but may the wind on my grave
    dance like a peasant in spring

—ADAPTED BY W. S. MERWIN

PRAYERS FOR THE FIRST FORTY DAYS OF THE DEAD

3

Have you seen
running in the plain
on shoes of cast metal
the train hiding in the lake mists
blowing down its iron nostrils

А за ним
По большой траве,
Как на празднике отчаянных гонок,
Тонкие ноги закидывая к голове,
Скачет красногривый жеребенок?

Милый, милый, смешной дуралей,
Ну, куда он, куда он гонится?
Неужель он не знает, что живых коней
Победила стальная конница?

Неужель он не знает, что в полях бессиянных
Той поры не вернет его бег,
Когда пару красивых степных россиянок
Отдавал за коня печенег?
По-иному судьба на торгах перекрасила
Наш разбуженный скрежетом плес,
И за тысячи пудов конской кожи и мяса
Покупают теперь паровоз.

1920

Я последний поэт деревни,
Скромен в песнях досчатый мост.
За прощальной стою обедней
Кадящих листвой берез.

Догорит золотистым пламенем
Из телесного воска свеча,
И луны часы деревянные
Прохрипят мой двенадцатый час.

На тропу голубого поля
Скоро выйдет железный гость.
Злак овсяный, зарею пролитый,
Соберет его черная горсть.

Неживые, чужие ладони,
Этим песням при вас не жить!
Только будут колосья-кони
О хозяине старом тужить.

and behind him
galloping over the high grasses
as though in the wild races at a fair
flinging his thin legs toward his chin the colt
with the red mane

the darling
the little idiot
where does he think he's running
Doesn't he know that all his kind
have lost to the steel cavalry
Doesn't he know there's no racing
in unnoticed fields that can bring back
the time when they'd trade
to the north of the Black Sea
for the right horse
two beautiful girls from the plain country
The fate of markets has troubled the face
of our still waters
waking them with the gnashing of iron Now
for a locomotive it would cost you tons
of the meat and skins of horses

—ADAPTED BY W. S. MERWIN

I am the last poet of the villages
the plank bridge lifts a plain song
I stand at a farewell service
birches swinging leaves like censors

The golden flame will burn down
in the candle of waxen flesh
and the moon a wooden clock
will caw caw my midnight

On the track in the blue field
soon the iron guest will appear
his black hand will seize
oats that the dawn sowed

In a lifeless and alien grip
my poems will die too
only nodding oats
will mourn for their old master

Будет ветер сосать их ржанье,
Панихидный справляя пляс.
Скоро, скоро часы деревянные
Прохрипят мой двенадцатый час!

1921

Да! Теперь решено. Без возврата
Я покинул родные поля.
Уж не будут листвою крылатой
Надо мною звенеть тополя.

Низкий дом без меня ссутулится,
Старый пес мой давно издох.
На московских изогнутых улицах
Умереть, знать, судил мне бог.

Я люблю этот город вязевый,
Пусть обрюзг он и пусть одрях.
Золотая дремотная Азия
Опочила на куполах.

А когда ночью светит месяц,
Когда светит ... черт знает как!
Я иду, головою свесясь,
Переулком в знакомый кабак.

Шум и гам в этом логове жутком,
Но всю ночь напролет, до зари,
Я читаю стихи проституткам
И с бандитами жарю спирт.

Сердце бьется все чаще и чаще,
И уж я говорю невпопад:
«Я такой же, как вы, пропащий,
Мне теперь не уйти назад».

Низкий дом без меня ссутулится,
Старый пес мой давно издох.
На московских изогнутых улицах
Умереть, знать, судил мне Бог.

1922–1923

The wind will take up their neighing
they will all dance in the morning
soon the moon a wooden clock
will caw caw my midnight

—ADAPTED BY W. S. MERWIN

It's done. I've left the home fields.
There'll be no going back.
The green wings all over the poplars
will never ring again.

Without me the hunched house sinks lower.
My old dog died long ago.
I know God means I'm to die
among the bent streets of Moscow.

I like the city, in its old script,
though it's grown fat with age.
The gold somnolence of Asia
dozes on the cupolas.

But at night when the moon shines, shines,
shines, the devil knows how,
I take a side street, head down,
into the same tavern.

A lair full of din and roaring,
but all night till daylight
I read out poems to whores
and drink with cutthroats.

My heart beats faster and faster,
I pick the wrong moments
to say, "I'm like you, I'm lost,
I can never go back."

Without me the hunched house sinks lower.
My old dog died long ago.
I know God means I'm to die
among the bent streets of Moscow.

—ADAPTED BY W. S. MERWIN

Снова пьют здесь, дерутся и плачут
Под гармоники желтую грусть.
Проклинают свои неудачи,
Вспоминают московскую Русь.

И я сам, опустясь головою,
Заливаю глаза вином,
Чтоб не видеть в лицо роковое,
Чтоб подумать хоть миг об ином.

Что-то всеми навек утрачено.
Май мой синий! Июнь голубой!
Не с того ль так чадит мертвячиной
Над пропащею этой гульбой.

Ах, сегодня так весело россам,
Самогонного спирта—река.
Гармонист с провалившимся носом
Им про Волгу поет и про Чека.

Что-то злое во взорах безумных,
Непокорное в громких речах.
Жалко им тех дурашливых, юных,
Что сгубили свою жизнь сгоряча.

Где ж вы те, что ушли далече?
Ярко ль светят вам наши лучи?
Гармонист спиртом сифилис лечит,
Что в киргизских степях получил.

Нет! таких не подмять, не рассеять.
Бесшабашность им гнилью дана.
Ты, Рассея моя . . . Рас . . . сея . . .
Азиатская сторона!

1923

They are drinking here again, brawling, sobbing,
to the amber woes of the accordion.
They curse their luck and they hark back
to a Russia—a Moscow—of other days.

For my part, I duck my head,
my eyes foundering in wine,
rather than look fate in the face,
I think of something else for a while.

There is something that we have all lost forever.
My dark blue May, my pale blue June,
that must be why the corpse smell
dogs this frantic carousal.

Oh, today's a great day for the Russians
the homemade vodka's flowing
and the noseless accordionist's singing
of the Volga and the secret police.

They're grumbling that bony October
caught them all in its blizzard
courage has gone back to whetting
the knife from its boot.*

A hatred shifts in the eyes
rebellion grates in the raised voices
and they pity the young and foolish
whose blood flamed up and burned away.

Where are you now and why so far?
Do we shine brightly for you?
The accordionist's on a vodka cure
for his clap caught in the Civil War.

No, the lost Russia will not be silenced.
On all sides the rot feeds a wild courage.
Oh Russia, my Russia,
rising in Asia.

—ADAPTED BY W. S. MERWIN

* This stanza is usually omitted in Soviet editions of Yesenin's works.

Nikolai Alexeevich Zabolotsky (1903–1958)

Spirit of Autumn, give me a voice!
The structure of the air is like a diamond.
A bull is hiding
Around the corner, and the sun,
A misty ball
Hovers and bloodies the edge of the earth.

Rolling a round, lidded eye
A large-size bird flies by:
Man himself may be felt in its movement.
Or is it simply that he hides—
An embryo between wide wings?
A beetle has opened the door of its leafy retreat.

Nikolai Zabolotsky, "Autumn," 1932

NIKOLAI ALEXEEVICH ZABOLOTSKY, born in 1903, belonged to the talented but ill-fated generation of Russian writers that was all but destroyed by political catastrophe and by World War II. Zabolotsky himself spent several years in a prison camp in Siberia. He was released shortly after Stalin's death and settled in Peredelkino, the writers' colony near Moscow, and later in the provincial town of Tarusa, where Marina Tsvetayeva had been born and spend part of her childhood. He lived in Tarusa until his death, amid the melancholy, tender Russian landscape that he particularly liked.

Zabolotsky's themes, mostly philosophical meditations on nature, as well as his forms are in the old Russian tradition, yet in his poetry they are always fresh. Despite his classicism, he was a poet completely attuned to our violent times. He never wrote directly about the events which took place in the U.S.S.R. under Stalin (if he had, he probably would not have lived). However, his poetry is a ringing assertion of man as an individual. For Zabolotsky, man is confronted with one riddle only: the insoluble one of his own presence at the heart of the natural world. It took great faith in humanity to probe this theme at a time of fear and bloodshed.

Zabolotsky identified the process of poetic creation with nature:

> Words glow like lanterns of the fireflies;
> Turn away, distracted, they seem to wink out. . . .

But if you look at them in a Black Sea spring
While oleanders sleep at dusk in solemn blooms,
The firefly words shine, spindrift into night
And fly in waves on the shore, in endless dooms.

—ADAPTED BY JAMES SCHEVILL

A growing feeling of compassion marks Zabolotsky's literary evolution. He started his career as a hermetic poet, a member of the Oberiuti, a brilliant avant-garde group. His first volume of poems, *Columns,* published in 1930, was strange and beautiful. Set in part in the animal kingdom, with seedy, rundown sections of Leningrad as a backdrop, it was full of the heavy, startlingly realistic imagery typical of this movement, which blended Surrealistic and Expressionistic techniques:

The coachman sits as on a throne,
His armor is made of cotton,
And his beard lies there,
Clanking with icon-like coins!

But the poor horse waves his arms,
And he stretches out like a fish,
And again eight legs are flashing
Inside his shiny belly.

1927

In these rich poems, Zabolotsky had not yet quite found his voice. Later his tone was one of majestic humility—his very own. This solemnity can be found only in the nineteenth-century Russian poet Tyutchev, and earlier in the founder of Russian poetry, the eighteenth-century scientist-poet Lomonosov. In this he was helped in part by his background, which was, unlike that of many Russian poets, without any foreign influence. He was one of six children in a family of exceedingly poor, first-generation intellectuals. His grandfather was a peasant, his father an agronomist. Zabolotsky drew harmoniously from two life-giving Russian traditions often considered to be at odds—that of the earth and that of the intelligentsia.

Shortly before his death at fifty-five, Zabolotsky experienced a great surge of inspiration. He had fallen in love with a woman much younger than himself. It was an anguished love, but it coincided with the general elation which followed Stalin's death, and it inspired some of Zabolotsky's best poems. He died of a heart ailment at the height of his poetic powers. But he had seen the beginning of Russia's awakening from the Stalinist nightmare. His faith in man and in Russia had not been betrayed.

In the peaceful town of Tarusa, Zabolotsky's spirit still lingers. Today, this artists' and writers' colony is a symbol of the survival of the Russian intelligentsia. Set in a landscape of soft hills and birch groves and open fields, Tarusa is still a nineteenth-century town. Perched on a high bank of the meandering river Oka, it has very wide streets and log houses set behind carved wooden fences. It looks like the setting for a Chekhov story, intimate and nostalgic and surrounded by countryside. Daily walks in the woods, long conversations punctuated by tea drinking, poetry readings—these are the pleasures of Tarusa.

This is how a friend of Zabolotsky, the writer Nikolai Stepanov,* describes the poet's last days in Tarusa:

Nikolai Alexeevich did a lot of work in Tarusa. He translated a Siberian folk epic and he was composing new poems. In Tarusa he wrote his poem "Rubruk." He often told me that nowhere did he work as well as in Tarusa. He usually worked from morning till noon; in the afternoon he rested, took walks and conversed with friends. Sitting on the terrace or under an apple tree he spent hours thinking and observing the garden around him. Many of his best poems were written there, inspired by this garden, the quiet life of the town, the landscape.

* From *Pages from Tarusa*, Kaluga, U.S.S.R., 1961.

At that time Nikolai Alexeevich was already very sick and was living through a painful personal dilemma. Nevertheless, he was full of such stability and wise understanding and love of people, as well as interest in life, that I forgot about the deadly threat which hung over him. He never spoke about sickness and never complained; he only tried to do as much as he could and finish all that he had undertaken. He was a person of meticulous order in everything, and even in his difficult situation he tried to cling to orderly ways. Sitting on his open terrace, Nikolai Alexeevich could look for a long time at the commotion among the hens and roosters and was amused by the biggest and handsomest rooster, who often emerged from battle with a torn tail and bloodied crest. He was most attached to a small furry dog, which had a little beard and the vague look of an ancestor. This little dog sat patiently for whole days on the terrace and looked adoringly at Nikolai Alexeevich. It was lively and barked loudly at unknown visitors. Its name was Druzhok, and it was immortalized in the poem "The Little Town." Nikolai Alexeevich loved to converse with Druzhok. One morning he read me "The Little Town," slightly squinting his myopic eyes, smiling that humorous smile which made his face particularly lovable—somehow peasantlike. He loved jokes more than anyone, but he always joked with a most serious expression on his face, assuming a simple-minded, dumb look.

From the garden one could see the roofs of the houses descending to the Oka in a sea of greenery. All was stillness except for the rare whistle of a river steamer, reminding us of the fact that Tarusa was not at the end of the world, but only three hours from Moscow.

Nowadays, young poets from Moscow often come to Tarusa for long stays. Local inhabitants, like the novelist Konstantin Paustovsky and the short-story writer Yuri Kazakov, keep alive Zabolotsky's and Tsvetayeva's memories, and the wide fields and trees evoke their poems.

Ивановы

Стоят чиновные деревья,
почти влезая в каждый дом;
давно их кончено кочевье—
они в решетках, под замком.
Шумит бульваров теснота,
домами плотно заперта.

Но вот—все двери растворились,
повсюду шопот пробежал:
на службу вышли Ивановы
в своих штанах и башмаках.
Пустые гладкие трамваи
им подают свои скамейки;
герои входят, покупают
билетов хрупкие дощечки,
сидят и держат их перед собой,
не увлекаясь быстрою ездой.

А мир, зажатый плоскими домами,
стоит, как море, перед нами,
грохочут волны мостовые,
и через лопасти колес—
сирены мечутся простые
в клубках оранжевых волос.
Иные—дуньками одеты,
сидеть не могут взаперти:
ногами делая балеты,
они идут. Куда идти,
кому нести кровавый ротик,
кому сказать сегодня «котик»,

у чьей постели бросить ботик
и дернуть кнопку на груди?
Неужто некуда идти?!
О, мир, свинцовый идол мой,
хлещи широкими волнами
и этих девок упокой
на перекрестке вверх ногами!
Он спит сегодня—грозный мир,
в домах—спокойствие и мир.

THE IVANOVS

Trees like government clerks
trying to enter every house,
you may have been gypsies once—
that was a long time ago,
now there are wire fences around you.
And you make a lot of noise,
narrow streets,
closed in by rooftops.

Suddenly doors open,
a whispering—
the Ivanovs
in their shoes and trousers
have gone out to work.

The fast empty streetcars
give up their benches to the Ivanovs
and our heroes climb aboard
buying fragile tickets,
sitting with the cardboard
held in front of their eyes.
They are not excited
by the speed or the smooth ride.

A world with flat houses
running up its sides
rushes past them
like a sea.
Waves on the road
chop and splash
and sirens flow under the cars,
their orange hair spinning
on the water wheels.

And country girls
who won't sit inside
follow along making ballet figures
with their white legs.
"Where shall I go? Who wants my blood-red mouth?
Who wants to hear me say 'darling' today?
Where's the bed I can put my little shoes under,
and who will unsnap my blouse?
Is there really nowhere to go?"

Ужели там найти мне место,
где ждет меня моя невеста,
где стулья выстроились в ряд,
где горка,—словно Арарат,
повитый кружевцем бумажным,
где стол стоит и трехэтажный
в железных латах самовар
шумит домашним генералом?

О, мир, свернись одним кварталом,
одной разбитой мостовой,
одним проплеванным амбаром,
одной мышиною норой,
но будь к оружию готов:
целует девку—Иванов!

1928

Метаморфозы

Как мир меняется! И как я сам меняюсь!
Лишь именем одним я называюсь,—
На самом деле то, что именуют мной,—
Не я один. Нас много. Я—живой.
Чтоб кровь моя остынуть не успела,
Я умирал не раз. О, сколько мертвых тел
Я отделил от собственного тела!
И если б только разум мой прозрел
И в землю устремил пронзительное око,
Он увидал бы там, среди могил, глубоко

O world,
my leaden idol,
pour out solace
with your heavy waves
for these girls at the crossroads
standing on their heads,
legs in the air!
Yet my terrible world doesn't threaten me today,
and there are normal houses somewhere.

Will I really find that place
where my betrothed waits for me?
Chairs lined up in a row,
the tall sideboard like Mount Ararat
and trimmed with lace paper,
there is a table
and an iron armor three storeys high
that is a samovar
grumbling like a general
who orders the house.

O world
fold up your buildings into one block,
one rutted street,
one storeroom with spit and dirt on the floor,
one mousehole—
but get ready for an explosion
when Ivanov
kisses his girl!

—ADAPTED BY BARBARA GUEST

METAMORPHOSES

As the world changes, I change!
My name does not name me.
One death only would be strange,
I was born to be the unity
Of many people. My blood would never cool.
How many dead skins
I have torn away from my body!
What is it that wins?
If only my mind were clairvoyant
I could stare deep into graves

Лежащего меня. Он показал бы мне
Меня, колеблемого на морской волне,
Меня, летящего по ветру в край незримый,—
Мой бедный прах, когда-то так любимый.

А я все жив! Все чище и полней
Объемлет дух скопленье чудных тварей.
Жива природа. Жив среди камней
И злак живой и мертвый мой гербарий.
Звено в звено и форма в форму. Мир
Во всей его живой архитектуре—
Орган поющий, море труб, клавир,
Не умирающий ни в радости, ни в буре.

Как все меняется! Что было раньше птицей,
Теперь лежит написанной страницей;
Мысль некогда была простым цветком;
Поэма шествовала медленным быком;
А то, что было мною, то, быть может,
Опять растет и мир растений множит.
Вот так, с трудом пытаясь развивать
Как бы клубок какой-то сложной пряжи,
Вдруг и увидишь то, что должно называть
Бессмертием. О, суеверья наши!

1937

Все, что было в душе

Все, что было в душе, все как будто опять потерялось,
И лежал я в траве, и печалью и скукой томим,
И прекрасное тело цветка надо мной поднималось,
И кузнечик, как маленький сторож, стоял перед ним.

И тогда я открыл свою книгу в большом переплете,
Где на первой странице растения виден чертеж.
И черна и мертва, протянулась от книги к природе
То ли правда цветка, то ли в нем заключенная ложь.

And see me buried there, buoyant,
Rising, floating on the waves,
Sailing in the wind to an unknown port,
My body that was loved by people of every sort.

But I am still alive!
My spirit embraces the living world.
Growing through stones, the plant in my house is a hive,
A small mold of the world's forms
That fill sea, sky, and land
With the architecture of music, invisible sounds
Changing color in an orchestra of endless forms
That shakes the earth with joy even in storms.

How everything changes!
The wingèd bird will lie down in the next hour
On a page peaked with words like mountains;
That thought was once a simple flower;
That poem, a placid, stationary ode,
Begins to crawl through the city with the ants,
And the lost part of myself in my house
Grows and multiplies in the cells of plants.
Straining to unravel my metamorphoses
In the weaving of their complex changes,
Suddenly I perceive the meaning of immortality . . .
Oh superstition that we claim to see!

—ADAPTED BY JAMES SCHEVILL

ALL THAT WAS IN THE SOUL

All of the shapes of the soul seemed somehow lost.
Sad and bored, I lay in the grass. Above me tossed
The beautiful flesh of a flower I could touch
Beside which a small guard, a cricket, stood watch.

Opening my book in its heavy old age
I discovered a flower drawn on the first page.
Dead and black it reached for the living plant.
Was it the flower's truth or a lie it would grant?

И цветок с удивленьем смотрел на свое отраженье
И как будто пытался чужую премудрость понять.
Трепетало в листах непривычное мысли движенье,
То усилие воли, которое не передать.

И кузнечик трубу свою поднял, и природа внезапно
проснулась,
И запела печальная тварь славословье уму,
И подобье цветка в старой книге моей шевельнулось
Так, что сердце мое шевельнулось навстречу ему.

1936

Поэт

Через бор за этим старым домом,
Перед домом—поле да овсы.
В небе серебристым комом
Облако невиданной красы.
По бокам туманно-лиловато,
Посредине грозно и светло,—
Медленно плывущее куда-то
Раненого лебедя крыло.
А внизу на стареньком балконе—
Юноша с седою головой,
Как портрет в старинном медальоне
Из цветов ромашки полевой.
Щурит он глаза свои косые,
Подмосковным солнышком согрет,
Выкованный грозами России
Собеседник сердца и поэт.
А леса, как ночь, стоят за домом,
А овсы, как бешеные прут...
То, что было раньше незнакомым,
Близким сердцу делается тут.

1953

With surprise, the flower stared at its reflection
Trying to understand the wisdom of selection.
Thoughts on leaves took away all possible rest
In an effort of will that cannot be expressed.

The cricket sounded his trumpet as if to find
That he was singing sweetly to my mind
And the image of flowering in the old book
Moved, as my heart moved into the flower's look.

—ADAPTED BY JAMES SCHEVILL

THE POET*

Black woods behind the old house,
In front a sloping field of oats;
Above a cloud curves in soft sky
Like a silver ball; centered
Against the cloud, beating with
Severe, painful clarity,
The wing of a wounded swan;
Below on the old wooden balcony
A young man with white hair,
His face the enigma of time
Like a portrait in an old medallion.
He narrows his oblique eyes,
Warmed by the light Moscow sun,
Hammered by the heavy Russian storms,
Poet who writes the heart's dialogue.
Behind the house the woods grow into night,
And wild oats fly crazed in dream . . .
Unknown until this time,
He has become a knowledge of the heart.

—ADAPTED BY JAMES SCHEVILL

*Boris Pasternak.

251

Чертополох

Принесли букет чертополоха
И на стол поставили, и вот
Предо мной пожар и суматоха
И огней багровый хоровод.
Эти звезды с острыми концами,
Эти брызги северной зари
И гремят и стонут бубенцами,
Фонарями вспыхнув изнутри.
Это тоже образ мирозданья,
Организм, сплетенный из лучей,
Битвы, неоконченной пыланье,
Полыханье поднятых мечей.
Это башня ярости и славы,
Где к копью приставлено копье,
Где пучки цветов, кровавоглавы,
Прямо в сердце врезаны мое...
И простерся шип клинообразный
В грудь мою, и уж в последний раз
Светит мне печальный и прекрасный
Взор ее неугасимых глаз.

1956

У гробницы Данте

Мне мачехой Флоренция была,
Я пожелал покоиться в Равенне.
Не говори, прохожий, о измене,
Пусть даже смерть клеймит ее дела.

Над белой усыпальницей моей
Воркует голубь, сладостная птица,
Но родина и до сих пор мне снится,
И до сих пор я верен только ей.

Разбитой лютни не берут в поход,
Она мертва среди родного стана.
Зачем же ты, печаль моя, Тоскана,
Целуешь мой осиротевший рот?

THE THISTLES

A bouquet of thistles! Is that possible?
Brought in, set on the table like flowers
And look! Fire, confusion,
A scarlet dance of flame;
Stars, glittering with sharp needles,
Flare like supernatural lanterns
Lighting the fury of Creation,
The flames of an endless battle.
These are the spiked towers of rage and glory
Guarded by spears, where the bloody heads
Of flowers cut into my heart. . . .
While their ancient, barbed guardians
Stick in my flesh with the memory of her love,
Her eyes shine through the thistles of time,
Beautiful, sad, enduring.

—ADAPTED BY JAMES SCHEVILL

AT DANTE'S TOMB

Florence was my stepmother of violence,
So I chose to lie in this tomb at Ravenna.
Passer-by, do not speak of treason,
Let death seal up the city with silence.

Time raised this white monument here
Over which the dove coos, quiet, sweet bird
Who seeks to sing me to rest, but I dream
Only of my country, my faith, my lost fear.

Exile, that broken lute, is immune to travel;
Years and languages away, it dies at home.
Oh, my sadness, Tuscany, your kiss of memory is
A web of flesh that death cannot unravel.

А голубь рвется с крыши и летит,
Как будто опасается кого-то,
И злая тень чужого самолета
Свои круги над городом чертит.

Так бей, звонарь, в свои колокола!
Не забывай, что мир в кровавой пене!
Я пожелал покоиться в Равенне,
Но и Равенна мне не помогла.

1958

Frightened, the dove darts from the tomb's roof
As the shadow of a wingéd machine,
High and deadly, draws strange lines
Over the city, white lines of war, evil, aloof.

O bell-ringer, your heavy bell will not cease
Ringing that the world still foams with blood!
I chose Ravenna's sanctuary for my death,
But even Ravenna brings no peace.

—ADAPTED BY JAMES SCHEVILL

BORIS

YULIANOVICH

POPLAVSKY

(1903–1935)

Europe, O Europe in youthful mourning,
How slowly your flags unfurl in moonlight!
Legless people are laughing at war. From the park
A rocket is launched to the moon.

Boris Poplavsky, "Pitying Europe," 1930

During the thirties, the majority of my parents' friends were Russians living in Paris. Not that France was inhospitable; we had French friends too, and during the war years we were especially close to them. Yet I grew up in an essentially Russian atmosphere. On Sundays, many of my parents' friends came for the day to our house in Le Plessis, twenty kilometers to the south of Paris — poets and painters who often traveled from Paris on their bicycles. We took long walks in the countryside. In the fall we went mushroom-gathering; in the summer we became berry pickers. There was afternoon tea-drinking, conversations that lasted late into the night, and poetry readings which I could overhear from my room after I had been put to bed. I loved to hear poetry recited. My father reads beautifully — his own verse and classical poetry—and so did Marina Tsvetayeva. Boris Poplavsky, perhaps the most original among the poets who formed the Russian school of Paris and as yet undiscovered by literary critics, read his verse with a singing, nasal voice:

> On a summer day above the white sidewalks,
> Paper lanterns were suspended.
> A trumpet's voice rasped. Over the avenue
> Flags dreamt on their long poles.
>
> A wave of heat and they were trembling,
> The sea was somewhere near.

258

> The air was dreamless like Lethe.
> We wept with sorrow for the flags.
>
> A flag flapping, a soul departing,
> Trembling like my love for you.
> Answer, darling, have you ever wanted
> Slowly to die, rolled in a flag?

This was the title poem in *Flags,* Poplavsky's first book, published in Paris in 1931.

Sometimes Poplavsky arrived at our house on foot, having walked all the way from Paris to Le Plessis. He usually wore knickers and a snap-brim plaid cap. Dark glasses protected his very pale blue eyes, which looked strained from reading or staying up late. I was always happy to see him. I remember him and the poet Nicholas Tatichtev, a friend who often came with him, admiring the drawings I had done with the tinted paper and pastels my father had given me.

I heard learned, lengthy conversations on all sorts of esoteric subjects, incomprehensible to me then, but captivating in their vagueness. Poplavsky had read everything, including the most peculiar and sometimes arcane books — Nostradamus, Jules Verne, and treatises on the cabala. He was a bohemian and had many friends, mostly Russian artists from around Montparnasse, who are still fanatically devoted to Poplavsky's memory. He died in the mid-1930's of an overdose of narcotics, probably accidentally. He took drugs in the company of a friend and apparently this man, who was bent on suicide, didn't hesitate to involve the poet.

Poplavsky was the only Russian poet of the Paris School to be directly influenced by the French poetry of that period, notably by Surrealism. Russia never figures literally in his poems, while Paris is always there, a fanciful, nostalgic city. He was a kind of Russian Guillaume Apollinaire, dead too soon, and there is a legend around his name, as if his poems and himself were of one essence. As a child, I thought that he was the perfect incarnation of a poet.

Nicholas Tatichtev dedicated himself to preserving Poplavsky's poems and manuscripts. He edited two post-humous collections of his verse in Russian, *The Snowy Hour* (1936) and *Last Poems* (1965), and these were published in Paris. This is how Tatichtev evokes his friend in a recent conversation:

"Poplavsky never held a paying job anywhere for more than three days in a row. He lived with his parents in a working class section of Paris, Porte d'Italie. (Both his parents were dedicated musicians. Before the Revolution, in Moscow, they had been well-to-do.) His father gave Poplavsky ten francs a day for food; sometimes the poet managed to collect unemployment compensation. When this happened, he would invite me to spend the evening with him — to go to the movies, or to the Closerie des Lilas, the café where the poets of Paris gathered then. Even better, we would go for a long walk into the Parisian suburbs, very far out of town, beyond the last subway stop. Poplavsky particularly liked the dull winter evenings around Paris — the snow, the fog, the poor people without overcoats and the rich ones with coats, who are so sad-looking.

"Now we are leaving Porte d'Italie and walking in the twilight, under the pillars of the elevated subway. Then we follow small dark streets; we are crossing the old fortifications lines, those of 1870. Poplavsky tells me that a generation ago, people took walks here in the winter — Guillaume Apollinaire and the Douanier Rousseau, and before them Charles Baudelaire and Corot . . . We cross Châtillon and Malakoff and find a beautiful white eighteenth-century country house in an abandoned wintry park. Crows sit on a tall blue fir by the house. A dim light burns in one of the windows. For a long time we

260

stand there and look into the park for signs of life, but there are none.

"Now in a lost *faubourg* we are sitting in a small café which will soon be closing. There is nothing outside but falling snow, a silent stream of snow. Two men are sitting near us, playing cards, like those two in Cézanne's painting. They softly speak to each other. 'They must be speaking about life and death,' Poplavsky says. 'There cannot be any other conversation . . .' "

Мистическое рондо III

Кошкам холодно. Они зевают
Да. Да.
А над башней мира тихо пролетают
Бабочки года.

Ангелы кирпич таскают белый
Строят дом,
А другие спят в лесу без дела
Золотом.

Дева осень их околдовала
Синевой
В нежный детский лоб поцеловала
Под горой.

Кто там ходит в бездне напевая?
Спать пора,
В синеве песок переливают
Два царя.

Царь дневной тщедушен хил и нежен
Смотрит он,
Как песок спадает белоснежный
На балкон.

Ищет в книге он святые звуки
Книга спит.
Белые сложив страницы-руки
На груди.

А ночной король на солнце ходит
С мертвой головой,
Бабочек он тонкой сеткой ловит
Голубой.

И тогда стекает время жизни
Как вода,
Что несет Офелию к отчизне.
Навсегда.

1927—1930

MYSTIC RONDO III

The cats are cold. They are yawning.
Yes. Yes.
The butterfly years fly gently over
the tower world.

Angels are carrying white stones,
building a house,
while others are slumbering idly
in the golden woods.

The autumn maiden enchanted them
with deep blue,
she has kissed their tender, childlike foreheads
under the hill.

Who walks there in the chasm singing?
It's time to sleep;
in the deep blue two kings pour sand
back and forth.

The Day King is frail and weak and tender;
he watches
how the sand tumbles white like snow
to the balcony.

He looks in the book for sacred sounds,
the book sleeps,
having closed its white hand pages
over its breast.

And the Night King wanders in the sun
with a death's head;
he catches butterflies with a fine
blue net.

And then, like water, the time of living
drains away,
that bears Ophelia down to her home
forever.

—ADAPTED BY HENRY CARLISLE

Дух воздуха

Анне Присмановой

Дева осень вышла из рая.
Небо сине до самого края.

Тихо в вышних морях светлооких
Тонет белый корабль одиноких.

Под березою в желтом лесу
Спит прекрасный лесной Иисус.

Кроткий заяц стоит над ним
Греет лапу о желтый нимб.

Дева осень ты хороша,
Как погибшая моя душа.

Ты тиха, как рассветная мгла,
В которой она от земли ушла.

Боже Господи, как легко,
Как глубоко, как от земли далеко.

В темном доме она жила.
Никому не сделала зла.

Много плакала, много спала.
Как хорошо, что она умерла.

Если Бога и рая нет,
Будет сладко ей спать во тьме.

Слаще, чем жить в золотом раю,
Куда я за ней никогда не приду.

1927–1930

Рукопись, найденная в бутылке

Мыс Доброй Надежды. Мы с доброй надеждой тебя
покидали,
Но море чернело, и красный закат холодов
Стоял над кормою, где пассажирки рыдали,
И призрак Титаника нас провожал среди льдов.

SPIRIT OF THE AIR

(to Anna Prismanova)

The autumn maiden went out of heaven.
The sky is blue to its distant end.

The blanched bark of men alone
Sinks softly into the clear-eyed foam.

Beneath a birch in the forest deeps
The beauteous silvan Jesus sleeps.

A gentle rabbit stands over Him
Warming a paw on His halo's rim.

You are as good, o autumn maid
As that soul of mine, eternally strayed.

You are as still as the morning's hand,
There where it wandered beyond the land.

O Lord, how lightly, how deep,
How far it wandered away from me.

Long in a shadowy house it lived
And never was evil. Fugitive!

Much it slumbered and much it cried,
What an excellent thing that at last it died.

If God and Heaven do not exist,
Sweet shall be its sleep in the mist.

Sweeter than lying in Heaven's gilt
Where I shall never go after it.

—ADAPTED BY HENRY CARLISLE

MANUSCRIPT FOUND IN A BOTTLE

Cape of Good Hope, we left you in good hope . . .
But soon the sea grew black, a gleam
of obsidian knives; the red sunset
chilled over the bows, where weeping passengers
clustered. The ghost of the Titanic
veered after us, following us through the ice.

265

В сумраке ахнул протяжный обеденный гонг.
В зале оркестр запел о любви невозвратной.
Вспыхнул на мачте блуждающий Эльмов огонь.
Перекрестились матросы внизу троекратно.

Мы погибали в таинственных южных морях,
Волны хлестали, смывая шезлонги и лодки.
Мы целовались, корабль опускался во мрак.
В трюме кричал арестант, сотрясая колодки.

С лодкою за борт, кривясь, исчезал рулевой,
Хлопали выстрелы, визги рвались на удары,
Мы целовались, и над Твоей головой
Гасли ракеты, взвиваясь прекрасно и даром.

Мы на пустом корабле оставались вдвоем,
Мы погружались, но мы погружались в веселье.
Розовым утром безбрежный расцвел водоем,
Мы со слезами встречали свое новоселье.

Солнце взошло над курчавой Твоей головой,
Ты просыпалась и пошевелила рукою.
В трюме, ныряя, я встретился с мертвой ногой,
Милый мертвец, мы неделю питались тобою.

Милая, мы умираем, прижмись же ко мне.
Небо нас угнетает, нас душит синяя твердь.
Милая, мы просыпаемся, это во сне.
Милая, это неправда. Милая, это смерть.

Тихо восходит на щеки последний румянец.
Невыразимо счастливыми души вернутся ко снам.
Рукопись эту в бутылке, прочти, иностранец.
И позавидуй с богами и звездами нам.

1927–1930

At twilight the dinner gong echoed a long time.
The orchestra tuned up in the lounge to play love songs.
St. Elmo's Fire was seen between mast and funnel.
The sailors crossed themselves—oh, three times over:
the wildfire remained, a sickly gleam.

We were perishing in the mysterious
down-under ocean. Steep seas began to sweep away
deckchairs, boats . . . As the ship slumped into the dark
we turned to each other. Slowly kissed.
In the hold the prisoners howled and shook their chains.

We saw the Captain put off in a small boat.
Screams, the sound of blows, a ring of shots.
We kissed; behind your head—your
curly head—up went the beautiful, useless, disaster flares.
In what intimacy we were left to go down!

The decks were bare. What gaiety filled us!
The endless water blossomed with pink morning,
the sea sheathed its knives. With tears
we celebrated our housewarming. The deck
sloped like a hill behind us.

Slowly the sun rose (over your curly head).
You woke, turning at once to touch me again.
Diving into the hold, I met a leg
floating. Dear cadaver! You gave us
a week more of life.

Now we are dying. Come close; closer.
The sky is against us, its hard azure is crushing us.
Dearest, we are awaking, this is a dream.
Dearest, this is not true.
Dearest, this is death.

Slowly a last blush
mounts to your cheek.
Souls return to their dreams: that is happiness.
—Stranger, read this letter sealed in a bottle,
and envy us, as you envy Gods and the stars.

—ADAPTED BY DENISE LEVERTOV

YEVGENY

ALEXANDROVICH

YEVTUSHENKO

(1933–   )

At dawn I awaken
My two-wheeled friend.
Mother calls sleepily:
"Don't ring in the stairs!"
He bounds on the steps.
The way that I jump
On him
Has never been seen!
Fearlessly I race
And I ring,
      and I ring,
           and I ring!

Yevgeny Yevtushenko, "The Bicycle," 1954
—ADAPTED BY HENRY CARLISLE

From an interview in *The Paris Review,* 1966:

THE HOPES for a general literary revival in Russia, which were so strong in Moscow when I first went to Russia in 1960, have not been fulfilled; the events following Khrushchev's denunciation of modern art, at the Manège show in late 1962, marked the end of these hopes. Today the prevailing mood in Russian intellectual circles is a mixture of impatience and fatigue; yet it is not without a secret intensity. The literary scene is marked by a superficial calm, due to the oppressive (but not repressive) tactics of the authorities; beneath this calm there are men of talent and passion producing often unpublished, but fortunately not always unread, manuscripts.

In 1965, and then again in 1967, Yevtushenko told me that he still believes that a renewed Marxism might be reconciled with literary integrity; that the present system is not incompatible with human and artistic growth. This is an uncomfortable position today in Moscow, where a stifling Social Realism is the only sanctioned esthetic doctrine. To hold his own view requires a heroism which has become Yevtushenko's trademark. He needs this heroism, for in the post-Khrushchev era he has against him not only the official dogmatists, but many of his younger followers, who now criticize this leader of only a few years ago as not radical enough.

I first met Yevgeny Yevtushenko during that winter of

1960, when many new poetic voices were being heard in Moscow. Although Stalin had been officially denounced, one still came upon his masklike effigy here and there. However, people averted their eyes from his portraits and avoided speaking his name. The existence of concentration camps under the Stalinist regime was never mentioned except in small circles of friends behind closed doors; yet one could sense that everyone was engaged in a kind of private probing, a secret sorting out of fact from falsehood.

Intellectuals were becoming increasingly conscious of the vacuous climate in which they had been living for so long. In their meetings with me, my new acquaintances sometimes seemed to be breaking through some of their old fears for the first time: the fear of associating with a stranger, of evoking the past, of speaking one's mind. It was a rather awesome atmosphere — but also one filled with hopefulness.

At that time Yevgeny Yevtushenko was already well known in Moscow literary circles, but his face and personality were not yet familiar to millions of people in the U.S.S.R. and the West. Shortly before my trip, I had read some of his poems in Soviet literary magazines. They were outspoken and threw off a special aura of youthfulness — a kind of swingy, joyful poetic journalism, altogether free of the stock clichés about Soviet life.

Soon after my arrival in Moscow I took advantage of my father's acquaintance with the poet and telephoned him. I invited him to have tea with me one afternoon, and also mentioned that my father had requested an inscribed volume of his poems. Yevtushenko accepted my invitation and was very friendly on the telephone, but I gathered that he found my father's request naïve. "Olga Vadimovna," he said, "clearly you are a newcomer to Moscow! Printings of poetry are sold out at once in our country. The twenty thousand copies of my most recent book of selected poems disappeared in two days. Not a single copy left. But I'll recite some of my new verse to you," he added with warmth.

I was staying at the Hotel Metropole in the center of Moscow, which was then buried under a particularly heavy snowfall. In the somber, enormous hotel, I occupied a suite of rooms furnished in Victorian style. It was paneled and heavily curtained in a manner perfectly appropriate to the Metropole's long-standing reputation as an establishment where foreigners and their guests were closely watched by the hotel's personnel, and perhaps even spied upon. But on the late afternoon of Yevtushenko's visit, as he arrived, removing his overcoat, shaking the snowflakes off his gray astrakan fur hat and presenting me with a large bunch of hothouse lilacs, my suite brightened noticeably.

Yevtushenko is a very tall, ash-blond young man with a small head atop a long athletic body, pale blue, humorous eyes, a slender nose in a round face, and an open manner that was startling in the Moscow of those days. Oblivious of the oppressive surroundings, he sat down and without preamble talked about Russian poetry. He talked of himself, of the great poet of the twenties, Mayakovsky, and, at length, of contemporary Soviet poets. His generosity towards his fellow poets struck me at once; he named many, praising their poems, quoting whole stanzas of some. "Voznesensky and Akhmadulina are our most promising poets," he said. "Akhmadulina is in the great Russian tradition of women poets, of Akhmatova and Tsvetayeva. This is the tradition of high, unadulterated lyricism. She is my wife," he said, smiling, "and you must meet her. Alas, I myself belong to a less exalted poetic tradition. My verse is usually dictated by contemporary events, by sudden emotions — but such is the nature of my talent . . . When I am deeply moved, I am prompted to pour my feelings out at once in verse."

272

As he spoke, Yevtushenko got up, moved around the room, sat in turn in every one of various overstuffed armchairs, settling eventually on the dark blue velvet settee, his long legs crossed. But soon he stood up again to recite a poem of his own, one of several dedicated to Mayakovsky:

> What is it destroyed Mayakovsky,
> Put a revolver in his hand?
> To him with his great voice, his nobility,
> Let us offer some tenderness.
> —Living people are such a nuisance
> Tenderness is for those safely dead.

In the large sitting room, lit only by a desk lamp, Yevtushenko was an eccentric presence whose every movement was magnified in a play of huge shadows on the walls. While he recited, his pointed profile was curiously at odds with his round face and high cheekbones, his long hands punctuating the lines with occasional broad gestures. He declaimed with theatrical dash, and his sonorous voice gave life to the poems, disguising their occasional thinness under a wave of emotion. His voice filled the room as he looked distantly over my head, creating in me an illusion of being in a vast auditorium among rows and rows of rapt listeners.

He recited from memory a long fragment of a poem he especially liked: "An Ugly Little Girl," by Zabolotsky. Like his own poem to Mayakovsky, it is a plea for greater kindness in everyday life. Yevtushenko sat down, there was silence, and then he spoke again in a passionate crescendo of statements. "The need to restore warmth to people's lives is our most imperative task. This alone can save us, save the whole planet. Also, the Russian people have suffered too long. It is up to us to do something about this now—to create a climate of kindness, to let people open up and flower again. How will we ever make up for the injustice, the stupidity and the blood if we don't start now? There is nothing in our Communist society to prevent this flowering. Quite the contrary; but first we must conquer our inner fears . . . Many poets have done this, there is nothing blocking their inspiration any longer; all the great themes of our times are theirs. The prose writers have a harder time. Russian prose has suffered from years of stifling censorship which affected poetry less insofar as it circulates orally with the greatest of ease. However, there are several promising prose writers in my generation: Dudintzev's *New Year Tale* shows clearly that he has matured since the days of *Not by Bread Alone*. Then there is Yuri Kasakov, whom you should read at once; in my opinion he is the best prose writer of the younger generation. He writes in a renewed, yet deeply Russian tradition, that of Anton Chekov; compassion is his theme . . ."

Disdaining detailed explanations, Yevtushenko expected me to understand, perhaps to share his convictions, which he expressed in flowing sentences full of old-fashioned metaphors. Yet for all his rhetoric, he wasted no time on conversational amenities. He seemed possessed by an urge to get directly to the truth, and in this he reminded me a little of certain New York beatniks. "We have entered a new age. In the name of Communism we are looking for truth—in ourselves, in others. We often find it in simpler people," he added, voicing a traditional Russian conviction. "Truth is as delicate as a tender plant. It has survived a harsh winter and now will grow."

Yevtushenko was fascinated by the idea of the old Russian intelligentsia, particularly by its spirit of universality. "This spirit," he said, "the world has to recapture if it is to survive." He spoke of the birth of a new intelligentsia in the U.S.S.R.: "It is like trying to catch a stream of water in the palm of your hand," he said.

274

"Most of it flows out but a little is retained in the cup of the hand. This is happening now. We and our children will eventually retain this little amount of water as against the mainstream — but of course the ever-increasing mainstream is our first concern. The fact that the Soviet government has been able to open the world of good books to the masses of people gives us faith in the future of Russia . . ."

Throughout our conversation (which at times seemed to me a sort of morality play — Yevtushenko speaking in the name of a dynamic and purified Soviet Union and I taking the part of the West), the poet would return to the problem of discovering unifying ideas which would insure the happiness and peace of Russia and the rest of the world. I had the feeling that through me, he wanted to be heard by Western intellectuals. He was intensely curious about Western intellectual life, the latest movements in painting and writing, and asked many questions about the Beat poets and the New York action painters.

Tea was brought, and our conversation turned to the special role of poetry in Russia today. Yevtushenko spoke of the huge spellbound crowds who listened to the young poets, of huge printings of their works sold out in a day. I was never to hear him so eloquent as on this first tea-drinking meeting. At a moment of increasing political tolerance he was himself sizing up the power of poetry — more specifically, of his own poems — and of his own personality. The force of verse expressing the long bottled-up emotions of a crowd was then a relatively new discovery to him. At that time, through an ever-growing number of public readings given by himself and other young artists, poetry was just beginning to carry a promise of honesty all over Russia. It was the first wedge to be driven into a monolithic system of stereotyped ideas and reactions.

275

Yevtushenko was in the process of becoming a national symbol: the denunciation of Stalinism was started in literature, and notably in poetry. By the end of my long conversation with him, I knew I had heard a persuasive public voice, a spokesman for a whole generation. Here was someone bigger and brighter than life, but also a kind of conventional romantic hero. Yevtushenko imitated Mayakovsky, or rather an image coined by Mayakovsky — that of a flamboyant, proletarian young poet of the Revolution. The emphatic directness of his whole style gave great weight to whatever he said, even if the flamboyance was something of a pose. For Yevtushenko has a special talent for improvisation in real life, just as in his poetry; when he chooses to, he can write a poem on a designated theme in one afternoon.

On each of my subsequent encounters with Yevtushenko, there were displays of his sparkling imaginativeness. Usually the center of attention, he instinctively recognized the dramatic possibilities in situations and provocative ideas. He would seize on them avidly, as actor, as poet, intent on giving through his personality a memorable stamp to ephemeral events. He acknowledges this bent for performance, relating it to Pasternak's, who "nobly acted out his life" (Pasternak, "Hamlet"), although Yevtushenko's acting is more studied than Pasternak's ever was. In Leningrad later that winter, drinking champagne among friends, he made an enchanting, elaborate toast to the glory of Pushkin, whose city we were then visiting: "To Pushkin, who smells of snow and champagne . . ." A year later in New York I saw him at an academic reception where, after reciting his breezy, optimistic "The Bicycle," he answered many thorny political questions, disarming the hostile, solemnly anti-Soviet audience with his suave shrewdness. In a taxicab in Moscow in the carefree spring of 1962, he recited his "Ballad of the Beatniks." Four of us were on our way to the Mos-

cow Artists' Union, where, as a result of the relaxed political mood of that period, Yevtushenko's friend, the
painter Yuri Vasiliev, was to speak on his ideas about
experimentation in art. The "Ballad of the Beatniks" elec-
trified Yevtushenko's audience, including the taxicab
driver, who pulled over against the curb momentarily,
"so that I may fully taste the beauty of art without en-
dangering your lives," as he explained it. The not overly
sophisticated Russian rhymes sounded marvelous as he
recited:

> The twentieth century dumfounded us.
> Lies were heavy as taxes.
> Like dandelion seeds
> Ideas blew away from living breath
> And our hands laughed applauding
> And our feet grinned and danced...

In Moscow during the spring of 1962 I saw Yevtushenko often. The city had undergone great changes since
my first visit there. It was gayer, busier, now hard to get
around in; Moscovites struggled energetically for the
available taxis, whose fares had been lowered. A holiday
atmosphere prevailed for several weeks; that year the
first-of-May celebration and Orthodox Easter coincided.
The weather was warm, and the streets were crowded
with shoppers from out of town. Peasant women carried
shopping bags bursting with the staples purchased from
well-stocked stores — everything needed to prepare the
traditional Easter *paskha* (dessert made of pot cheese
and fruits) and *kulitch* (decorated yeast cake). The
women in their kerchiefs and wide skirts and round
faces looked as if they came out of the depths of Russia.
It was very much of a political occasion too; Lenin's portraits were to be seen everywhere, and the city was hung
with innumerable red and pale blue flags. The two cele-
brations didn't seem incompatible, quite the contrary;

most Moscovites were planning to make the most of both festivities.

As friendly and open as ever, Yevtushenko now glowed with success; he was the semiofficial spokesman of the liberal-minded youth. He had traveled to the U.S., to Europe, and as a *Pravda* correspondent to Cuba, where he had been befriended by Fidel Castro; it was rumored that he was on the eve of being admitted to the Party. He had been divorced from the brilliant, mercurial poetess Bella Akhmadulina, and was now happily married to blue-eyed Gallya. Slightly older than Yevtushenko, Gallya is a poised intelligent brunette who is reputed to have first-rate taste in literary matters.

Yevtushenko and Gallya had just moved into a flat situated in a large new complex of buildings planned expressly for members of the Writers' Union and their families. It is far from the center of town along the wide Kiev highway, in a fast-growing new district where tall brick developments are erected next to old suburban log houses. The area hadn't been landscaped, and the dug-up streets were still unnamed. Inside the buildings, the apartments were not yet numbered.

The Yevtushenkos' place was already decorated in a particular Moscow fashion: a dash of contemporary Scandinavian and a little folk art — lovely Ukrainian ceramic toys — were mixed with objects apparently out of the twenties: armchairs full of unfunctional angles and complicated geometric patterns. All in all, the effect was gay and hospitable.

These were hectic days for the poet and his wife. They were about to leave for London on an official tour. Gallya was packing for the trip, and the telephone, which had just been connected, rang incessantly. The apartment was the scene of constant comings and goings. Friends of the Yevtushenkos dropped in to say good-bye. Many also came to look at their collection of paintings. Yevtushenko, who is very proud of this collection, had just finished hanging it. Like the apartment's decor, it had a vague 1920's look, the majority being rather crude Surrealistic works by Moscow painters. But there was some good painting as well: a handsome, monumental canvas by Nikonov of men playing cards, a set of working drawings by the sculptor Ernst Neizvestny, and several abstractions that Yevtushenko had brought back from Cuba.

Despite the chaos Yevtushenko agreed to be interviewed for *The Paris Review.* I had dinner there on the evening set for the interview. It was still daylight when we sat down to a supper of steak and small ripe tomatoes, the latter being one of Yevtushenko's favorite foods. There was a huge platter of them, and they matched the bright decor created by the versatile Yuri Vasiliev, who had used painted wooden spoons and popular Ukrainian motifs to relieve the standardized proportions of the kitchen where we ate. Through the window, a smell of *cheremoukha* came into the kitchen; this is the alder blossom that appears so often in Russian poetry, which has a heavy fragrance unknown to me until that spring. The sun was slowly setting behind a landscape of foamy green trees and huge construction cranes.

The Yevtushenkos were in an excellent mood, and we celebrated the occasion with champagne. Thus, like many of Yevtushenko's undertakings, the interview was something of a glamorous improvisation and was preceded by much animated conversation and elaborate toasts, an important part of festive Russian dining. Finally, when the table was cleared and Gallya was packing in the next room, Yevtushenko and I moved into the living room. The poet's desk, of a handsome Scandinavian design, stood there. On it stood a huge photograph of Hemingway in his middle years and an inscribed portrait of Castro — two bearded dieties presiding over our exchange. We continued to drink the sweet, mellow Soviet champagne.

Yevtushenko declined to answer those questions which particularly intrigued me then about international trends in literature, or the possible comparisons between certain Soviet poets and the younger generation of American writers. But he was obviously delighted to answer other questions, especially those dealing with art. We were surrounded by works of Vasiliev and Neizvestny, and it was about them that Yevtushenko spoke first. Then, as we proceeded with the interview, he sat down at his desk and typed out his answers, sometimes interrupting himself to recite a poem which emphasized the point he wanted to make. He was relaxed and gay, at times rising to walk around the room and look out the window, displaying the same restless energy that I remember from my first meeting with him.

"Happy changes are taking place in our lives right now," he said, "and they are felt in many realms. In the realm of literature, it is in poetry that they manifest themselves most clearly. There are many new poetic trends in Russia now. Like many horses galloping and racing each other, they overturn the mossy cobblestones of past thinking . . .

"Of course some people continue to think cobblestone thoughts, but in my opinion to view Russian poetry with irony and skepticism today is almost a crime. Where else in the world does poetry have the impact it has in the Soviet Union? Where else do poets express their country's deepest aspirations?"

Then Yevtushenko told me about the Day of Poetry, a yearly festival which has progressively grown in scope, and which is marked now by the publication of an annual anthology of the works of the poets participating.

"Some years ago when the poet Vladimir Lugovskoy proposed that a public recital of poetry be held every year

280

in the fall, not everyone believed in its success. But the Day of Poetry is now part of Russian life, an institution, an occasion for popular rejoicing . . . On this day, poets climb on counters in bookstores; they sell their autographed books, they read their verse and meet their readers. This takes place all over the country, but in Moscow it has a special amplitude. In the evening Moscovite poets assemble near Mayakovsky's statue and read again, this time in front of a huge crowd of eight or ten thousand people. The listeners stand for hours on end, even though the October wind blows hard. There have been years when snow fell that day, but the crowd did not disband; it stood listening in the storm."

I ventured to say that lack of popular entertainment might partly account for the following the poets commanded.

"No, no," protested Yevtushenko, "those readings are *not* organized frivolity. No artistic activity as esoteric as poetry can have a massive following unless it has something mature to say. Go to a Moscow bookstore, try to buy the poetic works of Akhmatova, Bella Akhmadulina, Boris Slutsky, or Andrei Voznesensky. The booksellers will only shrug their shoulders at you.

"In my opinion, two factors may explain this. First, the poets I just named are true poets: the time when courtiers flattered their master through verse writing and called themselves poets is over. But we also have many excellent readers, attentive and discriminating. This is not to say that the artists I have just mentioned — and many others, excellent poets whose names would mean nothing to Westerners — adapt themselves to the taste of the readers, however cultivated this taste may be. On the contrary, those poets contribute to the sharpening of public taste; they form and widen this taste, and this is their most important function.

"Incidentally, all the poets I speak of could not be more

different from one another. Voznesensky has a kind of 'atomic style', full of breathtaking, rhythmic pirouettes. Akhmadulina is restrained; she is a painstaking jewel-smith of words, yet she is lyrical, completely of our time. Boris Slutsky, on the other hand, is altogether deprived of atomic surge; he is a poet as virile as a stonecutter. Martynov can be cryptic, an inventor of charades. In his verse, profound philosophical themes are hidden under a graceful melodic disguise.

"Among the older poets, Alexander Tvardovsky stands out, but now he moves us less than he used to.* In my opinion he is a magnificent poet, but his verse lacks magic. However, such is his poetic gift. Under our eyes, what Mayakovsky once dreamt of is taking place:

> Only one thing to me is important:
> That there be poets,
> Many excellent, different poets!

"Traditionally, Russian poetry probes those questions which move us most, from intricate political queries to fine psychological points. Russian poetry was never ex-clusively descriptive, nor psychological, nor didactic, nor melodic. (I am speaking now about good poets only; they alone are representative.) Russian poetry is made up of all those elements, but it also usually contains a measure of serious political thought.

"Without exception, all our better poets today con-tinue this tradition. This is why they are loved. This is why windowpanes burst in the public meeting halls where poetry recitals are held. The militia has trouble containing the crowds eager to hear us. The audience is intense, responsive, often enthusiastic. But there is noth-

---

* Tvardovsky is one of the editors of the liberal literary periodical, *Novy Mir*, and the author of the anti-Stalinist satirical poem, "Tyorkin in the Other World," published in 1963, a sequel of his World War II "Vasily Tyorkin."

ing subversive or scandalous in those readings, as is sometimes suggested . . . Our audience is not an hysterical fringe. It is made up of workers, of students, of scientists. We poets feel that their interest and trust in us is in some measure a step forward into the future. We shall try not to disappoint them."

I asked Yevtushenko who he considered his literary ancestors.

"I always try to take anything that interests me from anyone, and yet try to remain myself. As you see, I go back to my notion of an eclectic art — yet one solidly centered, held together by the force of one's personality. Let me say, however, that Pushkin is my favorite figure in Russian letters. Also I love Blok, Mayakovsky, Pasternak . . . Yesenin influenced me. All have helped me in various, often evident ways. I would be happy to know that even one of my own lines will serve a poet in the future. In fact, this is how I would state my artistic ambition: to be able to write such a line . . . Incidentally, I love Walt Whitman. I also have a predilection for Paul Verlaine because of the melodic aspect of his verse. It may seem quaint to you, but I once wrote a poem under the direct influence of 'Chanson d'automne.' " *

What about contemporary Western influences? I inquired.

"As I see it, Hemingway is the strongest influence here," said Yevtushenko. "Early works by Remarque are also widely read. St. Exupéry has reached us only lately; one finds elements suggested by him in contemporary Soviet writings. Catcher in the Rye is a great success. We are very much open to Western writers, and occasionally we may borrow their techniques. These borrowings are only sporadically successful; they often turn out to be

---

* During his New York visit in 1966, Yevtushenko recited with great feeling part of this poem to Mrs. J. F. Kennedy when she indicated that she was particularly fond of Verlaine.

sterile. On the other hand, they sometimes lead to something organic which helps us grow.

"One Soviet poet, for example, is much influenced by the poetic intonation of Jacques Prévert, but in his verse this intonation is transformed into something entirely new and Russian. In Voznesensky there is a curious mixture of the Rimbaud of 'Le bâteau ivre' with the clash and dissonances of an Allen Ginsberg, but Voznesensky remains a completely original poet . . ."

There was a ring at the door. Friends had arrived to wish the Yevtushenkos a good journey, bringing presents and several bottles of champagne. This meant the end of the interview, and though we had several more conversations in 1962, and again in 1965, Yevtushenko did not substantially alter the opinions expressed on this first occasion.

That night the guests stayed on and on, talking into the spring night, the windows open on a dark, balmy Moscow. The conversation dealt with Russia and the West, with poetry and painting. Yevtushenko's visitors were artist and poets, and they all rejoiced in his good fortune at making the trip; I was struck by their great yearning for intensified exchanges with foreign countries. Now, years later, little still is done to allow visits abroad by the most talented Soviet artists and painters; instead, official-minded and unimaginative writers are all too often sent on cultural exchanges.

Yevtushenko, who has deliberately tried to overcome Soviet cultural provincialism, has time and again reiterated his faith in the existence of a "community of good people" throughout the world, regardless of their political or national allegiances. In the winter of 1962–1963, an official campaign was launched to squelch this view, which is held to be unorthodox from the Communist standpoint. In an effort to discredit Yevtushenko in

284

the eyes of his young Soviet contemporaries among whom he is so popular, another prestigious young man was called on: the cosmonaut Yuri Gagarin. Gagarin denounced Yevtushenko's want of patriotism in publishing abroad his autobiography without the sanction of the Writers' Union. Needless to say, the aviator's voice was not strong enough to smother Yevtushenko's. The young generation led by Yevtushenko has been heard across the Soviet Union and has thrilled the Soviet public. The young poets have become known internationally, showing just how anachronistic the wall of Soviet cultural isolationism is.

Yevtushenko has demonstrated something else — unexpected not only in Russia but anywhere today — that a dashing young poet speaking for freedom might command the same sort of popular audience now as Lord Byron and Victor Hugo did in the days of Romanticism. Like those artists, Yevtushenko's power is to be found in his whole personality, rather than in literary achievement alone.

Yevtushenko has helped earn the possibility of surviving for himself and other members of his generation. If it were not for the years of his shrewd yet generous public performances, he and those he has praised might all have been crushed in the 1962–1963 drive against nonconformity in Soviet art. Yet, because of the unchanging, ideological dogmas still prevailing in Russia today, from which he has never completely broken away, and also because of his own artistic limitations, Yevtushenko is unable to satisfy fully the Soviet public's urge for freedom of expression — a freedom, ironically, which he himself was the first to initiate. Such is often the fate of innovators. Today a new, more demanding generation of readers often finds Yevtushenko too superficial in his themes, too much in love with his own image, too ready to alter a line at the demand of an editor.

285

But no one has yet replaced Yevtushenko on the literary scene in terms of sheer popularity—not even Andrei Voznesensky, who is both a close friend and a rival. Yevtushenko's leadership does, however, show signs of fading. In the uncertain atmosphere now prevailing in Moscow, there seems on the part of the public an ever-increasing urge for truth, and on the part of the functionaries who control literary matters, the same old fear of it.

Не разглядывать
              в лупу
эту мелочь
          и ту,
как по летнему лугу,
я по жизни иду.
Настежь—
         ворот рубашки,
и в тревожных руках
все недели—
          ромашки
о семи лепестках.
Ветер сушит мне губы.
Я к ромашкам жесток.
Замирающе:
           «Любит»,—
говорит лепесток.
Люди,
      слышите,
            люди—
я счастливый какой!
Но спокойно:
           «Не любит»,—
возражает другой.

1953

Я шатаюсь в толкучке столичной
над веселой апрельской водой,
возмутительно нелогичный,
непростительно молодой.
Занимаю трамваи с бою,
увлеченно кому-то лгу.
и бегу я сам за собою
и догнать себя не могу.
Удивляюсь баржам бокастым.
самолетам,
          стихам своим . . .
Наделили меня богатством.
Не сказали, что делать с ним.

1954

Don't look too near
At this trifle or hear
That as over spring meadows
I walk across life,
Shirt collar open
Eager hands full of daisies
Every week new ones
With seven petals.
Lips dried by the weather
I am cruel to the petals,
Says one, dying, "She loves me . . ."
Oh, everyone see
How my happiness rises.
". . . Not," whispers another.

—ADAPTED BY HENRY CARLISLE

I roam through the packed city,
Over gay April waters,
I'm revoltingly erratic
And unforgivably young.
I fight my way onto trolleys,
I get carried away in lies,
And I run like mad
Never catching up with myself.
I marvel at the big-hipped barges,
At airplanes
           at my own verses.
I am given a great treasure
And no one explains its purpose.

—ADAPTED BY HENRY CARLISLE

Мне говорят, качая головой:
«Ты подобрел бы . . .
                    ты какой-то злой!»
Я добрый был.
               Недолго это было.
Меня ломала жизнь
               и в зубы била.
Я жил подобно глупому щенку.
Ударят—
          вновь я подставлял щеку.
Хвост благодушья,
               чтобы злей я был,
я сам
     одним ударом
                    отрубил!
И я вам расскажу сейчас о злости.
Когда перед собраньем шепчут:
                              «Бросьте!
Вы молодой, и лучше вы пишите,
а в драку лезть покамест не спешите . . .»
А я не уступаю ни черта:
быть злым к неправде—
                         это доброта!
Я коммунист по сущности своей.
Мне коммунизм велит
                    быть злей и злей
к тому, что на пути его стоит,
и с толку я советами не сбит.
И нету во мне робости былой,
и—
    интересно жить, когда ты злой.

1961

Бабий Яр

Над Бабьим Яром памятников нет,
Крутой обрыв, как грубое надгробье.
Мне страшно.
               Мне сегодня столько лет,
как самому еврейскому народу.
Мне кажется сейчас—
                    я иудей.

People tell me with solemn demeanor:
"Be sweeter,
        you're getting meaner and meaner."
Once I used to be nice,
        but not any more.
Life was hitting me,
        and breaking me up,
While I went around like a friendly pup:
Crack,
        and I'd wag my tail.
But one fine day,
        with a single blow
I severed the tail of kindliness—so!
And now let me tell you about badness.
Before a meeting you hear them hiss:
"Go home, go back to your writing.
You'll get more than you want if you look for fighting."
But I won't give a single foot.
Being mean to falseness is like being good.
I am a Communist to the last
And Communism insists I be nasty
To those who stand in its way.
By good advice I shall never be swayed,
All my old timidity is gone,
        and I'm glad,
For it's interesting just to be born when you're bad.

        —ADAPTED BY HENRY CARLISLE

BABI YAR

There are no monuments on Babi Yar,
A steep ravine is all, a rough memorial.
Fear is my ground—
Old as the Jewish people, a Jew myself it seems,
I roam in Egypt in her ancient days,
I perish on the cross, and even now
I bear the red marks of nails.

Вот я бреду по древнему Египту.
А вот я, на кресте распятый, гибну,
И до сих пор на мне следы гвоздей.
Мне кажется, что Дрейфус—
                это я.
Мещанство—
          мой доносчик и судья.
Я за решеткой.
              Я попал в кольцо.
Затравленный,
          оплеванный,
                  оболганный.
И дамочки с брюссельскими оборками,
визжа, зонтами тычут мне в лицо.
Мне кажется—я мальчик в Белостоке.
Кровь льется, растекаясь по полам.
Бесчинствуют вожди трактирной стойки
и пахнут водкой с луком пополам.
Я, сапогом отброшенный, бессилен.
Напрасно я погромщиков молю.
Под гогот:
          «Бей жидов, спасай Россию!»
Лабазник избивает мать мою.
О, русский мой народ!
              Я знаю—ты
по сущности интернационален.
Но часто те, чьи руки нечисты,
твоим чистейшим именем бряцали.
Я знаю доброту моей земли.
Как подло,
          что и жилочкой не дрогнув,
антисемиты пышно нарекли
себя союзом—«Союзом русского народа»!
Мне кажется—
          я это Анна Франк,
прозрачная, как веточка в апреле.
И я люблю,
          и мне не надо фраз.
как мало можно видеть,
                обонять!
Нельзя нам листьев и нельзя нам неба.
Но можно очень много—
              друг друга

I am Dreyfus, detested, denounced,
Snared behind prison bars:
Pettiness
Is my betrayer and my judge.
Shrieking ladies in fine ruffled gowns
Brandish their umbrellas in my face.

And now a boy in Bielostok,
I seem to see blood spurt and spread over the floor.
The tavern masters celebrate:
Under the smell of vodka and of onions
And of blood.
Kicked by their heavy boots I lie
Begging in vain for pity.
The rampant pogrom roars
"Murder the Jews! Save Russia!"
A man is beating up my mother.

> O Russian people,
> I know your heart
> Lives without bounds
> But often men
> With dirty hands abuse
> The body of your clear name.
> Shamelessly,
> Without the quiver of a nerve
> These pompous anti-Semites call themselves
> "The union of the Russian people."

Anne Frank, I am she,
A translucent twig of April
And I am filled with love that needs no words.
We are forbidden the sky and the green leaves
But in this dark room we can embrace.
Love, do not fear the noise—it is the rushing
Of spring itself.
Come, let us kiss . . .
The sounds of thawing ice change to pounding on
    the door.

это нежно
друг друга в темной комнате обнять.
Сюда идут?
            Не бойся—это гулы
самой весны—
            она сюда идет.
Иди ко мне,
            дай мне скорее губы.
Ломают дверь?
            Нет—это ледоход...
Над Бабьим Яром шелест диких трав,
Деревья смотрят грозно,
            по судейски.
Все молча здесь кричит,
            и шапку сняв,
я чувствую, как медленно седею.
И сам я?
            как сплошной беззвучный крик,
над тысячами тысяч погребенных.
Я—
Каждый здесь расстрелянный старик.
Я—
каждый здесь расстрелянный
            ребенок.
Ничто во мне
            про это не забудет!
«Интернационал»
            пусть прогремит,
когда навеки похоронен будет
последний на земле антисемит.
Еврейской крови нет в крови моей.
Но ненавистен злобой закорузлой
я всем антисемитам,
            как еврей.
И потому—
            я настоящий русский!

1961

Wild grasses rustle over Babi Yar,
The trees stare down, stern as my judge,
Silent the air howls.
I bare my head, graying now,
And I am myself an endless soundless howl
Over the buried
Thousands and thousands of thousands,
And I am every old man shot down here
And every child.
In no limb of my body can I forget.

Let the Internationale
Be sung
When the last reviler of the Jews is dead.
No Jewish blood is mixed in mine, but let me be a
    Jew
For all anti-Semites to hate, to spit upon.
Only then can I call myself
Russian.

—ADAPTED BY ROSE STYRON

Памяти Ахматовой

1

Ахматова двувременной была.
О ней и плакать как-то не пристало.
Не верилось, когда она жила,
не верилось, когда ее не стало.

Она ушла, как будто бы напев
уходит в глубь темнеющего сада.
Она ушла, как будто бы навек
вернулась в Петербург из Ленинграда.

Она связала эти времена
в туманно-теневое средоточье,
и если Пушкин—солнце, то она
в поэзии пребудет белой ночью.

Над смертью и бессмертьем, вне всего,
она лежала, как бы между прочим,
не в настоящем, а поверх него,
лежала между будущим и прошлым.

И прошлое у гроба тихо шло
не вереницей дам богоугодных.
Седые челки гордо и светло
мерцали из-под шляпок старомодных.

Да, изменило время их черты,
красавиц той, когдатошней России,
но их глаза—лампады доброты—
ни крутоверть, ни мгла не загасили.

Шло будущее, слабое в плечах.
Шли мальчики. Они себя сжигали
пожаром гимназическим в очах
и в кулаках тетрадочки сжимали.

И девочки в портфельчиках своих
несли, наверно, дневники и списки.
Все те же—из блаженных и святых—
наивные российские курсистки.

TO THE MEMORY OF AKHMATOVA

I

Akhmatova belonged to the old days and to our day
I don't know how to speak at her funeral

It is amazing she should have lived,
amazing she should have died,
Left, as if having forever
gone back to Petersburg from Leningrad.

If Pushkin was our sun
she was poetry's white night.

She was waiting here awhile so casually
holding the old horizon and the sky
together in a misty, shadowy knot.
Their faces had altered, yes,

under their graying bangs,
under their queer, old-fashioned hats,

Yes, the times had altered the faces
of the beauties of one-time Russia

but their eyes
kind as little church candles

did not go dead in the noise and the darkness.
White night all around us!

Old belle of no time, no place,
returned to Petersburg for the last time

the way the last bit of a song
or the light on a white

dress drifts into
the depths of a darkening garden

И ты, распад всемирный, не убий
ту связь времен,—она еще поможет.
Ведь просто быть не может двух Россий,
как быть и двух Ахматовых не может.

1966

Третья память

У всех такой бывает час:
тоска липучая пристанет,
и, догола разоблачась,
вся жизнь бессмысленной предстанет.

Подступит мертвый хлад к нутру.
Но чтоб себя переупрямить,
как милосердную сестру,
зовем, почти бессильно, память.

Но в нас порой такая ночь,
такая в нас порой разруха,
когда не могут нам помочь
ни память сердца, ни рассудка.

Уходит блеск живой из глаз.
Движенья, речь—все помертвело.
Но третья память есть у нас,
и эта память—память тела.

Пусть ноги вспомнят наяву
и теплоту дорожной пыли,
и холодящую траву,
когда они босыми были.

Пусть вспомнит бережно щека,
как утешала после драки
доброшершавость языка
всепонимающей собаки.

And not a cluster of murmuring ladies
but the Past went softly alongside her,

and the future followed—weak in the shoulders—
a speechless student, with reams of poems.

—ADAPTED BY JEAN VALENTINE

The Third Memory

To everyone comes that time
when anguish clings and clings.
Life then in all its nakedness
becomes pointless as death.

Fearful, weak, suddenly
cold, we shrink, but perseveringly
call out, call out to memory
as we might summon a sister

of mercy. But still the desolation
in the night prevails. The memories
of reason and the heart are not
enough to save what wants

to live within the eyes,
what moves, what makes us speak.
Everything dies. Only
the body's memory survives.

My legs remember being bare
against the coolest grasses.
My feet cannot forget the soft
sting of sand across a road.

My cheek recalls (it was after
a fight) how tenderly a dog
with that kind roughness of his tongue
consoled my rage away.

Пусть виновато вспомнит лоб,
как на него, благословляя,
лег поцелуй, чуть слышно лег,
всю нежность матери являя.

Пусть вспомнят пальцы хвою, рожь,
и дождь, почти неощутимый,
и дрожь воробышка, и дрожь
по нервной холке лошадиной.

Пусть вспомнят губы о губах.
В них лед и огнь. В них мрак со светом.
В них целый мир. Он весь пропах
и апельсинами и снегом...

И жизни скажешь ты: «Прости!
Я обвинял тебя вслепую.
Как тяжкий грех, мне отпусти
мою озлобленность тупую.

И если надобно платить
за то, что этот мир прекрасен,
ценой жестокой—так и быть
на эту плату я согласен.

Но и превратности в судьбе,
но и удары, и утраты,
жизнь, за прекрасное в тебе
такая ли большая плата?!»

1966

Ресторан для двоих

Гонолулу,
на спине ты качаешься сонно в серебряно-черном нигде.
Гонит луны
вдоль зазывно русалочьих бедер твоих ветерок по воде.
Всюду блестки.
По-дикарски ты любишь стекляшки витрин и реклам.
Словно брошки,
пароходы приколоты к влажным твоим волосам.
Ты тасуешь

My brow remembers still
(and guiltily) how silently a kiss
revealed my mother's tenderness
and how in darkness I was blessed.

My fingers keep their memories
of rye, pine needles, rain,
and barely tangible, a sparrow's
shiver or the nervous quiver

down the withers of a horse.
My lips remember lips
of ice and flame, of dawn
and dark, of some lost world

that tastes of oranges and snow.
Then I can whisper, "Life,
forgive my anger at your secrets.
Forgive the guilt that blinded

me until I doubted you.
If you must ask a bitter
price each time you offer
me some relish of the earth,

so be it. Uncertainties,
defeats, the pains of loss—
are these too much to pay
for all that's beautiful in you?"

—ADAPTED BY SAMUEL HAZO

THE RESTAURANT FOR TWO

Honolulu,
you loll dreamily on your back in a silver-black nowhere.
The breeze moves moons
Across the waves and along your mermaidenly thighs.
Ubiquitous scintillation.
Like a savage you love glinting trinkets in shopwindows.
Like brooches
great ships ride pinned in your watery hair.
In heedless brown hands

австралийцев, японцев и янки в шальных шоколадных руках.
        Ты танцуешь,
и звенят золоченые рыбки в стеклянных твоих каблучках.
        Лорд-шотландец
в пестрой юбочке пляшет с тобою, пуская слюну,
        и, шатаясь,
лезет мокро под юбку (и, кажется, не под свою.)
        Но, как гномик,
дотянулся до звезд   на ходулях—на пальмовых сваях своих
        крошка-домик,
уникальный игрушечный храм—«Ресторан для двоих».
        Без антенны
его крыша из листьев—зеленый смешной колпачок.
        Его стены
из бамбука и тайны, а что там творится—молчок.
        Бой-малаец
на подносе эбеновом вносит по лесенке в дом,
        ухмыляясь,
запеченый акулий плавник в ананасе, насквозь золотом.
        Два прибора.
Две свечи. Два лица. Два сообщника. Два беглеца.
        Как в соборы,
от содома они убежали друг другу в глаза.
        Ненадежно,
как в фонарике елочном здесь, и, пожалуй, морально грешно.
        Вообщем, ложно,
Вообщем, призрачно это, а все-таки так хорошо.
        Трепет самбы,
лепет звезд, и раскаты прибоя у дамбы—все только для них.
драпанул с удовольствием в тот ресторан для двоих!
        Подлым харям
закричал бы я, в пальцах обрыдлый бокал раздавив:
        «По-ды-хаю
от тоски среди вас! Я хочу в ресторан для двоих»!
        Надо делать
то и это, а этого—ни при каких..?!
        На-до-ело!
Я смертельно устал. Я хочу в ресторан для двоих!
        Надо думать
и бороться за что-то? Пытался я, пробовал... Фиг!
        Надоумил
этот домик меня. Я хочу в ресторан для двоих!
        Пусть осудят —

you shuffle Yanks, Japs and cards from Down Under.
You dance,
and tiny gilded fish tinkle in your heels.
A Scots laird
in a multicolored kilt reels with you, drooling,
and lubriciously
slips his hand under somebody's skirt, not his own.
But a modest hut,
a "Restaurant à deux," on its pilings of palm
like a gnome on stilts
has attained to the stars, a unique toy temple.
No aërial
tops its comical cap of green leaves.
Within, the walls
are woven of bamboo and mystery, and what takes place
is *hush-hush.*
A "boy," Malayan, smirking, fetches up the stairway
baked shark's fin
steeped in pineapple, golden through and through.
Two places set.
Two candles. Two conspirators. Two fugitives.
Into each other's eyes
as if into cathedrals they have fled the world's bedlam.
It's shaky in here,
it's rickety as a Chinese lantern. Maybe it's wrong.
It's false, sure.
That is to say, it's substanceless—and still, so pleasant!
The samba's throb,
the stars' murmuring, the thunder from the breakwater—
all for these two.
Gladly I would beat it to that Restaurant à deux.
I would crush
my glass of flat champagne and shout to the
        sourpussed mob:
"*I am dying,*
you bore me so. I yearn for the Restaurant à deux."
Oh no, you say?
One must do this, do that, but never, never the other?
I am fed up.
I am tired to death. I want in to the Restaurant à deux.
Reconsider?
Struggle on, be committed? Oh, I gave it a whack—so what?

303

удеру! Но бежать—это только для трусов, трусих.
ЧТО ЖЕ БУДЕТ,
ЕСЛИ КАЖДЫЙ ЗАПРЯЧЕТСЯ В СВОЙ РЕСТОРАН
ДЛЯ ДВОИХ?!
Среди гнойных
всех нарывов эпохи не выход—бежать от тоски
в домик-гномик,
в чьи-то волосы, губы, ладони, колени, виски!
...В звездных безднах,
словно в хрупком кораблике, тихо сидят, нашалив,
двое беглых,
а внизу ожидает с овчарками жизнь, как шериф...
И малаец
на приступочке дремлет внизу—на заветной черте,
умиляясь
чуть презрительно чьей-то святой и пустой простоте.
Замечает,
что еще полчаса до закрытия, а дальше—катись,
и включает
для иллюзии рая на пленку записанных птиц...

Гавайские острова. Гонолулу
Декабрь 1966 года

That little hut
has shown me the answer, the exit, the Restaurant à deux.
Let them judge me!
I'm off! And yet, running away . . . is cowardly stuff.
WHAT WOULD HAPPEN
IF EVERYONE WERE TO HIDE IN A RESTAURANT À DEUX?!
That's no way out,
in an epoch of crying wounds, to seek shelter from ennui
in a gnome-home,
in the tresses and lips of another, in her knees and brow.
A demon's whisper
impels us to flee; we cannot comprehend
that after flight
it is worse than before to be a galley-slave.
. . . Amid the stars,
they sit as in a dainty boat, having had their fun, at peace,
two fugitives:
while below them life with its dogs like a sheriff waits.
The Malayan
daydreams at the foot of the sacrosanct stairway
and scornfully
feels a stir of pity for such hollow innocence.
He observes
a half-hour remains to closing time (then, scram!)
and switches on
the birdsong tape-recorded to lend the illusion of paradise.

—TRANSLATED BY JOHN UPDIKE

ANDREI

ANDREYEVICH

VOZNESENSKY

(1933–)

Our destruction is unthinkable,
More unthinkable what we endure,
More unthinkable still that a sniper
Should ever sever the quivering thread.

Andrei Voznesensky, "My Achilles' Heart," 1965
—TRANSLATED BY W. H. AUDEN

ANDREI VOZNESENSKY was born in Moscow on May 12, 1933. During the war he was evacuated with his mother to the Urals. His father, a professor of engineering, who is now a member of the Soviet Academy of Sciences, served on the Leningrad front; he was involved in the task of evacuating Soviet factories and reorganizing them behind front lines during the blockade of the city. The family was reunited in Moscow after the war. The young Andrei grew up in a warm, intellectually stimulating atmosphere. As an adolescent, he wanted to become a painter; later he attended the Moscow Architectural Institute. He started to write poetry in his teens, but his first poem was published only in 1958.

Voznesensky has never lost his intense interest in the visual arts. Many of his friends in Moscow are architects and artists. Others are atomic scientists; Voznesensky's wife Zoya was once married to a physicist, and the Voznesenskys are still close to the scientific complex of Dubna, one of the greatest research centers in the Soviet Union. Along with many scientists, Voznesensky foresees that technology will dehumanize us unless it is brought under control; specialization and categorization will result, he believes, in a fragmentation of the soul. These fears he has expressed in his epic "Oza" (1963), a long symbolic poem about love in the modern world. This extremely complex, uneven poem is a great favorite with young Soviet scientists.

Voznesensky has often been taken to task by Soviet critics for the "formalism" * that allegedly mars his work; nevertheless he has been published regularly. The worst attacks against him came after the Manège onslaught against modern art. Voznesensky's answer to the assembled board of the Writers' Union was typically tough and elusive:

"It has been said at this meeting that I must never forget Nikita Sergeyevitch's severe, stern words. I shall never forget them. I shall not forget, not only these severe words, but also the advice which Nikita Sergeyevitch gave me: he said: 'Work.'

"His words are a program for me. I will work. I am already working. I am thinking and understanding many things that have taken place in the Kremlin and which have been said there. I understand my immense responsibility before the people, before our epoch, before the Communist party. These notions are dear to me. I do not want to justify myself now. I want to say this: the most important thing for me today is to work, work, work. My work will show what my attitude is towards our country. Communism will show what I am." (As quoted in *Le Monde*, Paris, March 30, 1963)

Although Voznesensky's poetic tone is not easily captured in other languages, the modernistic forms of his verse—framing a unique blend of Soviet humor, melodic richness, and cryptic thought—are beginning to win him international literary recognition as more and more of his verse is being translated into Italian, French, and English. As a personality, the young poet is becoming well-known outside of Russia. He is popu-

* A highly derogatory term in the Social Realist jargon, "formalism" means undue attention given to form as against social or political content. The term derives from the Formalist school of criticism which flourished right after the Revolution. Professor Roman Jakobson, a world-famous linguist, was one of its members.

lar abroad because he is as articulate as he is imaginative. Today he has a definite cosmopolitan literary following. Among his friends are Jean-Paul Sartre, Pablo Neruda, W. H. Auden, and Arthur Miller.

In Voznesensky's manner one finds the same mixture of whimsy and seriousness which characterizes his poetry. He is anxious to discuss his writing at length. I interviewed him on this subject a number of times—in Paris in 1963 and more recently in Moscow and New York. Often our conversations took place out of doors because he is an avid sightseer. In Paris we paced the Louvre and ascended Notre Dame together, and wandered all around Montmartre. In New York we visited the Guggenheim Museum and explored Greenwich Village. In Moscow a springtime walk through the Kremlin was memorable. Vozenesensky is in love with ancient Russian art and architecture and as a result was a marvelous guide around his native city.

But there were other conversations, held indoors, when I jotted down notes as the poet explored the world of his own poetic creation with visible delight. He opened one such conversation by praising the beauty of the English language, which he speaks better every year. He has liked it since, as a boy of thirteen, he fell in love with his teacher of English, Elena Sergeevna. She taught him "Annabel Lee." Although he still holds Edgar Allan Poe in affection, today Allen Ginsberg and Robert Lowell are his favorite American poets.

Voznesensky first received literary encouragement from Boris Pasternak. He was close to the poet during the period preceding the Nobel Prize scandal. "But I became a poet only when I broke away from Pasternak's influence," he says. "We were very close for a while; I was truly his disciple, but one day I realized that my poems were exactly like poems he might have written. I destroyed these poems. It was a traumatic break, but it was a decisive, unavoidable step."

The necessity of breaking away from tradition and discovering one's identity as a person and artist is a constant preoccupation with Voznesensky. The discovery of inner liberty is the underlying theme of many of his poems. When pressed on this subject, he calls it—not without a touch of half-playful grandiloquence—"the ever-present revolutionary aspect of poetry." "Real art is always revolutionary!" he exclaims, and recites from his "Parabolic Ballad," a poem dedicated to Gauguin which is famous throughout the U.S.S.R.:

> Laughing at law with its warnings and paragraphs,
> Art, love and history race along recklessly,
> Over a parabolic trajectory.

—TRANSLATED BY W. H. AUDEN

This poet, who is a member of Komsomol and who has written several heroic poems dedicated to Lenin, has about him an air of freedom typical of a large segment of the generation of Russians young enough to be without personal guilt for Stalinism. This is in contrast to the attitude of the poets of the war generation who are obsessed by this responsibility.

A certain breezy cheerfulness is also characteristic of Voznesensky, and this goes with his youthful looks, his turned-up nose, his bright blue eyes. The way he recounts his switching from architecture to literature is an example:

"It was all an accident," he says, "but a very fortunate one. I have never studied literature in school and this has proved an advantage: I feel that other, parallel arts often give more to the poet than poetry itself.

311

The danger of imitating is thus eliminated; it is like taking a shortcut. To be too close to one's predecessors is like courting one's own grandmother. As a poet, I have been more profitably influenced by ancient Russian churches and by the works of Le Corbusier than by other poets.

"Some years ago I was still a student of architecture, doing a little painting on the side, but already poetry was growing in me, running like a river under ice. I didn't plan it, but one day to my own surprise I found myself a professional poet. This was all due to a kind of symbolic occurrence. I was about to graduate from the Architectural Institute; I had completed my graduate thesis — a very theoretical project of a snail-shaped building not unlike Frank Lloyd Wright's Guggenheim Museum. And then one day the Architectural Institute caught fire. Years of still ungraded work by the graduating class were destroyed, whole cities on tracing paper went up in smoke. For me it was more than a fire; it was a symbolic event, a sign. I felt that architecture had burned up inside me. Suddenly, from one day to another, architecture seemed a ponderous, ineffectual means of expression. Now I can carry my life work in my pocket."

Voznesensky is thoughtful when speaking about Russia's recent past:

"The Stalinist era as I recall it was a fog, a thick cloud of ignorance, an accumulation of things unspoken . . . 1953 was a turning point for us. We who were twenty years old wept on that early spring morning. There was a gigantic, silent crowd milling in the streets of Moscow. It was so dense that we had to walk on rooftops to reach the Hall of Columns near the Kremlin where Stalin lay in state. We climbed over high walls, and made our way across backyards. The crowd caught us on their shoulders so that we wouldn't break our backs as we tumbled down into the street. We knew nothing then, and we felt lost in 1956.* But little by little we overcame our feeling of loss, we grew up. Because of the past, I couldn't write a single line for which I wouldn't die—literally, bodily. Our responsibility to our public is too great."

He has definite ideas regarding the popularity of poetry in the Soviet Union:

"Russian poetry today affords a look *inside* man, and this is its much-needed, durable contribution. In front of a huge audience, whose reaction to poetry is highly emotional, almost sensual, one senses a collective soul, wide open. Some say that my own verse is obscure, deprived of feeling in favor of form. But when ten thousand people clearly respond to it and enjoy it, it becomes obvious that my poetry is not really an art for esthetes as some would have it. If it is—long live the ten thousand esthetes of Moscow!

"In the U.S.S.R. we are going through a period of reappraisal in many fields, and poetry is playing an enormous role in this process. When we, the younger poets, read in front of thousands of people—and this happens very often, several times a month—we are acting as catalysts in a real transformation. Today the Russian people are struggling for greater awareness, for more sensitivity. There is a tremendous thirst for poetry wherever we go. Even when we are on trips, when we try to take a vacation, readings are improvised at local workers' clubs, in schools, in sanatoriums.

"Scientists respond to poetry strongly—more strongly than anyone else today in Russia. Clearly they need the symbolic feeling of unity which poetry creates. The space scientists especially—those who build our sputniks and concern themselves with complicated scientific problems. Naturally they are not interested in a simpleminded art. They set the level for our poetry, which is often

* When Khrushchev first denounced some of Stalin's crimes during the Twentieth Party Congress.

quite complex in form and content. They are our best readers; in fact, they must be the greatest readers in the world. You have to bear in mind that for decades during the Stalinist regime the best minds of Russia went into the sciences, bypassing the humanities altogether because of the terrific ideological pressures in these fields. Not that scientists were entirely free of them (witness the Lysenko case), but on the whole these pressures were less frightening in the realm of science.

"However, workers respond to poetry extremely well, even to the works of Pasternak and Khlebnikov, and to my own — to what is erroneously considered 'difficult' poetry. I gave a recital at the huge Bratsk Electric Station in Siberia some years ago and the audience was overwhelmingly, tempestuously enthusiastic, although the great majority of the listeners did not have a secondary education . . . Please don't think me immodest in mentioning my triumphs. I speak of them in an attempt to provide you with an idea of the life of our country at present."

I told Voznesensky that during my last visit to Moscow (in 1967) I had the feeling that *estradnaya* (declamatory) poetry was becoming less fashionable in the U.S.S.R., at least among intellectuals:

"This is certainly true of a small circle," he answered. "It may now be said that poetry has made it on a grand scale. Alert readers (and sensitive poets!) begin to feel that poetry is in danger of losing its strength by becoming more and more exclusively a mass entertainment. The time has come for poets to try to deepen their appeal instead of broadening it. There is a new mood in poetry — a need for poems which can be whispered. Personally I yearn for intimacy — in life and in art.

"It is a burden to be successful. Success is well-being, and an artist must not be too comfortable to be able to work well. Thus, I do a lot of painting right now. It is a

314

medium which satisfies me. I am not too comfortable in it at a technical level; it is a silent, intimate endeavor; I will never be a famous painter! I especially love that tricky medium, water color.* But naturally I am a poet, above all — a public poet at that. I bear the cross of success bravely."

Voznesensky is as fascinated with the role played by poetry in contemporary life as with the nature of poetry itself:

"Clearly poetry doesn't need to be completely intelligible to be enjoyed. A kind of powerful cement, it holds together the soul. Like the natural world, it gives birth not only to ideas, but also to sensations. Poetic thoughts are never completely rational. This is evident in our time: even in scientific matters, contemporary thought often proceeds by analogy, through associations which would have been termed as 'unscientific' in the nineteenth century. The second half of the twentieth century is the most magnificent time of all to be alive in: paradoxically, the atomic age has put within our reach the brotherhood of men. The atomic scientist has broken down the natural world to its particles; it is up to the poet to recreate its unity."

I expressed the fear that mankind would be destroyed before brotherhood was achieved, but Voznesensky protested.

"I simply cannot imagine another general war taking place," he said. "If it did, certainly any notion of heroic action such as flourished in World War II would fade; there could only be death, and infinite grieving. But ac-

---

* In Moscow in 1967 I was able to visit Voznesensky in his spacious new apartment in a skyscraper overlooking the Moskva River. He showed me some of his watercolors—surprisingly tender scenes of everyday Moscow life. In these there is not a trace of Voznesensky's modernistic, "constructivist" spirit as a poet. These works, the cozily furnished apartment, Zoya Voznesensky's attentive hospitality —all reflect the poet's longing for privacy. Alas, an ever-ringing telephone dispels any hope of achieving it for the time being.

tion against war is possible in the present: we must help prevent it, and perhaps we will succeed. I remember the last war fairly vividly, although I was quite small when it started. My mother and I were refugees in a small village in the Ural mountains. My father was in Leningrad. We thought that he had died. We were hungry; near the village wolves howled at night. One day the door opened and my father came in. He was unshaven and wore an old black overcoat. He brought us a tin of canned meat and a book about Goya; he was on leave and had come to visit us briefly. Since that day — I was nine — Goya has become a symbol for me, the symbol of war. Even today, he reminds me of the partisans shot by the Germans, of wolves, of our neighbor who was mourning her dead son, of the sirens during the bombardments of Moscow. Today he makes me think of Vietnam. Goya is like a bell tolling—a Spaniard, but also, in a way, a contemporary Russian artist. It is up to the artists to explore the horrors of life in order to help wipe them out. Above all, Goya tells us that all serious artists must be concerned with the threat of a war."

"You mean as artists, not necessarily as social spokesmen?" I asked.

"There is no longer any distinction between 'art for art's sake,' and 'engaged art' today," Voznesensky replied. "Either it is art or it is nothing. An artist helps to prevent war by creating beauty. It is as simple as that — or as complicated. People who are touched by beauty, be it the Samothrace Victory or a Le Corbusier building, are purified by their experience. The only serious hope that we have for the future lies in the fact that so many people, their numbers increasing in a geometric progression both in the West and in Russia, are becoming receptive to art. I love the faces of young people strolling in museums — in our Kremlin, in your Louvre. They help one realize that, just as the quarrel of 'engaged art' versus 'pure art' is absurd, 'new art' simply does not exist as opposed to the old-fashioned kind. There is only talent or lack of it. That which is talented is necessarily new. Often modernistic forms hide a lack of talent which is as old as the hills. In his late works, Pasternak returned to extremely traditional poetic forms. But he had lost none of his talent, and none of his newness. I would also equate talent with realism. No matter what form it takes, the lack of talent always yields unreal results. A talented artist will recognize things as they *are* and be able to express them. In the field of contemporary art, Picasso and Miró are in my opinion the greatest realists of all."

"Doesn't the making of contemporary art necessitate a search for new means of expression?" I asked.

"No, not really. An authentic artist will find new forms instinctively — or rather they will find him. As I walk, I am unconcerned about just how I do it; when I am in a hurry, I run. It's the *movement* which creates new forms — naturally, inevitably. Eluard and Rimbaud were far more revolutionary than Victor Hugo, who concerned himself expressly with burning political issues. Russian poetry more than any other has been traditionally revolutionary — and this is not to say that only those poets who threw themselves into social action were revolutionary."

"Aren't you giving the word 'revolutionary' an extremely general meaning?" I inquired.

"Why not," Vosnesensky answered. "And in this sense love is the most revolutionary of all happenings! When it is authentic, love endlessly reinvents itself. If a poet knows how to listen to its whispering, his poetry will always be new. The love of two people, an intimacy which seems to enclose them and to isolate them, also paradoxically opens them wide to the world:

Laughing at law with its warnings and paragraphs,
Art, love and history race along recklessly,
Over a parabolic trajectory.

Voznesensky likes to punctuate a conversation with passages from his own poems. When he is in a good mood he will recite a whole poem that is his favorite at the time — the "Parabolic Ballad" in 1963, and more recently poems out of *My Achilles Heart*, his last collection of verse. But *The Triangular Pear* remains his favorite. This cycle of poems, the most original to have been written in Russian since Pasternak's *Poems from Doctor Zhivago*, was inspired by a brief trip the young poet made to the United States in June, 1961: the triangular pear is the bare light bulb glaring in a New York subway. For Voznesensky, his first taste of New York was an intense experience; the young Soviet citizen fell in love with the city. (Later, he loved Paris, but with less wholehearted rapture.)

My own friendship with Voznesensky started in New York that year. Together with Yevgeny Yevtushenko, who was also on his first visit to the U.S.A. and who had introduced us, we walked at night in the Village in search of a good striptease show. I proved to be an incompetent guide in the matter, but we did find a café where Sarah Vaughn was singing, and she delighted Voznesensky.

On that trip the young poet was lucky; he was not yet well known in the West. He was free to wander around the city for several days, absorbing its sights and its sounds. In the meantime his traveling companion, Yevtushenko, better known at that time, was invited to Harvard to give a reading and reap his first American laurels.

More even than Paris and New York, Voznesensky loves traveling. Breathlessly he declaims his poem about Kennedy Airport at night:

> How frightening it is
> When the sky stands still
> In the fiery runways
> Of fantastic cities!

"My whole life is a voyage," Vosnesensky has said. "One might say that a poet has to be in a constant state of flight today. My long poem *Longjumeau*, about Lenin in Paris, opens with the description of a flight, when the earth seems to lie on its back — silent, springlike . . . For me a plane seat is the best of studies — what privacy it affords; no telephone, no interruptions. But then there are other travels, those of the heart, trips that one takes through other people's souls. And also the souls of animals, of things . . . Cities, too, have souls. Someday I'd like to put together a collection of my poems on the theme of the 'Cities Inside Myself.' New York, Paris, Rome, Moscow — harsh yet tender — these great cities are generous to the poet. He is an eternal traveler, an explorer . . ." I asked Voznesensky to elaborate on his definition of the poet:

"Above all the poet must have the dynamism necessary to be an explorer of souls," he said. "And of course there is no such thing as a 'pure' poet. One must always distinguish between the everyday person and the artist: it is as if two people resided alongside in one body. The everyday person is no more than a pair of shoes, a suit of clothes, which are inhabited by the artist. The everyday person may be a most insignificant creature, but inside him, like a shadow, dwells this other, visionary being — the poet. Sometimes these beings live together in harmony — or at least with a reasonable degree of harmony — but they also may clash. Sometimes they clash mortally and this is the tragic end of many poets, like Mayakovsky, for example, or Yesenin. Usually the everyday man does not know where the poet will take him, what he will undertake, what souls he will explore . . . I am not trying to *épater le bourgeois* when I say in "Autumn in Sigulda":

> Glad that into my transparent shoulder blades
> genius thrust itself
> like the ruddy fist of a man into a rubber glove.

"When I write poems, someone else takes the place of my daily *I*. When Mayakovsky wrote, he was not Volodya Mayakovsky, but another, a prophet. In the ideal Communist society of which Mayakovsky was dreaming, all the *chinovniks* [the functionaries] were to be transformed into poets. May antiheads* vanish from the face of this earth!"

> I love my carping critics
> On the neck of one there sits,
> naked
> And sweet-smelling
> a gleaming antihead!

* See "Antiworlds," page 325.

Ночной аэропорт в Нью-Йорке

Автопортрет мой, реторта неона, апостол
                              небесных ворот—
Аэропорт!
Брезжат дюралевые витражи,
Точно рентгеновский снимок души.
Как это страшно, когда в тебе небо стоит
В тлеющих трассах
Необыкновенных столиц!
Каждые сутки
                    тебя наполняют, как шлюз,
Звездные судьбы
Грузчиков, шлюх.
В баре, как ангелы, гаснут твои
                              алкоголики
Ты им глаголишь!
Ты их, прибитых,
                    возвышаешь!
Ты им «Прибытье»
                    возвещаешь!

Ждут кавалеров, судеб, чемоданов, чудес . . .
Пять «Каравелл»
              ослепительно
                              сядут с небес!
Пять полуночниц шасси выпускают устало.
Где же шестая!
Видно, допрыгалась—
                              дрянь, аистенок, звезда! . . .
Электроплитками
                    пляшут под ней города.
Где она реет,
              стонет, дурит?
И сигареткой
              в тумане горит?
Она прогноз не понимает.
Ее земля не принимает.

Худы прогнозы. И ты в ожидании бури,

322

The Airport at Night

The following seven poems are part of *The Triangular Pear* cycle.

My self-portrait, neon alembic, apostle of heaven's door—
Airport!
In their aluminum frames the windows
Gleam like X-ray pictures of the soul.
How frightening it is
                    when the sky stands still
in the fiery runways
of fantastic cities!
Twenty-four hours a day
                  through your sluice doors
      pour starry destinies,
      porters, whores.
      In the bar, like angels, your alcoholics are fading
           away.
      You speak to them.
They who were beaten down
              you elevate.
You announce an Arrival!

One waits here for boy friends, miracles, bags, careers,
And dazzlingly
      five Caravels
           set down from the skies!
Five carousers wearily lowering their landing gears.
Where is the sixth?
It looks like she's wandered too far,
             wicked storkling,
Little star.
Beneath her the electric cities
          play leap-frog.
Oh, where does she roam
         and sigh and frolic,
Like a cigarette
       burning in the fog?
She doesn't understand the forecast.
The earth is not receiving her.

The forecast is bad, and to await the storm

Как в партизаны, уходишь в свои вестибюли
Мощное око взирает в иные мира.
Мойщики окон
                слезят тебя, как мошкара,
Звездный десантник, хрустальное чудище,
Сладко, досадно быть сыном будущего,
Где нет дураков
                и вокзалов-тортов—
Одни поэты и аэропорты!
Стонет в аквариумном стекле
Небо,
            приваренное к земле.

Аэропорт—озона и солнца
Аккредитованное посольство!
Сто поколений
                не смели такого коснуться—
Преодоленья
                несущих конструкций.
Вместо каменных истуканов
Стынет стакан синевы—
                без стакана.
Рядом с кассами-теремами
Он, точно газ,
                антиматериален!
Бруклин—дурак, твердокаменный черт.
Памятник эры—
Аэропорт.

1961

Антимиры

Живет у нас сосед Букашкин,
Бухгалтер цвета промокашки,
Но, как воздушные шары,
Над ним горят
                Антимиры!
И в них, магический как демон,
Вселенной правит, возлежит
Антибукашкин, академик,
И щупает Лоллобриджид.

You retreat like guerillas to the gate areas.
The powerful eye searches other worlds.
The window washers
                              make your eyes water,
Sidereal parachutists of the crystal monster.
How sweet and annoying
                              to be of the future generation,
Where there'll be no fools
                              or gingerbread stations—
Only poets and airports!
The sky moans in its aquarium glass,
Welded to the earth.

Airport—you are the accredited embassy
of ozone and sun!
A hundred generations
                              dared not reach for this—
The triumph over mass in construction.
Instead of stone idols
                              a glassful of azure
Cools—with no glass.
Around the check-in rows
You are as antimaterial as gas!
Brooklyn Bridge, old fool, grim stone fort,
The monument of this age
is the Airport.

—ADAPTED BY HENRY CARLISLE

ANTIWORLDS

Mr. Beetle lives nearby (he's our neighbor).
He's a clerk
                    the color of blotting paper.
But over his head like great balloons
Glow
          Antiworlds!

And up among them like a magic fiend
          serene and
                    academic

Но грезятся Антибукашкину
Виденья цвета промокашки.

Да здравствуют Антимиры!
Фантасты—посреди муры.

Без глупых не было бы умных.
Оазисов—без Каракумов.

Нет женщин—
    есть антимужчины.
В лесах ревут антимашины.
Есть соль земли. Есть сор земли.
Но сохнет сокол без змеи.

Люблю я критиков моих.
На шее одного из них,
Благоуханна и гола,
Сияет антиголова!

...Я сплю с окошками открытыми.
А где-то свищет звездопад.
И небоскребы
    сталактитами
На брюхе глобуса висят.
И подо мной
    вниз головой,
Вонзившись вилкой в шар земной,
Беспечный, милый мотылек,
Живешь ты,
    мой антимирок!

Зачем среди ночной поры
Встречаются антимиры?
Зачем они вдвоем сидят
И в телевизоры глядят?

Им не понять и пары фраз.
Их первый раз—последний раз.

Сидят, забывши про бонтон.
Ведь будут мучиться потом.

Mr. Anti-Beetle
                    is feeling
Lollobrigida.

(While through this bittersweet romance
Visions of blotting paper dance.)

So let the Antiworlds be praised,
The fantastic in our humdrum days!

Who would be sane if it weren't for the mad?
Where's the oasis if it wasn't for sand?

There are no women
                    just antimen.
Antimachines bellow in their jungle dens.
Where there's salt of the earth there are faults of the earth,
And the hawk perishes
                    deprived of its prey.

I love my carping critics.
On the neck of one there sits,
                              naked
And sweet-smelling,
                    a gleaming antihead!

I sleep with windows open.
Somewhere a star whistles by,
And skyscrapers hang down
                          like stalactites
From the underbelly of the earth,
Where, head down,

Stuck like a fork in the globe,
You live,
          my dear carefree little moth,
My antiworld!

Tell me why do antiworlds meet
                              in the night

And sit watching TV perfectly delighted
When they can't even understand the words?
They think the first time is the last;
Yet they sit there forgetting their manners.
Of course they'll hate themselves
                              afterwards.

И ушки красные горят,
Как будто бабочки сидят ...

... Знакомый лектор мне вчера
Сакзал: «Антимиры?—Мура!...»
Я сплю, ворочаюсь спросонок.
Наверно, прав научный хмырь.

Мой кот как радиоприемник
Зеленым глазом ловит мир.

1961

Еще вступительное

Открывайся, Америка!
Эврика!

Корoную Емельку,
                        открываю, сопя,
В Америке—Америку,
В себе—
           себя.

Рву кожуру с планеты,
                        сметаю пыль и тлен,
Спускаюсь
           в глубь
                        предмета,
Как в метрополитен.

Там груши—треугольные,
                        ищу в них души голые.
Я плод трапециевидный
                        беру не чтоб глотать—

Чтоб стекла сердцевинки
Сияли, как алтарь!

(Look, their little red ears are aglow
As they sit there like butterflies.)

Yesterday a lecturer I know
Said, "Antiworlds? Utter nonsense!"
I toss and turn in my sleep.
The world of science is dead right.

And like a radio my cat lies
Tuned in to the world through her green eyes.

—ADAPTED BY HENRY CARLISLE

An Opening

Open up, America!
Eureka!

Finally crowning Peter Three,*
I enter: a reek, a
Scent in America of—America,
And in myself—
                    of me.

Brushing off ashes and dust
                    I unpeel the planet around
And descend
              to the depths
                    of the thing,
Like a ride in the Underground.

Inside each triangular pear
                    I seek the spirit bare;
I would not eat, but I pluck
                    this bright isosceles fruit

That the clear panes of the core
May glow like an altar.

*Pugachov, Cossack leader of a revolt in the eighteenth century, executed before he could fulfill his aspiration to be crowned Tsar Peter III.

329

Исследуйте, орудуйте,
              не дуйте в ус,
Пусть врут, что изумрудный,—
Он красный, ваш арбуз!
Вгрызаюсь, как легавая,
              врубаюсь, как колун...

Художник хулиганит?
Балуй,
       Колумб!

По наитию
          дую к берегу...

Ищешь
      Индию—
Найдешь
       Америку!

                        1961–1962

Стриптиз

В ревю
          танцовщица раздевается, дуря...
Реву?...
Или режут мне глаза прожектора?

Шарф срывает, шаль срывает, мишуру.
Как сдирают с апельсина кожуру.

А в глазах тоска такая, как у птиц.
Этот танец называется «стриптиз».

Страшен танец. В баре лысины и свист,
Как пиявки
          глазки пьяниц налились.
Этот рыжий, как обляпанный желтком,
Пневматическим исходит молотком!
Тот, как клоп,—
            апоплексичен и страшон.
Апокалипсисом воет саксофон!

Keep searching—not lurching,
                    never losing your head;
It's a lie that the cores are all emerald
—No, they're watermelon red!
O, to gnaw at it, to chop,
                    axlike, into something columnar . . .

Is poetry only posies?
Come on, it's all funsville,
                    Columbus!

Not in search of much
                    we rush down to the beach . . .

So you want to
                    discover Indies?
It's America
          you reach!

                    —ADAPTED BY JOHN HOLLANDER

STRIPTEASE

A hall:
          In the dance, she fools around some while she strips.
A howl?
          Is it mine? Are these my eyes the spotlight rips?

She unpeels her shawl and scarves and glitter, in
Just the way you'd strip an orange of its skin,
But the sorrows of the birds are in her glance . . .
Note that "striptease" is the name they give this dance.

Frightening dance . . . Dipped heads and whistles in the
     bar . . .
Like a leech
          each bloodshot eye will drink its fill;
As if smeared with yolk of egg, one of these heads
Is emitting laughs like some pneumatic drill;
Like a bug
          another, apoplectic, one . . .

Now the sax with its apocalypse screams out.

Проклинаю твой, Вселенная, масштаб,
Марсианское сиянье на мостах,
Проклинаю,
        обожая и дивясь,
Проливная пляшет женщина под джаз!...

«Вы Америка?»—спрошу, как идиот.
Она сядет, сигаретку разомнет.

«Мальчик,—скажет,—ах, какой у вас акцент!
Закажите мне мартини и абсент».

1961–1962

Еще вступительное

Обожаю
Твой пожар этажей, устремленных к окрестностям рая!
Я—борзая,
        узнавшая гон наконец, я—борзая!
Я тебя догоню и породу твою распознаю.
По базарному дну
        ты, как битница, дуешь, босая!

Под брандспойтом шоссе мои уши кружились,
        как мельницы,

По безбожной,
        бейсбольной,
            по бензоопасной Америке!

Кока-кола. Колокола.
Вот нелегкая занесла!

Ты, чертовски дразня, сквозь чертоги вела и задворки,
И на женщин глаза
        отлетали, как будто затворы!

Мне на шею с витрин твои вещи дешевками вешались.
Но я душу искал,
        я турил их, забывши про вежливость.

O I damn you, universe, your awful scale,
As above our bridges Martian sparklings flash!
O I damn you
           as I worship and adore;
See, the dancer overflows into the jazz!

"You're America?" I'll ask her, like a dope;
She'll sit down with me and twist her cigarette,

She'll say, "Kid, that's a wild accent that you've got—
How about a nice Martini with Pernod?"

—ADAPTED BY JOHN HOLLANDER

ANOTHER OPENING

I adore
Your sparks flying upward from high floors into the districts
    of Heaven!
I, a hound
           who has finally learned to hunt, I—a hound . . .
I'll catch you and find out what breed you are
As you run like some shoeless chick
                    on the floor of a shopping bazaar.

Under the overpass' hoselike spasm
                    my ears like windmills churned
Over the godless
            baseballed
                    treacherous American chasm.

Coca Cola. Carillonola.
What ill wind has drawn me here?

You, fiendishly teasing, have dragged me past alleys and
    palaces,
Past women whose eyes came unhinged like opening clasps.

From shop windows shoddy objects grabbed me around the
    neck,
But no, I was out for Soul, and rudely shoved them away.

333

Я спускался в Бродвей, как идут под водой с аквалангом.
Синей лампой в подвале
                        плясала твоя негритянка!
Я был рядом почти, но ты зябко ушла от погони.
Ты прочти и прости,
                        если что в суматохе не понял...

Я на крыше, как гном, над нью-йоркской стою планировкой.
На мизинце моем
                        твое солнце—как божья коровка.

                                                    1961–1962

Отступление об отступлениях

Болен я. Живу у моря.
Нет «Америки». Умора!

Я живу, счастливый пленный
Обнаглевших отступлений.

Муза мне чаек мешает,
Помогает и мешает.

Ждет редактор Косолапов...

Берег кляксами заляпав,
Мое море отступает,
Точно сцену обнажает—
Душу,
        водоросли,
                    песок,

А потом на берег шпарит,
Как асфальтовый каток!

                                                    1961–1962

As if sealed in a diving suit, I was lowered down into Broad-
    way—
Like a blue lamp in a cellar a black girl danced.
You were almost run to earth
                        but you finally outfoxed me;
Read this and forgive it—I must
                        have missed much in the
   midst of it all.

A gnome, I stand over the great street-grid of New York,
Your sun, on my little fingernail
                    is perched, like a ladybug.

                —ADAPTED BY JOHN HOLLANDER

A DIGRESSION ABOUT DIGRESSIONS

I'm sick. I live beside the sea.
There's no America. Tee-hee!

A happy prisoner, I lurk
Among digressions gone berserk.

The Muse brews up a pot of tea,
And as she helps, she hinders me.

Bungle awaits (my editor)

My inkstains dripped along the shore;
My sea recedes now, past my reach
As if a stage were being cleared:
Now you see soul
             seaweed
                and sand

The sea, steamrolling up the beach,
Lays blacktop roadbed on the strand.

              —ADAPTED BY JOHN HOLLANDER

Рублевское шоссе

Мимо санатория
Реют мотороллеры.

За рулем влюбленные—
Как ангелы рублевские.

Фреской Благовещенья,
Резкой белизной
За ними блещут женщины
Как крылья за спиной!

Их одежда плещет,
Рвется от руля,
Вонзайтесь в мои плечи,
Белые крыла.

Улечу ли?
        Кану ль?

Соколом ли?
Камнем?

Осень. Небеса.
Красные леса.

1961–1962

Вечернее

Я сослан в себя
        я—Михайловское
горят мои сосны смыкаются

в лице моем мутном как зеркало
смеркаются лоси и пергалы

природа в реке и во мне
и где-то еще—извне

три красные солнца горят
три рощи как стекла дрожат

RUBLYOV TURNPIKE*

Past the sanatorium
Motorscooters roar,
Lovers, like Rublyov angels
Ranged behind handlebars.

Fiercely as white as in an
Old Annunciation
Women behind them flash,
Following them like wings.

Up from the handlebars
They take off, clothes a-splash.

White wings,
Pierce my shoulders!

Then I'll fly?
                    Or submerge then?
Hawklike?

Like a stone?

Fall. Sky overhead.
The forest all in red.

—ADAPTED BY JOHN HOLLANDER

NIGHTPIECE

I was sent into exile inside me,
Consequently, I'm all Mikhailovskoye. **
My pine forests crumple in fire.

In my face, clouded up like a mirror,
Deer and villas are sinking to darkness.

And within me as here in this river,
Nature courses along, and beyond me.

Three red suns are afire, and trembling
Like three bright panes of glass are three pine groves.

*Andrei Rublyov (1370–1430), the greatest of Russian icon paint-
ers; a turnpike near Moscow is named for him.
** Pushkin was exiled here.

три женщины брезжут в одной
как матрешки—одна в другой

одна меня любит смеется
другая в ней птицей бьется

а третья—та в уголок
забилась как уголек

она меня не простит
она еще отомстит

мне светит ее лицо
как со дна колодца—кольцо

1961–1962

Автопортрет

Он тощ, точно сучья. Небрит и мордаст.
Под ним третьи сутки
                    трещит мой матрац.
Чугунная тень по стене нависает.
И губы вполхари, дымясь, полыхают.

«Приветик,—хрипит он,—российской поэзии.
Вам дать пистолетик? А может быть, лезвие?
Вы—гений? Так будьте ж циничнее к хаосу...
А может, покаемся?...
Послюним газетку и через минутку
свернем самокритику как самокрутку?...»

Зачем он тебя обнимает при мне?
Зачем он мое примеряет кашне?
И щурит прищур от моих папирос...

Чур меня, чур!

SOS!

1963

338

And three women are rattling in one
Like a nest of dolls, one in another.

One of them loves me. She's laughing
While another inside of her twitters.

But the last of them hides in a corner
Like a tiny, radiant ember,

She who will never forgive me,
The one who will yet have her vengeance;

And her face blazes out at me, gleaming
Like a ring in a well, at the bottom.

—ADAPTED BY JOHN HOLLANDER

SELF-PORTRAIT

Dry as a dead tree.
Hasn't shaved. Snout of a nose.
Three days and nights with no sleep.
A cast-iron shadow

looms on the wall there, hinged mouth
burning out—"Morning, Russian Poetry.
Want a gun? a knife?
You're a genius? oh, then all this

won't matter—but maybe, for now—
Here, let's take stock. 'The Work of Voznesensky.'
Let's roll up a newspaper, spit on it,
roll our own—"

How can he kiss you like that in front of me?
Why is he putting on my coat?

Get away, get out!

SOS!

—ADAPTED BY JEAN VALENTINE

339

Замерли

Заведи мне ладони за плечи,
обойми,
только губы дыхнут об мои,
только море за спинами плещет.
Наши спины, как лунные раковины,
что замкнулись за нами сейчас.
Мы заслушаемся,
                                   прислонясь.
Мы—как формула жизни двоякая.
На ветру мировых клоунад
заслоняем своими плечами
возникающее меж нами—
как ладонями пламя хранят.
Если правда, душа в каждой клеточке,
свои форточки отвори.
В моих порах
                         стрижами заплещутся
души пойманные твои!
Все становится тайное явным.
Неужели под свистопад,
разомкнувши объятья, завянем—
как раковины не гудят?
А пока нажимай, зав_аруха,
на скорлупы упругие спин!
Это нас погружает друг в друга.
Спим.

1965

DEAD STILL

Now, with your palms on the blades of my shoulders,
Let us embrace:
Let there be only your lips' breath on my face,
Only, behind our backs, the plunge of rollers.

Our backs, which like two shells in moonlight shine,
Are shut behind us now;
We lie here huddled, listening brow to brow,
Like life's twin formula or double sign.

In folly's worldwide wind
Our shoulders shield from the weather
The calm we now beget together,
Like a flame held between hand and hand.

Does each cell have a soul within it?
If so, fling open all your little doors,
And all your souls shall flutter like the linner
In the cages of my pores.

Nothing is hidden that shall not be known.
Yet by no storm of scorn shall we
Be pried from this embrace, and left alone
Like muted shells forgetful of the sea.

Meanwhile. O load of stress and bother,
Lie on the shells of our backs in a great heap:
It will but press us closer, one to the other.

We are asleep.

—ADAPTED BY RICHARD WILBUR

*This poem was translated in collaboration with Max Hayward and is reprinted from *Antiworlds* by Andrei Voznesensky, edited by Patricia Blake and Max Hayward, published by Basic Books, 1966.

Морозный ипподром

В. АКСЕНОВУ

Табуном рванулись трибуны к стартам,
В центре—лошади, вкопанные в наст.
Ты думаешь, Вася,
     мы на них ставим?
Они, кобылы, поставили на нас.

На меня поставила вороная иноходь.
Яблоки по крупу—е-мое ...
Умеет крупно конюшню вынюхать.
Беру все финиши, а выигрыш—ее.

Королю кажется, что он правит.
Людям кажется, что им они.
Природа и рощи на нас поставили.
А мы—гони!

Колдуют лошади, они шепочут.
К столбу Ханурик примерз цепочкой.
Все-таки 43° ...
Птица замерзла в воздухе, как елочная игрушка.
Мрак, надвигаясь с востока, замерз посредине неба,
         как шторка

у испорченного фотоаппарата.
А у нас в Переделкине в Доме творчества были
        открыты 16 форточек.

У каждой стоял круглый плотный комок
         комнатного воздуха,
Он состоял из сонного дыхания, перегара,
        тяжелых идей.

Некоторые закнопливают фортки марлей,
чтобы идеи не вылетали из комнаты,
как мухи.
У тех воздух свисал тугой и плотный,
        как творог в тряпочке.

Взирают лошади в городах:
Как рощи в яблоках о четырех стволах ...

WINTER AT THE TRACK

(to Vasily Aksyonov)

The stands go stampeding to the starting post
Down to where the horses paw the ground.
And, Vasya, you think we're betting on them?
They're betting on us—it's the other way round.

That black mare has put all her money on me—
Just look at her dappled rump;
A hot tip tells her who to pick;
And I always win, but the take is hers.

So the rulers think it is they who rule,
While the people think they rule the rulers.
The woods and the hills have gambled on us;
So what can we do but race like hell?

The horses whisper, chafing at the bit.
Barfly pisses on the post, linked to it
By a frozen yellow chain:
                              it is forty below.
A Christmas-tree ornament, a bird freezes up there.
Night, moving in from the east, is caught congealed in
     midair,
The shutter of a broken camera.
But at Peredelkino, in the Writers' Club,
Sixteen windows are open a crack.

In front of each hangs a chunk of frozen air—
Congealed hot air.
Some writers cover the windows with gauze
So their portentous ideas won't escape like flies.
And the air balloons, sagging, thick and slimy,
As with curds in a cloth.

Horses gaze about them, penned up in cities
Like groves of dappled four-trunked trees.

Свистят Ханурику.
                    Но кто свистит?
Свисток считает, что он свистит.
Сержант считает, что он свистит.
Закон считает, что он свистит.

Планета кружится в свистке горошиной,
но в чьей свистульке? Кто свищет? Глядь—
упал Ханурик. Хохочут лошади—
кобыла Дунька, Судьба, Конь Блед.

Хохочут лошади.
Их стоны жутки:
«Давай, очкарик! Нажми! Бодрей!»
Их головы покачиваются,
                          как на парашютиках,
на паре, выброшенном из ноздрей.
                    Понятно, мгновенно замерзшим.

Все-таки 45°...
У ворот ипподрома лежал Ханурик.
Он лежал навзничь. Слева еще пять.
Над его круглым ртом,
            короткая, как вертикальный штопор,
открытый из перочинного ножа, стояла
                                замерзшая
                                      Душа.
Она была похожа на поставленную торчком
                          винтообразную сосульку.
            Видно, испарялась по спирали,
                    да так и замерзла.
И как бывает в сосульку вмерзает листик или веточка,
внутри ее вмерзло доказательство добрых дел,
взятое с собой. Это был обрывок доноса на соседа
за невыключенный радиоприемник.
Над соседними тоже стояли Души, как пустые
                                      бутылки,

Между тел бродил Ангел.

Он был одет в сатиновый халат подметальщика.
Он собирал Души, как порожние бутылки.
                              Внимательно

Now they're whistling at Barfly,
But who is whistling?
The whistle thinks the whistle's whistling.
The policeman thinks that he is whistling.
The law thinks that it is whistling.

The planet twirls, a pea in a whistle,
But in whose whistle? Who's whistling—wait!
Look, Barfly's down. And the others laugh—
Russian Filly, Pale Horse, Fate.

The horses laugh,
Making terrible sounds:
"Come on, Egghead, let's go! Get a move on!"
While their heads sway on tiny parachutes
Of steam exhaled from their nostrils
And frozen at once.

It is forty-five below:
Barfly lies at the starting post—
On his back: to the left, five others.
Above his open mouth, blunt as a corkscrew
Sticking up from a penknife, his frozen soul,
A screw-shaped icicle protruding into the air;
It has spiraled and condensed.
And as a leaf or twig freezes in an icicle,
Frozen within is its final Certificate of Good Deeds;
(In reality, the denunciation of a neighbor for not turning
    off his radio.)
Souls like empty bottles are poised above the other horses,
While among their bodies wanders an angel.
In a street cleaner's smock, it strolls along,
Collecting the souls, the empty bottles,
Drawing its finger carefully over each to see if it is broken,

проводил пальцем—нет ли зазубрин.
Бракованные скорбно откидывал через плечо.
Когда он отходил, на снегу оставались отпечатки следов
                                    с подковками...

...А лошадь Ангел—в дыму морозном
ноги растворились,
                    как в азотной кислоте,
шейку шаловливо отогнула, как полозья,
сама, как саночки, скользит на животе!...

1967

Sadly tossing the rejects over its shoulder,
Leaving behind the print of horseshoes in the snow . . .

And the Angel Horse, in the frozen haze,
Legs dissolving as in nitric acid,
Playfully arches its neck like the curved runner of a sleigh,
And then, on its belly, slides away.

1967

—ADAPTED BY WILLIAM JAY SMITH

THE
BARACHNI
POETS

A LITERARY OUTGROWTH of the contemporary oral *blatnoi* trend (that of the thieves' songs), *barachni* poetry is written today primarily by young poets. Like a considerable body of Soviet poetry, it circulates in typescript only. The term *barachni* derives from the word *barracks* (*baraki*)—those of concentration camps and of slum areas surrounding big cities. Marked by a certain urban ultra-realism, *barachni* poetry may be regarded as a manifestation of the vast international movement which reflects the discontent and anxiety of people facing the crumbling of yesterday's values, whether Christian morality or Marxist ideology.

A kind of crude Expressionistic satire, *barachni* poetry is one reaction to the atmosphere of uneasiness and fear which prevailed in Russia during the Stalinist regime. Above all, it satirizes contemporary Soviet life. This same approach may also be found in the prose of such writers as Tertz, as well as in painting. Oscar Rabin, to whom one of the poems quoted below is dedicated, is the best-known among the *barachni* painters of Moscow.

Barachni poetry is popular in Moscow literary circles. Though not anonymous, its poets are relatively obscure. One may hear their verse at small literary evenings held in Moscow by groups of intimates; Sabgir and Holin, for instance, are quite influential among "subterranean" Muscovites. These two, who are close friends, are credited with coining the term *barachni*. Now in their late

350

thirties, they are said to have a following of young poets who for the most part are also unpublished.

Artists and poets with a *barachni* turn of mind are particularly interested in such Western Expressionistic artists as Kafka, Klee, and Becket, though few examples of their work are readily available in the U.S.S.R. But the *barachni* movement is not alien to Russian literature; parts of Mayakovsky's *Bedbug* anticipate it.

The singer Galich writes songs in a *barachni* mood. A successful engineer, a man nearing fifty who sings his own compositions to a guitar accompaniment, he is one of Russia's most fashionable artists at this time. He too is totally nonofficial: his songs circulate on tape and are sung all over the U.S.S.R., but they are never recorded nor printed. His lyrics, often employing a grotesque "pop" use of Soviet slogans, are the creations of a real poet. They are apolitical and asocial in a virulent way, poignant, ironic mixtures of contemporary Soviet street talk, of camp lore, and of a pervasive, bittersweet nostalgia typical of Russian folklore. Galich is a good example of the flowering of Soviet folk songs, whose popularity surpasses even that of poetry today, as if, even for intellectuals, songs were a better means of expression for the *malaise*, the feeling of *nausée* — in Sartre's sense of awareness of the absurd — so characteristic of contemporary life.

Here is one of Galich's* lyrics:

> Clouds float by, white clouds, white clouds,
> They float slowly by as they do in the flicks.
> I eat fried chicken and drink cognac
>
> To try keep warm, as warm as the clouds.
> Because I am cold—I am always cold
> Having spent twenty years scraping ice in a camp.

* The critic Kornei Chukovsky credits him with a remarkable sense of contemporary street talk.

I've spent twenty years scraping ice in a camp.
White clouds on your wall to the Kalima camp
Tell the Kalima ice that I now have new teeth,

Now I sit in a bar like a lord, a boss,
And I order pineapple and I drink Cognac,
Dreaming of clouds, white clouds by floating by. . . .

The following instances of *barachni* poetry are not dated. As far as we know they were written in the early sixties. Their principal merit is to be extremely typical of a certain Soviet mood today — one reminiscent of American contemporary "beat" trends.

ИГОРЬ ХОЛИН

Кибернетический век
Человек
Пришел на вокзал
Вам куда
В Кабул
Нет
На созвездие Ориона
Хорошо
Проходите в кабину
Сейчас
Мы вас
Разложим на электроны
И направим
В космос
В виде
Радиосигналов
Товарищ Мачалов
Включите ток
Так
Готово
Орион
Принимайте Иванова
Все в порядке
Цель путешествия
Хочет
Купить
Сыну
Перчатки

У бара
Незабудка
Курсирует
Автомат
Проститутка
Подмигивает прохожим
Фарой
Она
Опусти сотню
В щелку
Изображу

IGOR HOLIN

The age of cybernetics
a man
came to the station
    Where to, Mac,
    Kabul?
    No
    Orion
    OK
    Step into the cabin
    In a sec
    we'll break you down
    into electrons
    and send you
    into space
    as a radio beam
    Comrade Machalov
    turn on the juice
    Ready
    Roger
    Orion
    Take over Ivanov
Situation normal
Purpose of the voyage
He wants
to buy
a pair of mittens
for his kid
—ADAPTED BY ALEXANDER ANDREYEV

Near the bar
"Forget-me-not"
an automation whore
is cruising
winking at the passers-by
with her headlight
She:
Drop a ten-spot
in my slot
I'll act like
a cherry

Целку
Он
Пойдем в подворотню
Там
Темно
Она
Давай тут
Не все ли равно
Он
Стыдно
Она
Чепуха
Он
Ладно
Заворачивай кожуха

ГЕНРИХ САБГИР

Икар

(Оскару Рабину)

Скульптор
Вылепил Икара.
Ушел натурщик,
Бормоча: «Халтурщик!
У меня мускулатура,
А не части мотора».
Пришли приятели.
Говорят: «Банально!
Лишь женщины увидели,
Что это—гениально.
— Какая мощь!
— Вот это вещь!
— Традиции
древней Греции…
—Сексуальные эмоции…
— Я хочу иметь детей—
от коробки скоростей!
От коробки скоростей!
Зачала—и в скорости
На предельной скорости,
Закусив удила́,

He:
Let's go where
it's dark
She:
Let's do it here
Who gives a crap
He:
But I'm embarrassed
She:
Nonsense
He:
All right
roll up your casing

—ADAPTED BY ALEXANDER ANDREYEV

HENRI SABGIR

ICARUS

(to Oscar Rabin)

The sculptor
made a statue of Icarus
His model stalked out
grumbling: "Lousy hack!
I have muscles
not parts of a motor."
His buddies came
and said: "It's trite."
Only women saw,
a work of genius.
    What power!
    A real masterpiece!
    In the tradition
of ancient Greece . . .
    Sexual emotions:
    I'd like my children to be sired
by a gear box!
She conceived—and speedily
in overdrive
gnawing at the bit
gave birth

Родила
Вертолет.
Он летит и кричит
Свою маму зовет.
Вот уходит в облака ...

Зарыдала публика:
ТАКОВО ВОСПИТАТЕЛЬНОЕ ЗНАЧЕНИЕ ИСКУССТВА!
Раскланялся артист.

На площади поставлен бюст—
Автопортрет,
Автофургон,
Телефон—
Автомат.
ТАКОВО ВОСПИТАТЕЛЬНОЕ ЗНАЧЕНИЕ ИСКУССТВА!

Суд

Беседую, как с другом,
С Богом.
Но верю лишь своим
Ногам.
Они несут меня, несут
На площадь—
На Великий Суд.
— Что случилось?
Кого собираются вешать?
Отвечайте же скорее!
— Говорят,
Казнят
Еврея.
Спрашиваю одного героя:
— Неужели всех
Врачей?—
(Смех)
— Рабиновича?
— Рабиновича.
— Абрамовича?
— Абрамовича.

to a chopper
He's flying and crying
calling for his mammy—
disappears in the clouds . . .

The public weeps:
SUCH IS THE EDUCATIONAL MEANING OF ART!
The artist bows.

In the square
a bust
is erected:
self-portrait,
truck,
telephone booth.
SUCH IS THE EDUCATIONAL MEANING OF ART!

—ADAPTED BY ALEXANDER ANDREYEV

THE TRIAL

I talk to God
like a friend
but I only believe
in my legs.
They carry me
to the square
to the Last Judgment
"What happened
Who are they hanging?
Answer!"
"They are executing
Jews."
"Not all the doctors,
surely?"*
(Laughter)
    "Rabinovich?"
    "Rabinovich!"
    "Abramovich?"

*A reference to the anti-Semitic Doctors' Plot invented by Stalin
shortly before his death. Seventeen doctors, most of them Jews, were
accused of plotting the dictator's death.

— А Гуревича?
— И Гуревича.
И Петрова Ивана Петровича...
(Странные творятся вещи.)
Покосился этот тип
Зловеще—
Холодный пот
Меня прошиб.
— Ты сам случайно
Не сектант?
Товарищи,
Интеллигент!—
Тут окончилась война
И началась такая бойня,
Что даже Бог—
Мой лучший друг
Никого не уберег.
У Бога есть один дефект!
Его смущает интеллект.

Чудо!
В городке открылась «Мебель и посуда».

Иван и диван

Иван
Купил диван-кровать,
Чтобы с женой вольготней спать.
У забора грузовик.
— Ничего, говорит, я привык.
Тут народ помог
Ивану,
Взвалил диван
Ему на спину.
Идет Иван,
На нем—диван.
Жара.
Гора.

"Abramovich!"
"And Gurevich?"
"Yes, Gurevich."
"And Petrov, Ivan Petrovich?"
Odd.
The fellow stares
ominously.

I break out
in cold sweat.
"You wouldn't by chance
belong to a sect?
Comrades,
An intellectual!"
The war ended then
—the carnage began.
It got so bad that
God my best friend
couldn't help anyone.

God does have one great defect:
he is embarrassed by intellect.

—ADAPTED BY ALEXANDER ANDREYEV

Miracle! A new Furniture & Crockery
store opened in town.

IVAN AND THE DIVAN

Ivan
Bought a convertible divan,
All the merrier to sleep with his wife.
There's a truck near the gate.
It's okay, he says, I'm used to it.
The people around helped
Ivan
Load the divan
on his back.
Off goes Ivan
Sporting—a divan.
It's hot.
Up the hill.

Барак.
Река.
До села рукой подать—
На тот берег.
А до моста—
Ворота!...
У воды
В песке—диван,
На нем—Иван.
Трясогузка
Цвирк—
И села на диван.
Брысь—
Прогнал ее Иван.
Перышко смахнул с обивки...
С откоса увидали девки:
Иван и диван
Переходят реку вброд.
Поплыл диван!
Бежит народ!
Спасен
Иван.
Утонул диван.
— Без дивана нам не жить!—
Голосит жена Ивана.
Дома—голая стена.
Мужик
Напился самогона,
Начал песни распевать:
— Пропадай диван-кровать!

Past the shack.
The river.
His village is right there
On the other side.
But to the bridge—
It's a mile!
Near the water
In the sand—the divan
resting on it is Ivan.
A goldfinch
Chirped—
And sat on the divan.
Shoo—
Go away, says Ivan.
Brushed a feather from the upholstery.
From up the hill the girls saw suddenly
How Ivan and the divan
Started to ford the river
The divan's afloat!
People running to get a look!
Ivan is safe.
The divan sank.
Life is death without a divan!
Wails the better half of Ivan.
Poor Ivan!
He got drunk on moonshine booze
And started making up blues:
Convertible divan—
                bad news!

—ADAPTED BY ALEXANDER ANDREYEV

Bella
Akhatovna
Akhmadulina
(1937–   )

There are lots of us going. Maybe four of us.
Racing like hell in a car
driven by a girl with copper-colored hair—
white arms—a Paris dress—

Bella, you fatal show-off,
you angel from another world!
that beautiful, bratty tilt of your chin—
the light-edged line of your profile—

The cops in Hell will wipe their lips
and send out their best men to the gates
when, puffing on a Gauloise, yawning,
you break their last law.

O Bella! foot to the floor of the car,
in that voice pure as a church chorale,
you'll say: "Oh hell! it's so sad—
they've taken my license away!"

> Andrei Voznesensky, "To Bella Akhmadulina," 1964
>
> —ADAPTED BY JEAN VALENTINE

Oₙₑ ᴏꜰ ᴛʜᴇ most agreeable literary occasions I attended in Moscow in the winter of 1964 was a small, informal soiree given by a middle-aged historian and his wife. The poet Bella Akhmadulina was among the twelve or fifteen guests. Her presence at the party completely overshadowed mine as a Russian-speaking visitor from the United States, a circumstance that might otherwise have been intriguing.

At thirty, Miss Akhmadulina is one of the best-known young women in Moscow today. Her beauty, as well as her social position as the wife of the successful writer Yuri Nagibin. are matched by her literary talent. She is one of the most unconventional poets in the U.S.S.R. today. Hers is a resolutely feminine lyricism. Her verse is classic in form, but the emotion which underlies it is always deeply felt, always dynamic. She is the author of a collection of verse, *Struna (The Music Chord),* published in 1962, and of several long poems, among which "Poems to Pasternak" (1962) and "Rain" (1964) are the best known.

Dressed in a low-cut red dress, elegant but aloof, Bella was silent during the first part of the evening, as the other guests mingled, drinking white Caucasian wine and discussing such matters as the relative merits of Hemingway and Faulkner. (*The Hamlet* had recently been published in Moscow in a careful, sensitive translation.)

We were gathered in the living room of a tiny apartment in the Aeroport section of Moscow, where many writers and intellectuals live. A cocktail table was laden with glasses, canapés and cakes. On the wall, several seventeenth-century icons were oddly but effectively mixed with strong, expressionistic drawings by the contemporary Soviet sculptor, Ernst Neizvestny. Neizvestny gained international attention at the time of his public altercation with Khrushchev at the Manège showing in 1963, when the Soviet Premier vented his outrage against modern art.

After an hour of social amenities, the hostess asked Bella to recite a few of her poems. There was silence as she went to one end of the room and stood against the icons on the wall. With everyone's attention on her, the retiring young woman became a dramatic interpreter of her poetry. She recited in an emotional manner, with absolute concentration, half closing her dark, slanting eyes — first a love elegy, then a long poem about her encounter with Boris Pasternak shortly before his death. One was struck by her fervor, by the feeling that she was performing a rite. Her reading seemed to echo that of Pasternak himself reciting his verse for a few friends at dusk in Peredelkino.

After her recitation Bella sat down, visibly exhilarated. The ice had been broken between her and the other guests. She acknowledged their enthusiastic response, smiling at the young mathematicians who had applauded loudest when she had finished. She joined in the general conversation, which had by now turned to Pasternak. Two of the guests, a young painter and his wife, were recounting their visit with the poet in 1958. Although they had never met him before, they had traveled to Peredelkino to pay homage to the poet after his exclusion from the Writers' Union. He had received them warmly and shown them his collection of his father's sketches.

A discussion followed regarding the merits of *Doctor Zhivago*, which by then every intellectual in Moscow had read in typescript. Pasternak has been progressively rehabilitated by the literary authorities, but *Doctor Zhivago* has not yet come out in the U.S.S.R. In Moscow, opinions are sharply divided about the book. Older readers often say that Pasternak's rendering of the past is too subjective to be truthful. The younger ones criticize the passiveness of Yuri Zhivago as a hero. But the novel also has its ardent devotees who consider it to be the great Russian novel of the century.

Two of the guests, a mathematician and an older man who was a literary critic, monopolized the conversation for a while. They argued about the future of the novel. Was the great psychological novel which had blossomed in the nineteenth century dead today? Perhaps the formal looseness of *Doctor Zhivago*, the vagueness of the French *nouveau roman*, were here to stay, new aspects of a renewed art form. To the disgust of the critic, the young mathematician vehemently asserted that the current Soviet realistic novel was a "dinosaur on the contemporary scene."

Around 11:30 the guests began to leave. By then Bella was the center of the conversation. After telling about her recent brief trip to Greece with her husband, she asked me many questions about American poets. When the party broke up, she offered to drive me back to the center of town.

Kiev avenue was quiet; in Moscow there is almost no traffic at that hour. It was winter and the street lights shone softly in the snow. As she drove through white, deserted streets, Bella continued to talk in long melodic sentences about the growing and beneficial role of poetry in Russian spiritual life, and about other poets whom she admired. I was moved by her lyricism and her wish to become acquainted with the world outside Moscow's literary milieu. Unlike some of my acquaintances, she didn't gossip about other writers. Rather, she wanted to share her love of parts of the U.S.S.R. which I didn't know, like Georgia:

> My dream about you, Georgia
> is deep,
> a mountain gorge...

And she wanted to hear all about America. She said, "One of the most frustrating experiences I ever had was an encounter which the Writers' Union organized for its younger members to meet John Steinbeck on his visit to Moscow. This meeting turned out to be such a banal affair despite Steinbeck's efforts to reach out to us! We young writers were like silent school children. We didn't know English, we lacked worldliness, we couldn't forget that this was an official function. There was this marvelous man just across the room from us — a hero, a great writer, and it was as if an ocean separated us. I could have cried for the sheer humiliation of it." *

Bella Akhmadulina was born and brought up in Moscow in a middle-class family. Despite her Moslem-sounding name she is Russian, and above all a Moscovite. She attended Moscow's Gorky Institute, the Soviet Union's leading school in literary matters, where many contemporary Soviet writers have studied at one time or another. There she met Yevgeny Yevtushenko, who was to become her first husband. Because of her indifference to political matters she had difficulties being elected to the Writers' Union; finally she qualified as a translator rather than as a poet, despite the fact that her poetry is

---

* This conversation preceded by some months Steinbeck's stand on Vietnam, which has made him a most unpopular figure in the eyes of Russian intellectuals.

widely read. She is typical of the younger generation of Soviet writers—outspoken, thirsting for contacts with the outside world, unafraid of foreigners. Her favorite writers are Boris Pasternak and Ivan Bunin, and she readily identifies with two Russian women poets, Anna Akhmatova and Marina Tsvetayeva.

There is no celebrity in the U.S.S.R. without professional achievement. Bella is the closest thing to a star to be found there today. Her poetic output is small, but her verse has literary merit and that quality which contemporary Soviet readers have come to value above all others —inner freedom. However, she is known not only for her poetical achievements but also for that imponderable element so rare in the U.S.S.R.—glamour. She photographs beautifully. Not long ago she acted in a movie; she was fetching in her role as a girl reporter in a lighthearted study of contemporary Soviet youth. Her black eyes give her a vaguely oriental air, and she has very white skin and dark hair that she tints red. Her reddish bangs are celebrated and imitated all over Russia, but they became famous through literature rather than through photography. Until she made her movie debut, Bella's picture seldom appeared in Soviet magazines. Her bangs were described in the love poems of her first husband, Yevtushenko. These verses to Bella were the sensation and sometimes the scandal of Moscow in the late fifties, and she is probably the only woman to have been personally and openly celebrated in contemporary Soviet poetry. Certain slightly—very slight by Western standards—suggestive details in Yevtushenko's poems thrilled and shocked Soviet opinion. Russian literature is traditionally chaste, and the Soviet sense of propriety is always ready to be outraged.

There is a mixture of helplessness and haughtiness in Bella's manner, a hint of vulnerability which brings out protectiveness in men. Far from feeling threatened by

370

her bright talent, her male colleagues shelter Bella and promote her gifts. When I first met Yevtushenko in 1960, he and Bella were on the eve of divorce by mutual consent. Nonetheless, Yevtushenko spoke of Bella both as a woman and as a poet with a rhapsodic admiration. Later, he was responsible for editing her first book of poems.

In Moscow, where women find it difficult to buy good-looking clothes, well-dressed Bella is considered fashion personified. Her arrival at the Writers' Union, escorted by Yuri Nagibin, sends a flurry of excitement throughout the sedate professional institution. As the couple settle down in the club's restaurant, other writers come up to their table to present their homage to Bella and kiss her hand. (Hand-kissing is a pre-Revolutionary custom which is still in use in certain Soviet circles, although now it is usually practiced with a touch of playfulness.) Before long, the Nagibins' table is surrounded by a group of admirers.

Yuri Nagibin, who is older than Bella by almost twenty years, is the epitome of Soviet literary and social success. He is a member of the Communist party, but his writings are apolitical—short stories in a traditional nineteenth-century vein, as well as literate movie scenarios which make a great deal of money. (He was the screen writer for the sensational movie *The President,* a study of the terrible social situations prevailing today in many communal farms in the Soviet Union.) He is handsome, witty, and devoted to Bella. He nurses his hypersensitive wife through an occasional period of nervous depression. Together, they are one of the most sought-after couples in the Soviet literary world. They divide their time between a Moscow apartment and a country *dacha* some twenty miles out of town. Yuri's parents live in the *dacha* permanently, and Bella and Yuri spend most of the week there reading and writing. In the country they entertain rarely. Each week they travel to Moscow for a day or two, usually for business and literary appointments. At that time, if they do not go out at night to some official function, movie premiere or poetry recital, they invite their Moscow friends to their apartment for cold supper and vodka and Caucasian brandy.

The Nagibins' guests are apt to be writers, actors, and painters. They may include the Yevtushenkos, the Voznesenskys, Ernst Neizvestny, or the actor Mikhail Ulianov, the recipient of a recent Lenin prize. Their parties blend gaiety with sophistication, and often last late into the night. Sometimes Bella gives them a Georgian quality by encouraging many elaborate toasts. In the U.S.S.R., Georgia stands for the warmest hospitality and the most uninhibited poetic inspiration. Dining in the Georgian style involves an intricate ritual, including speeches — and in this case the reciting of poetry — with which hosts and guests honor each other as the meal progresses. For most Soviet writers today, Georgia is the land of sun and wine, of handsome people, of great mountains and luminous beaches — a symbol of freedom. "I become more myself when I am in Georgia," Bella says. Since a poet of her reputation in Russia is invited to give poetry recitals all over the country, she often travels to Georgia "for a breath of freedom and friendship." She has many friends among contemporary poets there, who write in their native Georgian tongue and are among the very best in the U.S.S.R. Not long ago, the predecessors of these poets were translated by poets of the scope of Zabolotsky, Pasternak, and Akhmatova.

The distinct flavor of Bella's life is to be enjoyed best during an overnight visit at the Nagibins' *dacha*, where informality and coziness prevail. The Nagibins' apartment in town — two well-furnished rooms and a spacious kitchen — has that slightly abandoned look of places not regularly lived in. It shows plainly that Bella's interests do not lie in housekeeping, although she is not only an attentive hostess but an efficient one as well, always able to produce a meal at any hour of the day or night. But it is the *dacha*, the Nagibins' real home, which affords the foreign guest a glimpse of a traditional Russian way of life, modest and yet comfortable.

At the Nagibins', the day starts with a late breakfast of tea and bread with Yuri's parents, a charming, cultivated elderly couple, while Bella and Yuri work upstairs. Soon it is time for a long walk in the woods with the younger Nagibins before an informal lunch. Afterwards one reads, listens to music or sits and talks by the fireplace in Bella's room. A copious, lengthy dinner is served late. A walk before bedtime, even in winter, is customary. The walks are especially lovely on a mild winter night, when the woods surrounding the *dacha* are a fairyland of fluffy, snowy firs.

The Nagibins have that great rarity in the Soviet Union, an efficient young "home worker" who does all the housework under Yuri's mother's direction. The Nagibins go out of their way to keep her happy; a separate bungalow was recently built for her and her husband in the *dacha's* garden. Whatever is unavailable at the local stores — and Soviet provincial stores are notoriously ill stocked — can be purchased in Moscow when a member of the Nagibin family travels to the capital in the chauffeured car. Thus Bella is spared all the responsibilities of everyday life — a situation which is exceptional for a woman in Russia. She can devote herself unconditionally to her art, without any thought of its being acceptable for immediate publication. At present she is engaged in putting together a second, long-awaited book of poems for the foremost Moscow publishing house, the Soviet Writers' Publishing House.

Стихи о Грузии

Б. ПАСТЕРНАКУ

ГРУЗИНСКИХ ЖЕНЩИН ИМЕНА...

Там в море парусы плутали,
и, непричастные жаре,
медлительно цвели платаны
и осыпались в декабре.

Мешались гомоны базара,
и обнажала высота
переплетения базальта
и снега яркие цвета.

И лавочка в прибрежном парке
бела вставала и нема,
и смутно виноградом пахли
грузинских женщин имена.

Они переходили в лепет,
который к морю выбегал,
и выплывал, как черный лебедь,
и странно шею выгибал.

Смеялась женщина Ламара,
бежала по камням в воде,
и каблучки по ним ломала,
и губы красила в вине.

И мокли волосы Медеи,
вплетались руки в водопад,
и капли сохли и мелели,
и загорались невпопад.

И, заглушая олеандры,
собравшись все в одном цветке,
витало имя Ариадны
и растворялось вдалеке.

Едва опершийся о сваи,
там приникал к воде причал.
— Цисана!—из окошка звали.
— Натэла!—голос отвечал.

A CYCLE OF POEMS ABOUT GEORGIA
(to the memory of Boris Pasternak)
THE NAMES OF GEORGIAN WOMEN

There on the sea sails wandered,
And unconcerned by the heat
Sycamores blossomed at leisure,
Leaves for streets in December.

The market sounds intermingled;
On naked heights above
Basalt and snow wove light
Into rainbow prisms.

A kiosk in the park by the seaside
Stood empty and white and silent;
The syllabled names of Georgian women
Seemed to smell of grapes;

They became a chirruping
Breezing out to sea,
Sailing out like a black swan
Strangely reaching his neck.

Then a woman called Lamara
Ran down to the water
Where she broke her heel on the pebbles
Tinting her lips with wine.

Medea's hair was dark and wet;
Arms wove the waterfall;
Drying, drops on skin turned golden,
Sparkling at odd moments.

Stronger even than oleanders
Embraced into a cluster,
The name of Ariadne floated
And dissolved upon the skyline.

Swaying and barely touching the shoreline
A float poised on the water—
Tisana! called a voice from a window—
Natella! a voice answered.

СКАЗАННОЕ ВО ВРЕМЯ БОМБЕЖКИ

В той давности, в том времени условном
что был я прежде? Облако? Звезда?
Не пробужденный колдовством любовным
алгетский камень, чистый, как вода?

Ценой любви у вечности откуплен,
я был изъят из тьмы, я был рожден.
Я—человек. Я—как поющий купол,
округло и таинственно сложен.

Познавший мудрость, сведущий в искусствах,
в тот день я крикнул:—О земля моя!
Даруй мне тень! Пошли хоть малый кустик—
простить меня и защитить меня!

Там, в небесах, не склонный к проволочке,
сияющий нацелен окуляр,
чтобы вкусил я беззащитность точки,
которой алчет перпендикуляр.

Я по колено в гибели, по пояс,
я вязну в ней, тесно дышать груди.
О школьник обезумевший! Опомнись!
Губительной прямой не проводи!

Я—человек, и драгоценен пламень
в душе моей. Но нет, я не хочу
сиять заметно! Я—алгетский камень.
О Господи, задуй во мне свечу!

И отдалился грохот равномерный,
и куст дышал, и я дышал под ним.
Немилосердный ангел современный
побрезговал ничтожеством моим.

И в этот мир, где пахло, где желтело,
Смеркалось, пело, силилось сверкнуть,
я нежно вынес собственного тела
родимую и жалостную суть.

WORDS SPOKEN
BY PASTERNAK DURING A BOMBING*

In that ancient time—in eternity—
What was I then a cloud, a star?
Not wakened yet by love,
A mountain stone, clear like water?

Brought from eternity by desire
I was torn from the dark, I was born.
Now a man, I am a singing cupola,
Rounded and mysterious as a hull.

I have experience now, adept in the arts.
That day I cried out: Oh earth!
Give me shade, the smallest bush
Which will forgive and protect me!

There in the sky, implacably shines
The bombsight, so that I
May taste the helplessness of a dot,
Created by an avid perpendicular.

I am to my knees in doom, to my waist;
I struggle in quicksand, out of breath.
Oh, insane schoolboy, awake!
Do not draw this fateful line!

I am a man, and a precious nugget
Lies in my soul. Yet, I do not wish to gleam,
To glow—I am a mountain stone,
Soft and worn, and want to be invisible!

The even roaring faded;
The bush exhaled and grew, and I breathed
Under it. The pitiless modern angel
Winged away, despising my insignificance.

Into this world of fresh smells,
Where things turn gold with light,
Where they sing and sparkle, I carried my body,
That intimate and fragile thing.

*This is based on an episode related by Pasternak in his wartime reminiscences.

Заплакал я, всему живому близкий,
вздыхающий, трепещущий, живой.
О высота моей молитвы низкой,
Я подтверждаю бедный лепет твой.

Я видел одинокое, большое
твое лицо. Из этого огня
себя я вынес, как дитя чужое,
слегка напоминавшее меня.

Не за свое молился долговечье
в тот год, в тот час, в той темной тишине —
за чье-то золотое, человечье,
случайно обитавшее во мне.

И выжило оно. И над водою
стоял я долго. Я устал тогда.
Мне стать хотелось облаком, звездою,
алгетским камнем, чистым, как вода.

ГЛАВЫ ИЗ ПОЭМЫ

1

Начну издалека, не здесь, а там,
начну с конца, но он и есть начало.
Был мир как мир. И это означало
все, что угодно в этом мире вам.

В той местности был лес, как огород,—
так невелик и все-таки обширен.
Там, прихотью младенческих ошибок,
все было так и все наоборот.

На маленьком пространстве тишины
был дом как дом. И это означало,
что женщина в нем головой качала
и рано были лампы зажжены.

Там труд был легок, как урок письма,
И кто-то—мы еще не знали сами—
замаливал один пред небесами
наш грех несовершенного ума.

I cried, feeling close to all living things,
Sighing, pulsating, alive.
O my prayer, lowly yet so high,
I repeat your tender whisper.

Death, I have seen your blank,
Lonely features. I carried myself
Away from them like a strange child
Who vaguely resembled me.

I am not praying for my longevity!
But, as at that hour in gray silence,
For some human and flamelike unfolding
Which accidentally inhabited me.

It survived, and over the water
I stood for a long, long time, tired.
I wanted to be a cloud, a star,
A mountain stone—clear, like water.

CHAPTERS OUT OF A POEM

I

I will start my tale far back
I will start at the end—for us, a rebirth.
The world was itself, which means
That it wore its everyday, dull façade.

But in that region there was a forest
Like a vegetable garden, at once frugal and large,
And as in a child's game
Everything in it was right, and magical.

At a still patch in this wood
There was a house, which means
That a woman in it nodded her head
And the lamps were lighted early;

Like handwriting lessons, the work there was easy,
And someone—though we didn't know it then—
Was redeeming us in the sight of divinity
For our imperfect hearts.

379

В том равновесье меж добром и злом
был он повинен. И земля летела
неосторожно, как она хотела,
пока свеча горела над столом.

Когда же им оставленный пробел
возник над миром, около восхода,
толчком заторможенная природа
переместила тяжесть наших тел.

Объединенных бедною гурьбой,
врасплох нас наблюдала необъятность,
и наших недостоинств неприглядность
уже никто не возмещал собой.

В тот дом езжали многие. И те
два мальчика в рубашках полосатых
без робости вступали в палисадник
с малиною, темневшей в темноте.

Мне доводилось около бывать,
но я чужда привычке современной
налаживать контакт несоразмерный,
в знакомстве быть и имя называть.

По вечерам мне выпадала честь
смотреть на дом и обращать молитву
на дом, на палисадник, на малину—
то имя я не смела произнесть.

Стояла осень, и она была
лишь следствием, но не залогом лета.
Тогда еще никто не знал, что эта
окружность года не была кругла.

Сурово избегая встречи с ним,
я шла в деревья, в неизбежность встречи,
в простор его лица, в протяжность речи...
Но рифмовать пред именем твоим?
О, нет.

Он неожиданно вышел из убогой чащи переделкинских дерев
поздно вечером, в октябре, более двух лет назад. На нем был
грубый и опрятный костюм охотника: синий плащ, сапоги и бе-

This balance between evil and good
Was his doing: the world recklessly soared
Just as it wished, while a candle burned,
On his table a candle burned.

When the vacuum he left,
Departing from earth at sunset, jarred the universe,
Nature paused in its flight
And we felt again the weight of our bodies.

With bowed heads, gathered in a poor flock,
We seemed to stare at infinity
And see our unworthiness, our pettiness,
Now he was no longer redeeming us.

Many came to this house. These two boys
In striped shirts stepped boldly,
Going beyond the hedge, carrying raspberries
Which looked blue in the twilight.

In the dusk I looked at his house,
And with closed eyes I prayed for the house, the hedge,
For the raspberries, while
Not even daring to speak his name.

It was fall, a consequence of summer,
Not a promise, though we didn't know
That the circle of that year
Would never be closed.

Oh, I walked in the wood, an encounter
Unavoidable—with his spacious face,
His drawn-out, melodious voice.
But this I dare not say in verse.

Unexpectedly he stepped out of a humble thicket of Peredelkino trees, late one evening in October, more than two
years ago. He was wearing the rough but neat outfit of a

лые вязаные варежки. От нежности к нему, от гордости к себе я почти не видела его лица—только ярко-белые вспышки его рук во тьме слепили мне уголки глаз. Он сказал: «О, здравствуйте! Мне о вас рассказывали, и я вас сразу узнал». И вдруг, вложив в это неожиданную силу переживания, взмолился: «Ради бога! Извините меня! Я именно теперь должен позвонить!».

Он вошел было в маленькое здание какой-то конторы, но резко вернулся, и из кромешной темноты мне в лицо ударило, плеснуло яркой светлостью его лица, лбом и скулами, люминесцирующими при слабой луне. Меня охватил сладко-ледяной, шекспировский холодок за него. Он спросил с ужасом: «Вам не холодно? Ведь дело к ноябрю?»—и, смутившись, неловко впятился в низкую дверь. Прислонясь к стене, я телом, как глухой, слышала, как он говорил с кем-то, словно настойчиво оправдываясь перед ним, окружая его заботой и любовью голоса. Спиной и ладонями я впитывала диковинные приемы его речи—нарастающее пение фраз, доброе восточное бормотание, обращенное в невнятный трепет и гул дощатых перегородок. Я, и дом, и кусты вокруг нечаянно попали в обильные объятия этой округлолюбовной, величественно-деликатной интонации. Затем он вышел, и мы сделали несколько шагов по заросшей пнями, сучьями, изгородями, чрезвычайно неудобной для ходьбы земле. Но он как-то легко и по-домашнему ладил с корявой бездной, сгустившейся вокруг нас,—с выпяченными, дешево сверкающими звездами, с впадиной на месте луны, с грубо поставленными, неуютными деревьями. Он сказал: «Отчего вы никогда не заходите? У меня иногда бывают очень милые и интересные люди—вам не будет скучно. Приходите же! Приходите завтра». От низкого головокружения, овладевшего мной, я ответила почти надменно: «Благодарю вас. Как-нибудь я непременно зайду».

hunter: a sea-blue cape, boots, and white knitted mittens. Out of tenderness for him, pride towards myself, I hardly looked at his face—though the white flarings of his hands in the dark blinded the edges of my eyes. He said, "Oh, how do you do? I was told about you, and I recognized you at once." Suddenly he put into this the unexpected energy of an experience, and he pleaded, "For the love of God! Please forgive me. I have to telephone, right now." He was about to enter a booth by a small office, but brusquely he returned, and from the dark I was struck in the eyes and splashed with the brilliant glow of his face, brow, and cheekbones, luminescent in dim moonlight. I was seized with an icy sweetness, a Shakespearean apprehension for him. He asked with alarm, "You are not cold? For this is November." Then, suddenly embarrassed, he turned and clumsily made his way into the low doorway. Leaning against the cold wall, I heard with my body, like a deaf person, how he spoke with someone, as if insistently excusing himself, surrounding the person with the care and love of his voice. With my back and the palms of my hands I absorbed the extraordinary turns of his conversation, the insistent singing of the sentences, the kindly eastern muttering, which I felt now as indistinct pulsations, next as a boy's clattering along a picket fence; I and the shed and the bushes around were inadvertently caught up in the embrace of this rounded, loving, majestically subtle intonation. He came out, and we tramped a few yards across overgrown tree stumps, broken branches, and fallen fences, a terrain not made for strolling. But he managed easily, as if at home in the clumsy void which had thickened around us, below protuberant, tinsel-scintillating stars, the hole in a cloud where the moon should have been, the roughly-arranged, shaggy trees. He halted and said, "Why do you never stop by? I sometimes have very nice and interesting people. You will not be bored. Do come. Do come tomorrow!" Because of a shameful dizziness which had seized me, I answered, almost arrogantly, "I thank you. Someday I will certainly drop by."

Из леса, как из-за кулис актер,
он вынес вдруг высокопарность позы,
при этом не выгадывая пользы
у зрителя—и руки распростер.

Он сразу был театром и собой,
той древней сценой, где прекрасны речи.
Сейчас начало! Гаснет свет! Сквозь плечи
уже мерцает фосфор голубой.

— О, здравствуйте! Ведь дело к ноябрю—
не холодно ли?—вот и все, не боле.
Как он играл в единственной той роли
всемирной ласки к людям и зверью.

Вот так играть свою игру—шутя!
Всерьез! до слез! навеки! не лукавя!—
как он играл, как, молоко лакая,
играет с миром зверь или дитя.

— Прощайте же!—так петь между людьми
не принято. Но так поют у рампы,
так завершают монолог той драмы,
где речь идет о смерти и любви.

Уж занавес! Уж освещает тьму!
Еще не все:—Так заходите! завтра!—
О, тон гостеприимного азарта,
что ведом лишь грузинам, как ему.

Но должен быть такой на свете дом,
куда войти—не знаю! невозможно!
И потому, навек неосторожно,
я не пришла ни завтра, ни потом.

Я плакала меж звезд, дерев и дач—
после спектакля, в гаснущем партере,
над первым предвкушением потери
так плачут дети, и велик их плач.

2

Он утверждал—«Между теплиц
и льдин, чуть-чуть южнее рая,
на детской дудочке играя,

From between the trees, like an actor stepping from
The theater's wings, he suddenly emerged
With a noble gesture, without the audience's
Slightest complicity. He spread his arms.

He was both himself and the theater,
That ancient scene, where speeches are poetry.
The curtain is rising on silence. The lights dim;
Phosphorescence glows from the stage.

"It is a cold November night—are you
Not cold?" he said. How well he played
That unique role, of boundless kindness to
All that is living, to people and beasts and plants.

Thus one must play—like a game, yet
Seriously. To the point of tears. Without faking!
He played with the world like an animal or a child
Good-naturedly playing, drinking its milk.

"Farewell . . ." People do not speak like this,
For this is singing, such as resounds
On the stage, like the last lines
Of a classic drama full of love and blood.

The curtain lowers, the phosphorescence fades.
Yet the last words resound—this cannot be
The end: "Come back! Yes, tomorrow, please . . ."
Such warmth of heart is Georgian.

But there must be, somehow, one house
Which you cannot enter. Thus,
Improvident before eternity
I did not return—not tomorrow, never.

I wept among the stars, the trees, the houses
After the play was over, in the darkening theater,
With my first premonition of loss,
With my arms and head hanging, as a child weeps.

2

He asserted: "Halfway between hothouses
And floating icebergs, to the south of Eden
Where a child's flute trills

живет вселенная вторая
и называется—Тифлис».

Ожог глазам, рукам—простуда,
любовь моя, мой плач—Тифлис!
природы вогнутый карниз,
где Бог капризный, впав в каприз,
над миром примостил то чудо.

Возник в моих глазах туман,
брала разбег моя ошибка,
когда тот город зыбко-зыбко
лег полукружьем, как улыбка
благословенных уст Тамар.

Не знаю для какой потехи
сомкнул он надо мной овал,
поцеловал, околдовал
на жизнь, на смерть и наповал—
быть вечным узником Метехи.

О, если бы из вод Куры
не пить мне!
И из вод Арагвы
не пить!
И сладости отравы
не ведать!
И лицом в те травы
не падать!

И вернуть дары,
что ты мне, Грузия, дарила!
Но поздно! Уж отпит глоток,
и вечен хмель, и видит Бог,
что сон мой о тебе—глубок,
как Алазанская долина.

1961–1962

В опустевшем доме отдыха

Впасть в обморок беспамятства, как плод,
уснувший тихо средь ветвей и грядок,
не сознавать свою живую плоть,
ее чужой и грубый беспорядок.

386

There is a second universe
Whose name is Tiflis."

It burns the eyes and cools the hands,
My love, my tears—Tiflis!

Mist floated up before me
I was losing myself so fast,
As the city, tremulous
With distance, fell into a half-circle
Like Tamara's sudden, blessed smile.

I do not know for what playful reason
It closed its oval around me,
Kissed me, bewitching me then and forever,
For life, beyond death
To be, endlessly, the prisoner of Georgia.

Oh, if I had not drunk the water
Of your streams, Georgia, the water
Of the river Aragva
And had not known the nectar of your lotus,
And if I hadn't fallen face-down into this grass!

If only I could give back the gifts
You have given me,
But it is too late—
The first sip is taken
And the intoxication is forever

And, God be witness,
My dream about you, Georgia,
Is deep,
A mountain gorge, or the valley
Of Allazanskaya.

—ADAPTED BY STANLEY NOYES

IN THE EMPTIED REST HOME

To fall, like an apple, no mind,
no memory! To lie
on the soft ground, blank as an apple,
to not feel this body.

Вот яблоко, возникшее вчера.
В нем—мышцы влаги, красота пигмента,
то тех, то этих действий толчея.
Но яблоку так безразлично это.
А тут, словно с оравою детей,
не совладаешь со своим же телом,
не предусмотришь всех его затей,
не расплетешь его переплетений.
И так надоедает под конец
в себя смотреть, как в пациента лекарь,
все время слышать треск своих сердец
и различать щекотный бег молекул.
И отвернуться хочется уже,
вот отвернусь, но любопытно глазу.
Так музыка на верхнем этаже
мешает и заманивает сразу.
В глуши, в уединении моем,
под снегом, вырастающим на кровле,
живу одна и будто бы вдвоем—
со вздохом в легких, с удареньем крови.
То улыбнусь, то пискнет голос мой,
то бьется пульс, как бабочка в ладони.
Ну, слава богу, думаю, живой
остался кто-то в опустевшем доме.
И вот тогда тебя благодарю,
мой организм, живой зверек природы,
верши, верши простую жизнь свою,
как солнышко, как лес, как огороды.
И впредь играй, не ведай немоты!
В глубоком одиночестве, зимою,
я всласть повеселюсь средь пустоты,
тесно и шумно населенной мною.

1965

Немота

Кто же был так силен и умен!
Кто мой голос из горла увел!
Не умеет заплакать о нем
рана черная в горле моем.

An apple: muscles of moisture,
veins of color, all sorts of changes
crowding each other out.
The apple doesn't care.

Hopeless to care here,
it's war, whole gangs of orphans
run wild with real guns and knives,
and the water's rising.

And it's boring. I'm tired of looking at it
both ways, doctor and patient.
The same crackling heart, the same
tickling run of the molecules.

I'm ready to turn away,
but I don't turn away: I half stay,
the way you half listen to someone
whistling in the next apartment.

Solitude, distance. The snow keeps on rising
up on the roof. I'm too much alone,
it's as if there were two of us here,
the air in my lungs, the beat in my blood.

But my eyes can still see, my voice
squeaks, my pulse beats like a moth
in my closed hand: oh, thank God, my body,
little child, little mouse! Thank God

there's something alive in this house!
In the dead of winter, alone,
go on with your simple life, the life
of the black woods, the vegetable gardens, the sun.

—ADAPTED BY JEAN VALENTINE

MUTE

March: at last
things start to break up:
I want to praise every twig,
every simple drop,

Сколь достойны хвалы и любви,
март, простые деянья твои,
но мертвы моих слов соловьи
и теперь их сады—словари.

— О, воспой!—умоляют уста
снегопада, обрыва, куста.
Я кричу, но, как пар изо рта,
округлилась у губ немота.

Вдохновенье—чрезмерный, сплошной
вдох мгновенья душою немой.
Не спасет ее вдох иной,
кроме слова, что сказано мной.

Задыхаюсь, и дохну, и лгу,
что еще не останусь в долгу
пред красою деревьев в снегу,
о которой сказать не могу.

Облегчить переполненный пульс—
как угодно, нечаянно, пусть,
и во все, что воспеть тороплюсь,
воплощусь навсегда, наизусть.

А за то, что была так нема,
и любила всех слов имена,
и устала вдруг, как умерла,—
сами, сами воспойте меня.

1966

Сон

О, опрометчивость моя!
Как видеть сны мои решаюсь?
Так дорого платить за шалость—
Заснуть? Но засыпаю я.

И снится мне, что свеж и скуп
Сентябрьский воздух. Все знакомо:
Осенняя пригожесть дома,
вкус яблок, не сходящий с губ.

Но незнакомый садовод
возделывает сад знакомый

but my words that were bright
and flew, are dead. The blue-
gray dictionary
is their garden now:

the black wound in my throat
can't even break open to cry.
I stare at the snow,
the little bushes covered with snow,

the lips of the ravine.
I want to name their names
but nothing comes.
The mist of my own breath.

"Inspiration"—
the silent soul gulped air.
Another breath
won't save my soul. God,

to free the throbbing blood
some way, accidental or not!
Open forever, my body
broken, taken up

with the sap! And because I had no words,
and because I loved the names of all the words,
now that I'm suddenly dead, you sudden silver
drops of wet March, sing me.

—ADAPTED BY JEAN VALENTINE

A DREAM

It's all familiar,
the fall air, clear and sober,
the little house, the door half open,
the salty taste of our apples,

but a stranger is raking the garden.
He says he is the rightful owner now,
and asks me in. The brick floor, the blank
where the clock stood, that slant of light,

my rushed, uncertain steps,
my eyes that saw, and saw nothing,

и говорит, что он законный
владелец. И войти зовет.

Войти? Как можно? Столько раз
Я знала здесь печаль и гордость,
И нежную шагов нетвердость,
И нежную незрячесть глаз.

Уж минуло так много дней,
А нежность—облаком вчерашним,
А нежность—обмороком влажным
Меня омыла у дверей.

Но садоводова жена
меня приветствует жеманно.
Я говорю:—Как здесь туманно...
И я здесь некогда жила.

Я здесь жила лет сто назад:
— Лет сто? Вы шутите?
— Да нет же!
Шутить теперь? Когда так нежно
моим столетьем пахнет сад?

Сто лет прошло, а все свежи
в ладонях нежности к родимой.
Кора деревьев, запах дымный
Вокруг все тот же.

— Не скажи!—
промолвил садовод в ответ.
Затем спросил:—под паутиной,
со старомодной челкой длинной,
Не ваш ли в чердаке портрет?

Ваш сильно изменился взгляд
С тех давних пор, когда в кручине,
Не помню, по какой причине,
вы умерли—лет сто назад.

— Возможно, но жить так давно,
лишь тенью в чердаке остаться,
и все затем, чтоб не расстаться
с той нежностью? Вот что смешно.

1966

your tender voices . . . but the gardener's wife
is standing there waiting.

"It's so foggy here! I lived here too, once,
a hundred years ago . . .
it's all the same, that same
smoky smell over the garden,

the dog's fur still wet on my fingers . . ."
"You don't say," the gardener answers,
cocking his head, coming closer.
Then he smiles, and asks,

"Isn't it you, though, that picture
up in the attic? Isn't it her,
with the long, old-fashioned curls?
But your eyes have changed

since those terrible old days
a hundred years ago,
when you died, alone in the house here,
poor, without work or friends."

—ADAPTED BY JEAN VALENTINE

Прощание

А напоследок я скажу:
прощай, любить не обязуйся.
С ума схожу. Иль восхожу
к высокой степени безумства.

Как ты любил!—ты пригубил
погибели. Не в этом дело.
Как ты любил!—ты погубил,
но погубил так неумело.

Жестокость промаха, о, нет
тебе прощенья. Живо тело,
и бродит, видит белый свет,
но тело мое опустело.

Работу малую висок
еще вершит. Но пали руки,
и стайкою, наискосок,
уходят запахи и звуки.

1966

GOODBYE

And finally I'll say goodbye.
Don't feel you have to love.
I'm chattering, crazy,
or maybe coming into a crazier kind of peace.

How you loved! Your lips just grazing over disaster,
tasting nothing. But that doesn't matter.
How you loved! How you destroyed!
Offhandedly, like a great pale curious boy.

O coldness of failure, cold certainty,
there's no settling with you. The body
wanders around, sees light; sun and moon
shine through the glass pane.

The empty body goes on with its little task.
But the hands fall light and slack,
and like a small flock, sideways,
all sounds and smells graze off away.

—ADAPTED BY JEAN VALENTINE

JOSEPH

BRODSKY*

(1940–   )

To walk out of love on a bright sunny day with no return,
To hear the rustling of grass in the alleys which lead away,
In the warm cloud of the day, in the darkening evening,
  sleepily
To listen to the barking of dogs from under the square nests
  of sod.

Joseph Brodsky

* Brodsky's patronymic is not known to me.

THE WEST is acquainted with the name of Joseph Brodsky because of his well-known trial. In March, 1964, the Soviet police authorities made this young poet's plight into a cause célèbre by convicting him in a civil court in Leningrad on charges of vagrancy. He was a "social parasite" with no other occupation than the writing and freelance translating of poetry! Brodsky was sent to a *kolkhoz* (a collective farm) near Archangel, where, among other tasks, he shoveled manure.

The whole affair was an attempt on the part of a group of reactionary Leningrad writers to intimidate their independent-minded colleagues—those who have given up any thought of being published now in order to be able to write exactly as they choose. The case was publicized abroad thanks to a Communist, a courageous member of the Leningrad Writers' Union, Frieda Vigdorova. She attended the trial and, outraged at the insulting, arbitrary manner in which it was conducted, took down in shorthand a record of the proceedings. This verbatim record was subsequently published in the Western press, shocking public opinion deeply.

An outburst of indignation followed this attempt to discredit one part of the Soviet literary intelligentsia. At about the same time Brodsky's works were smuggled out of Russia. By then Brodsky was well known in the West; his poems were brought out at once by an émigré publishing house. It turned out that the "social parasite" was a young poet of brilliance and originality. And he was not actively anti-Soviet; like many of his Russian contemporaries—he is twenty-seven years old—Brodsky is essentially apolitical.

Brodsky is a Jew, and was born and brought up in Leningrad in the Soviet equivalent of a middle-class family. He is said to have left school at the age of fifteen, dedicating himself to the writing of poetry and to translating from the English and Polish languages. He was Akhmatova's favorite young poet. His trial was a blow to her, as it was to others. For the first time since the early thirties, protests were heard from Soviet intellectuals. This, combined with a flood of petitions from abroad, led to Brodsky's release in the winter of 1966, and he was allowed to return to Leningrad shortly before Akhmatova's death.

One cannot tell yet if Brodsky will become a major poet, as Akhmatova predicted. In his work, as in Voznesensky's, there is sometimes a tendency towards wordiness; a hollowness may be felt occasionally underneath the rhetoric. Perhaps what is absent is the nineteenth-century humanism, which had its last representatives in Pasternak and Akhmatova. Compared with them, many young Soviet writers have a certain simple-mindedness common to youths of many countries today. Like the hippies of America, they attempt to answer the world's problems through a return to immediate perceptions. But in the case of Brodsky, one feels that his interest in traditional literary and religious concepts has enriched his work and will continue to help him grow. (This can also be said of Akhmadulina, and for the same reasons, but Brodsky is less self-conscious and more profound a poet than she.)

Brodsky's poems are intensely personal. Most of them are about death—a private death. When they deal with life, his vision is somber. They echo Mandelstam's late poems, but on the whole Brodsky's literary ancestors are not easy to trace. Edward Arlington Robinson and Robert Frost are favorites of his, and at present he is engaged in translating John Donne into Russian. More than any other young Soviet poet today, he is under the influence of English classics and of contemporary American writers. But his perceptions are purely Russian:

> We are no harder of hearing,
> we have not aged, we say
> the same words, our coats are no brighter,
> the same women do not care for us,
>
> We still toy with the seasons
> in the amphitheaters of solitude,
> the same lanterns flare on our heads
> like exclamation marks of night.
>
> We live on the past as though it were the present,
> present unlike the future, again we stay awake
> all night, we forget those who sleep,
> we repeat the same labors.
>
> Humor, watch over the joyful young
> in the nocturnal rounds of light
> and shadow, make them great for the glory and shame,
> and good for the vanity of age.
>
> —ADAPTED BY W. S. MERWIN

Not long ago while in Moscow I heard Brodsky's voice on tape, reading his "The Great Elegy for John Donne." The voice was extremely youthful and frenzied with anguish. The poet was reciting the elegy's detailed catalogue of household objects in a breathless, rhetorical manner, in the tradition of the poets of the Revolutionary generation. His passion gave life to each thing enumerated, and this somehow made the very long poem seem short. There was a touch of Surrealism to this work—a new, Soviet kind of Surrealism—in the intrusion of everyday detail into the poem. However, Brodsky's Surrealism takes on a more metaphysical dimension in some of his short poems. These are as good as anything written in the sixties in Russia. (Incidentally, we are unable to date them exactly. They were made available to Western readers in 1965 without indication as to when they were written or how they were obtained. We may assume that they are the works of a poet in his early twenties.)

Большая элегия

ДЖОНУ ДОННУ

1

Джон Донн уснул, уснуло все вокруг,
Уснули стены, пол, постель, картины,
уснули стол, ковры, засовы, крюк,
весь гардероб, буфет, свеча, гардины.
Уснуло все. Бутыль, стакан, тазы,
хлеб, хлебный нож, фарфор, хрусталь, посуда,
ночник, белье, шкафы, стекло, часы,
ступеньки лестниц, двери. Ночь повсюду.
Повсюду ночь: в углах, в глазах, в белье,
среди бумаг, в столе, в готовой речи,
в ее словах, в дровах, в щипцах, в угле
остывшего камина, в каждой вещи.
В камзоле, в башмаках, в чулках, в тенях,
за зеркалом, в кровати, в спинке стула,
опять в тазу, в распятьях, в простынях,
в метле у входа, в туфлях. Всё уснуло.
Уснуло всё. Окно. И снег в окне.
Соседней крыши белый скат. Как скатерть
Ее конек. И весь квартал во сне,
разрезанный оконной рамой насмерть.
Уснули арки, стены, окна, всё.
Булыжники, торцы, решетки, клумбы.
Не вспыхнет свет, не скрипнет колесо . . .
Ограды, украшенья, цепи, тумбы.
Уснули двери, кольца, ручки, крюк,
замки, засовы, их ключи, запоры.
Нигде не слышен шопот, шорох, стук.
Лишь снег скрипит. Всё спит. Рассвет не скоро.
Уснули тюрьмы, замки. Спят весы
средь рыбной лавки. Спят свиные туши.
Дома, задворки. Спят цепные псы.
В подвалах кошки спят, торчат их уши.
Спят мыши, люди. Лондон крепко спит.
Спит парусник в порту. Вода со снегом
под кузовом его во сне сипит,
сливаясь вдалеке с уснувшим небом.

THE GREAT ELEGY FOR JOHN DONNE

I

Listen! John Donne
has fallen asleep
and all around him, fallen asleep:
the walls of his room,
the steps of a staircase,
floors, tables, clocks and old glass-
ware, bottles and porcelain
crockery, crystal,
breadknife and fresh-baked loaves, all still.
Night is everywhere, everywhere night,
in corners and eyes,
in papers in the drawer,
in the ever-ready sermon, her words, and there
in the garden,
in fire tongs and bellows,
each careless thing: a nightgown, the shadows
behind the mirror and
washbowl and bed,
the crucifix, the blizzard whirling outside.
All are asleep, asleep, asleep . . .
See, through the window
white snow and the white wood
house next door—the whole neighborhood
sleeps, cut off by the
guillotine
of the window's sash, the arches of stone,
the walls, grills.
Light will not flare
nor a wheel scrape nor a whisper flurry.
No silk-soft noise. Only the snow cries.
Everything sleeps.
No dawn reflects
the prison napping deep in its locks,
the scales of the fishmarket,
dogs on leashes,
cats in the cellar with still-pointed ears.
London's asleep.
A sail in her harbor

2

Джон Донн уснул. И море вместе с ним.
И берег меловой уснул над морем.
Весь остров спит, объятый сном одним.
И каждый сад закрыт тройным запором.
Спят клены, сосны, крабы, пихты, ель.
Спят склоны гор, ручьи на склонах, тропы.
Лисицы, волк. Залез медведь в постель.
Наносит снег у входов нор сугробы.
И птицы спят. Не слышно пенья их.
Воронний крик не слышен, ночь, совиный
не слышен смех. Простор английский тих.
Звезда сверкает. Мышь идет с повинной.
Уснуло всё. Лежат в своих гробах
все мертвецы. Спокойно спят. В кроватях
живые спят в морях своих рубах.
По одиночке. Крепко. Спят в объятьях.
Уснуло всё. Спят реки, горы, лес.
Спят звери, птицы, мертвый мир, живое.
Лишь белый снег летит с ночных небес.
Но спят и там, у всех над головою.

3

Спят ангелы. Тревожный мир забыт
во сне святыми—к их стыду святому
геенна спит и рай прекрасный спит.
Никто не выйдет в этот час из дому.
Господь уснул. Земля сейчас чужда.
Глаза не видят, слух не внемлет боле.
И дьявол спит. И вместе с ним вражда
заснула на снегу в английском поле.
Спят всадники. Архангел спит с трубой.
И кони спят, во сне качаясь плавно.
И херувимы все—одной толпой,
обнявшись, спят под сводом церкви Павла.

under its bow churns snow and water
blurring soft
into the distant sky.

2

Listen! John Donne
has gone to sleep
and the sea is asleep and the chalky cliffs—
the whole island is seized with the same
slumber. Each garden is closed
with a triple latch; maples and pines and
crabs and wolves and
foxes drowse,
the bear has crawled into his dream
and the snow piles up outside his lair
and the birds are still, the crows, still,
the English space is quiet.
A star sparkles. All the dead
lie in their coffins quietly sleeping
and in their beds the living sleep
in the seas of their nightshirts,
each alone, embracing.

3

The angels are silent;
the saints forget
the disturbed world in their holy sleep.
Gehenna sleeps and Paradise.
God is asleep and
earth alien.
Eyes and ears are senseless to pain.
Satan sleeps;
war is dumb on the English fields,
horses doze, the trumpeting archangel
and all the cherubs
crowd in sleep
under the dome of St. Paul's

4

Джон Донн уснул. Уснули, спят стихи.
Все образы, все рифмы. Сильных, слабых
найти нельзя. Порок, тоска, грехи,
равно тихи, лежат в своих силлабах.
И каждый стих с другим, как близкий брат,
хоть шепчет другу друг: чуть-чуть подвинься.
Но каждый так далек от райских врат,
так беден, густ, так чист, что в них—единство.
Все строки спят. Спит ямбов строгий свод.
Хореи спят, как стражи, слева, справа.
И спит виденье в них летейских вод.
И крепко спит за ним другое—слава.
Спят беды все. Страданья крепко спят.
Пороки спят. Добро со злом обнялось.
Пророки спят. Белесый снегопад
в пространстве ищет черных пятен малость.
Уснуло всё. Спят крепко толпы книг.
Спят реки слов, покрыты льдом забвенья.
Спят речи все, со всею правдой в них.
Их цепи спят. Чуть-чуть звенят их звенья.
Все крепко спят: святые, дьявол, Бог.
Их слуги злые. Их друзья. Их дети.
И только снег шуршит во тьме дорог.
И больше звуков нет на целом свете.

5

Но, чу! Ты слышишь—там в холодной тьме,
там кто-то плачет, кто-то шепчет в страхе.
Там кто-то предоставлен всей зиме.
И плачет он. Там кто-то есть во мраке,
Так тонок голос. Тонок, впрямь игла.
А нити нет ... И он так одиноко

4

Listen! John Donne
has fallen asleep
and all his images, all his rhymes.
Who can tell the weak from the strong?
Shame and sadness and sins are equally
quiet
encased in their own syllables.
Each verse murmurs close to its brother,
"Move over a bit."
Yet each is so remote from heaven's gate,
so humble, dense, and pure they
blend into one.
The sharp vaulting
Of the iambs sleep
and the trochees sleep standing like guards
to the right and left, and in them sleeps
the vision of Lethean waters.
Behind that vision, glory sleeps;
disaster and suffering somnolent lie,
good and evil embrace while the prophets
drowse. Snowflakes descend
seeking out small black
dots in the landscape.
Crowds of books and rivers of words
are glazed in the ice of oblivion.
Whole chains of speeches sleep encircling
their truths and lightly clinking.
Saints and devils and gods sleep heavily
next to their children,
their mean servants, their friends.
Only the snow rustles along the dark roads.
In the world
there is no other sound.

5

But swift in the cold darkness
someone comes weeping—
someone afraid in the power of winter—
his tears blur in the shadows,
his voice is thin as a threadless needle,
lonely, floating. Yet somewhere higher

плывет в снегу. Повсюду холод, мгла . . .
Сшивая ночь с рассветом . . . Так высоко.
«Кто ж там рыдает? Ты ли, ангел мой,
возврата ждешь, под снегом ждешь, как лета,
любви моей? Во тьме идешь домой.
Не ты ль кричишь во мраке?»—Нет ответа.
«Не вы ль там, херувимы? Грустный хор
напомнило мне этих слез звучанье.
Не вы ль решились спящий мой собор
покинуть вдруг. Не вы ль! Не вы ль?»—Молчанье.
«Не ты ли, Павел? Правда, голос твой
уж слишком огрублен суровой речью.
Не ты ль поник во тьме седой главой
и плачешь там?»—Но тишь летит навстречу.
«Не та ль во тьме прикрыла взор рука,
которая повсюду здесь маячит?
Не ты ль, Господь? Пусть мысль моя дика,
но слишком уж высокий голос плачет».
Молчанье. Тишь.—«Не ты ли, Гавриил,
подул в трубу, а кто-то громко лает?
Но что ж, лишь я один глаза открыл,
а всадники своих коней седлают.
Всё крепко спит. В объятьях крепкой тьмы.
А гончие уж мчат с небес толпою.
Не ты ли, Гавриил, среди зимы
рыдаешь тут, один, впотьмах, с трубою?»

6

Нет, это я, твоя душа, Джон Донн.
Здесь я одна скорблю в небесной выси
о том, что создала своим трудом
тяжелые, как цепи, чувства, мысли.
Ты с этим грузом мог вершить полет
среди страстей, среди грехов, и выше
Ты птицей был и видел свой народ
повсюду, весь взлетал над скатом крыши.
Ты видел все моря, весь дальний край.
И Ад ты зрел—в себе, а после—в яви.
Ты видел также явно светлый Рай
в печальнейшей—из всех страстей—оправе.
Ты видел: жизнь, она как остров твой.
И с Океаном этим ты встречался:

the night must be sewn with dawn.
Whose is the weeping?
Yours, my angel,
lying in snowfalls
awaiting my love like summer?
Home is a dark place.
Is it not you, moaning in the dark?
Silence. Or you, cherubs,
this sorrowful chorus your tears?
Do you leave my sleeping cathedral? Silence.
Could it be you, Paul, voice gone hoarse
from your strenuous sermons,
bowing your graying head in the night to weep?
Silence again. A beacon shines.
Ah, my Lord, is it not you? My guess
may be wild but the voice is high . . .
Silence. Gabriel, you?
A trumpet blows and a bark echoes.
So be it. I alone may have opened my eyes.
The riders are saddling their steeds.
All is lost in the clasp of perfect
darkness, and couriers rush
down from the heavens in crowds.
Gabriel, Gabriel, surely it's you
alone in the midst of winter,
your trumpet sobbing.

6

No. It is I,
your soul, John Donne.
Here alone on the heights of heaven
I brood, my senses heavy as chains.
Even encumbered you could fly
up through our lust and longings;
birdlike, beyond slant roofs you saw
your kin, the seas and far-off lands
You saw Hell, first in yourself, then
vast and true below.
And you saw Heaven
clear and luminous, set like a jewel—
the saddest of all our passions.
And you saw life: she was your island.

со всех сторон лишь тьма, лишь тьма и вой.
Ты Бога облетел и вспять помчался.
Но этот груз тебя не пустит ввысь,
откуда этот мир—лишь сотня башен
да ленты рек, и где, при взгляде вниз,
сей страшный суд почти совсем не страшен.
И климат там недвижен, в той стране.
Оттуда всё, как сон больной в истоме.
Господь оттуда—только свет в окне
туманной ночью в самом дальнем доме.
Поля бывают. Их не пашет плуг.
Года не пашет. И века не пашет.
Одни леса стоят стеной вокруг,
и только дождь в траве огромной пляшет . . .

Стихи о слепых музыкантах

Слепые блуждают
                     ночью.
Ночью намного проще
перейти через площадь.

Слепые живут
наощупь,
трогая мир руками,
не зная света и тени,
и ощущая камни:
из камня делают
                     стены.
За ними живут мужчины.
Женщины.
          Дети.
               Деньги.

Поэтому
несокрушимые

You met with the ocean, surrounded
by darkness and howling.
All around God you flew yet higher;
my weight keeps you from soaring.
From here the world is only a hundred
towers and the rivers ribbons.
From here the Last Judgment
seems less dreadful; the climate in all this land hovers,
everything dreams in a sick delirium,
and God is only a light in the window
of the most distant house
on a foggy night.
The fields are here
but all unplowed,
the years and the centuries, all unplowed.
Only the woods
stand like a wall and only the rains
dance in gigantic grass. . . .

—ADAPTED BY ROSE STYRON

THE BLIND MUSICIANS

The blind go their way
            by night
It's easier to cross
the squares
            at night.
The blind live
feeling their way,
brushing the world with their hands,
knowing neither shadow nor light,
and their hands drift over the stones
built into walls
of men, women,
children,
            money
walls that cannot be broken,
            better
to follow along them.
Against them the music
            hurls itself

411

лучше обойти
                        стены.
А музыка—в них
упрется.
Музыку поглотят камни.
И музыка
умрет в них,
захватанная руками.

Плохо умирать ночью.
Плохо умирать
                        наощупь.

Так, значит, слепым—проще...
Слепой идет
                        через площадь.

Глаголы

Меня окружают молчаливые глаголы,
похожие на чужие головы
                        глаголы,
голодные глаголы, голые глаголы,
главные глаголы, глухие глаголы.

Глаголы без существительных, глаголы—просто.
Глаголы, которые живут в подвалах,
говорят—в подвалах,
                        рождаются—в подвалах
под несколькими этажами
всеобщего оптимизма.

Каждое утро они идут на работу,
раствор мешают и камни таскают,
но, возводя город, возводят не город,
а собственному одиночеству памятник воздвигают.

И уходя, как уходят в чужую память,
мерно ступая от слова к слову,
всеми своими тремя временами
глаголы однажды восходят на Голгофу.

and the stones soak it up.
In them the music dies
under the hands.
It's hard dying at night, hard
to die feeling your way.
The way of the blind is
simpler, the blind
          cross the empty squares.

—ADAPTED BY W. S. MERWIN

THE VERBS

In the silence the verbs surround me
like faces of strangers,
          the verbs,
famished verbs, naked verbs,
essential verbs, deaf verbs,
verbs with no names, mere verbs,
verbs that live in caves
speak in caves,
are born in caves,
under the shifting level
of the univérsal optimism.

They go to work every morning,
mix cement, haul stones,
build the city . . . No, they erect
a monument to their own solitude.
They recede as we disappear from the memory
of someone else, they keep in step beside words,
and with their three tenses in line,
the verbs climb the hill Golgotha.

И небо над ними,
как птица над погостом,
и, словно стоя

перед запертой дверью,
некто стучит, забивая гвозди
в прошедшее,
в настоящее,
в будущее
время.

Никто не придет и никто не снимет.
Стук молотка
вечным ритмом станет.
Земли гипербола лежит под ними,
как небо метафор плывет над ними!

Воспоминания

Белое небо,
крутится надо мною.
Земля серая
тарахтит у меня под ногами.
Слева деревья. Справа
озеро очередное
с каменными берегами,
с деревянными берегами.

Я вытаскиваю, выдергиваю
ноги из болота,
и солнышко освещает меня
маленькими лучами.
Полевой сезон
пятьдесят восьмого года!
Узнаешь:
это—твое начало.

Еще живой Добровольский,
улыбаясь, идет по городу.
В дактилической рифме
еще я не разбираюсь.
Полевой сезон

The sky wheels above them
like a bird above a cemetery.
They stand upright
as though in front of a closed door
and a man lifts his arm and drives nails
into the past
into the present
into the future.

No one will ever come to bear witness.
The strokes of the hammer
become the rhythm of eternity.
Under the verbs stretches the hyperbole, earth,
and heaven, the metaphor, drifts above them.

—ADAPTED BY W. S. MERWIN

MEMORIES

Over me
the white sky turns.
The gray earth
grates under my feet.
Trees on my left. On my right
the next of many lakes,
with banks of stone,
banks of wood.

I drag, I
heave my leg out of the mire,
and the sun touches me
with its meager rays.
Harvest season
nineteen fifty eight.
Recognize this:
it is where you began.

Still alive. Dobrovolsky
walks the city, smiling.
And I am still struggling
to rhyme dactyls.
Harvest season

пятьдесят восьмого года.
Я к Белому морю
медленно пробираюсь.

Реки текут на север.
Ребята бредут—по-пояс—по рекам.
Белая ночь над ними
легонько брезжит.
Я ищу. Я делаю из себя
человека.
И вот мы выходим,
выходим на побережье.

Голубоватый ветер
до нас уже долетает.
Земля переходит в воду
с коротким плеском.
Я опускаю руки
и голову поднимаю,
и море ко мне приходит
цветом своим белесым.

Памятник

Поставим памятник
в конце длинной городской улицы
или в центре широкой городской площади,
памятник,
который впишется в любой ансамбль,
потому что он будет
немного конструктивен и очень реалистичен.
Поставим памятник,
который никому не помешает.

У подножья пьедестала
мы разобьем клумбу,
а если позволят отцы города,—
небольшой сквер,
и наши дети
будут жмуриться на толстое

nineteen fifty eight.
Slowly I open the road
leading to the White Sea.

The rivers flow toward the north.
Boys wade, waist-deep,
following the streams,
the white night over them
almost at daybreak.
I am searching. I want to make of myself
a man. And there, we emerge,
there, we emerge on the shore.

The blue wind
reaches us now.
The land buries itself in water
with a brief rustling.
My hands slip toward the ground,
I raise my head,
and the sea bears toward me
its bleak whiteness.

—ADAPTED BY W. S. MERWIN

THE MONUMENT

Let us set up a monument
in the city, at the end of the long avenue,
or at the center of the big square,
a monument
that will stand out against any background
because it will be
quite well built and very realistic.
Let us set up a monument
that will not disturb anybody.

We will plant flowers
around the pedestal
and with the permission of the city fathers
we will lay out a little garden
where our children
will blink

417

оранжевое солнце,
принимая фигуру на пьедестале
за признанного мыслителя,
композитора
или генерала.

У подножия пьедестала—ручаюсь—
каждое утро будут появляться
цветы.
Поставим памятник,
который никому не помешает.

Даже шоферы
будут любоваться его величественным силуэтом.
В сквере
будут устраиваться свидания.
Поставим памятник,
мимо которого мы будем спешить на работу,
около которого
будут фотографироваться иностранцы.
Ночью мы подсветим его снизу прожекторами.

Поставим памятник лжи.

Еврейское кладбище около Ленинграда.
Кривой забор из гнилой фанеры.
За кривым забором лежат рядом
юристы, торговцы, музыканты, революционеры.

Для себя пели.
Для себя копили.
Для других умирали.
Но сначала платили налоги,
                        уважали пристава,
и в этом мире, безвыходно материальном,
толковали Талмуд,
                оставаясь идеалистами.

at the great orange sun
and take the figure perched above them
for a well-known thinker
a composer
or a general.

I guarantee that flowers will appear
every morning
on the pedestal.
Let us set up a monument
that will not disturb anybody.
Even taxi drivers
will admire its majestic silhouette.
The garden will be a place
for rendezvous.
Let us set up a monument,
we will pass under it
                hurrying on our way to work,
foreigners will have their pictures taken
                standing under it,
we will splash it at night with the glare
                of floodlights.

Let us set up a monument to The Lie.

—ADAPTED BY W. S. MERWIN

THE JEWISH CEMETERY

The Jewish Cemetery near Leningrad:
a lame fence of rotten planks
and lying behind it side by side
lawyers, businessmen, musicians, revolutionaries.

They sang for themselves,
got rich for themselves,
died for others.
But always paid their taxes first;
        heeded the constabulary,
and in this inescapably material world
studied the Talmud,
        remained idealists.

Может, видели больше.
Может, верили слепо.
Но учили детей, чтобы были терпимы
и стали упорны.
И не сеяли хлеба.
                    Никогда не сеяли хлеба.
Просто сами ложились
в холодную землю, как зерна.
И навек засыпали.
А потом их землей засыпали,
зажигали свечи,
и в день Поминовения
голодные старики высокими голосами,
задыхаясь от холода, кричали об успокоении.

И они обретали его.
                    В виде распада материи.

Ничего не помня.
Ничего не забывая.
За кривым забором из гнилой фанеры,
в четырех километрах от кольца трамвая.

Maybe they saw something more,
maybe believed blindly.
In any case they taught their children
        tolerance. But
        obstinacy. They
sowed no wheat,
        never sowed wheat,
simply lay down in the earth
        like grain
and fell asleep forever.
Earth was heaped over them,
candles were lit for them,
and on their day of the dead raw voices of famished
old men, the cold at their throats,
shrieked at them, "Eternal peace!"
Which they have found
        in the disintegration of matter,
remembering nothing
forgetting nothing

behind the lame fence of rotten planks
four kilometers past the streetcar terminal.

—ADAPTED BY W. S. MERWIN

INDEX OF POETS

423

INDEX OF FIRST LINES OF POEMS IN ENGLISH

428

ABOUT THE AUTHOR

Born in 1930, OLGA ANDREYEV CARLISLE was brought up in Paris. During World War II she lived with her family on Ile d'Oléron, a small island off the Atlantic coast of France. In 1949 she came to the United States and attended Bard College.

Mrs. Carlisle comes from a well-known Russian literary family. Her grandfather was Leonid Andreyev and her father, Vadim, is a poet. Married to Henry Carlisle, also a writer, she divides her time between painting and writing when at home in Washington, Connecticut. Her first book, *Voices in the Snow* was published in 1963